Greek Cooking

For a delicious taste of Greece, that most
magical of European countries, this is the
Number One book to consult. Robin Howe's
recipes are renowned for their accuracy
of flavour and intense variety. Within
minutes she can fill your kitchen with the
smell of rosemary and thyme, and have your
mouth watering at the prospect of lamb
roasting on a spit, of garlic and melon and
pastry so flaky it will blow away like those
tantalising thoughts of *Bouzouki* music, *taverna*
food, and love . . .

Also by Robin Howe
in Mayflower Books

GERMAN COOKING

Greek Cooking

Robin Howe

Mayflower

Granada Publishing Limited
Published in 1972 by Mayflower Books Ltd
Frogmore, St Albans, Herts AL2 2NF
Reprinted 1973, 1975, 1976

First published by André Deutsch Ltd 1960
Copyright © Robin Howe 1960
Made and printed in Great Britain by
C. Nicholls & Company Ltd
The Philips Park Press, Manchester
Set in Monotype Times

Contents

Introduction

Almost everything Greek is controversial; the country, the politics, the economy, and naturally the cooking and wines.

The main controversy over Greek cooking is whether it is really Greek or of Turkish origin. For me to discuss this question is extremely difficult. I have written on both Greek and Turkish cooking. I enjoy both cuisines; I have both Greek and Turkish friends. When the subject is broached, and it often is in the two countries, then I try desperately to follow the non-alignment policy of Mr. Nehru.

The Greeks base their claims to their own cooking on an older civilization. They say that when they were inventing exquisite sauces the Turks were nomads grilling bits of meat on skewers and turning milk into yoghurt in gourds slung over their saddle bags. One impassioned Greek writer explained to me, 'Lucullus came to Byzantium and brought with him the cooking of the Romans – which they had earlier learnt from the Greeks. This was blended with Byzantine cooking. Then came the Turks – who knew nothing of cooking except what they could do from the saddle bag. They sent all their cooks to Balu (a town in the Turkish interior which boasts the best cooks in the country even today) and had them taught Greek dishes. They then returned to Constantinople, called this Turkish cooking and the myth has been played ever since.'

Ancient Greece was interested in food, very much so, and in their earliest writings there is frequent mention of food and cooking. There were many famous men who boasted of their culinary ability in those days. Thimbron of Athens was one; Soteriades was another – he was something of a faddist for he liked to cook different foods for different moods. There was the philosopher Archestratus, whose *Gastrology* was a culinary masterpiece. He wrote 'for immortal Greece' and stated his precepts with the zeal of a sublime legislator. He travelled widely in his search for new recipes and new luxuries to delight his table. One of the sadnesses of his life was that he could not eat the

things he liked all the year round, but he brightened up with the
thought that even so, there was nothing to prevent him talking
of all dishes all the year round. Many of his recipes, which must
surely be of the oldest in the world – he was writing around
350 B.C. – are said to be in use in Greece today.

The whole of the Western world owes much to Greek cooking.
We owe to them aristology or the art of dining. To the Greeks
belongs the honour of producing the sages of the kitchen:
Orion who invented white sauce; Lampriadas who discovered
brown sauce; Nereuse of Corinth who turned the conger eel
into a dish 'fit for the gods'; Agres of Rhodes who first thought
of filleting fish; Atlantus who invented the perfect restorative,
and finally there was Euthymus who is said to have created the
most exquisite vegetable dishes. There were others – Artemidorus
who commented on and made a collection of all the words used
in the kitchens of his time. Timachidas, another Rhodean, was a
cook and poet of high renown who composed an epic poem
on his art. Dionysius wrote of cooking and what constituted the
perfect cook in no uncertain terms:

> To roast some beef, to carve a joint with neatness,
> To boil up sauces, and to blow the fire,
> Is anybody's task; he who does this
> Is but a seasoner and broth-maker.
> A cook is quite another thing. His mind
> Must comprehend all facts and circumstances;
> Where is the place, and what the time of supper;
> Who are the guests, and who the entertainer;
> What fish he ought to buy, and where to buy it.

And so on.

And roughly a century later Atheneus, writing his *Banquet
of the Learned*, had a great deal to say on gastronomy, quoting
such dicta as:

> Know then the cook, a dinner that's bespoke
> Aspiring to prepare, with prescient zeal,
> Should know the tastes and humours of the guests

And:

> *All books of cookery, all helps of art,*
> *All critic learning, all commenting notes*
> *Are vain, if void of genius, thou wouldst cook.*

He also quotes Ana, the philosopher, who said, 'The master cook makes the nostril feel each scent distinct.'

Finally the chef's cap is said to be of Greek origin, being a white version of the Greek monk's hat. During days of persecution many famous cooks (who were also philosophers) sought refuge in the monasteries. These had a tradition of good food and wines. The cooks in their sanctuary carried on their proud art but felt that they were men above the ordinary monk, men apart, and asked permission to wear a white cap instead of the conventional black. They were given this distinction and, as all the world recognizes, the chef is known by his tall white cap.

The Greek Empire was finally eclipsed by the Roman – but even then the Greeks had their triumphs, for they took their culture and their culinary arts to Rome. One reads of peacock from Samos, crabs from Chios, Iberian chestnuts, cranes from Melos and Phrygian turkey. And yet, although the Romans inherited all the luxury of Greece, they never erected, as the Greeks did, a temple to Addephagia, the Goddess of Good Cheer.

This is the Greek case – and only part of it.

Today there is a great similarity between the food of the Greeks and the Turks – it is hard to distinguish it. The Greeks are, perhaps, tending to look more to the West these days and they use wine in their dishes, which the Turks as Moslems should not do. The grilled dishes are probably of Turkish origin, but what has actually happened is that the peoples of this region have become so intermingled as the results of succeeding conquests over the centuries that it is difficult to sort out the various national dishes. Oddly enough most Greeks are willing to concede that the Greek sweets are really Turkish – but since honey was such an important ingredient in Greek cooking, and one must not forget that it was the Greeks again who invented pastry (although the French perfected this art), I am inclined to think that they are of Greek origin.

But this is enough. Counsel, I feel, should rest at this stage of the argument.

I would not be honest if I did not admit that there are two distinct schools of thought regarding Greek food. For and against. There are no half measures. I belong, quite naturally, to the 'for' school of thought, but do realize that the 'against' have their points.

Greek food is apt to be served lukewarm and with too much oil for our taste. Many non-Greeks do not like olive oil but as it is an essential part of all Mediterranean cooking – there it is. I have lived long enough in olive oil producing countries to like it very much. But I do not like all my food smothered in oil. Some Greeks do. As far as this book is concerned I have given the Greek quantities and leave it for individual cooks to use as much or as little as they like.

Greek cooking is seasonal, there is not much refrigeration in the country nor is there much tinning or canning. I do not mean that you will not see tinned foods in the Greek delicatessen shops which, by the way, are so filled with food they always appear as if they will burst at the sides. But Greek housewives rely mainly on the fruit, vegetables, meat and fish of the season and look forward to the grapes, the strawberries and artichokes, not anticipating them in tins.

Greek meals are not as ours. They are less formal. Breakfast consists of a coffee – often black. Lunch is fairly late and is invariably followed by a siesta, then back to work until seven or eight o'clock. Dinner is always late. Most Greek men appear to eat out at least three times a week, women less often, although they spend quite a lot of time in the patisseries, which evens things out.

But Greeks do also appear to be eating all through the day. They start on their way to the office when they stop for a fresh roll from the street corner bakery-stand; then they send out for a slice of cheese pie, or nibble away at nuts and small eats. And although I know that Greeks do work – most of my Greek friends work very hard – I always wonder, when in Greece, where all the people come from who are sitting around the coffee houses sipping coffee and denouncing the world.

Food shopping in Athens is fun and can be accomplished at any time of the day or night – well – up to very late in the evening. You can even buy flowers and have them sent to a friend well after dark. Maybe this is bad for shop assistants but it is awfully nice for the customers.

Much of the shopping for the house is done at the door. Earliest to arrive is the baker's boy who comes with the fresh sesame rolls calling *'freska koulouria'* loudly as he rushes up the stairs or through the garden gate. And the house after his visit is filled with the sweet smell of hot bread. From then on the day is one long sales campaign. The fishmonger, the baker's boy, this time with the brown bread slung haphazardly over the handle-bars of his bicycle, the greengrocer, the butcher, all there on the doorstep, their goods carried either by donkey or donkey cart. The fish comes alive, the fishmonger yelling with vigour, *'Ap ti thalassa zondana'*, which means roughly, 'All alive-o, straight from the sea', since no Greek in his senses would buy a dead fish.

There are several markets. One of my favourites is in the centre of Athens where the stalls are piled high with the produce of the countryside brought from just outside the town. Tomatoes, 'as sweet as honey', ladies' fingers, aubergines, large and purple and highly polished, are displayed side by side with white cauliflowers. Small marrows, onions and sweet peppers in all their brilliant colours; black and red cherries, lemons, melons and grapes, grapes and more grapes. Further along there is the meat market with huge dripping carcasses of sheep and lamb, goat and kid – all very young. Greeks prefer always to see what they are buying and, where there is a cold storage, the notice telling the customers what they have in stock is very large. There are game birds in plenty, and round the corner is the fish market. In front of the entrance sit little old women selling lemons – for everyone knows that if you buy fish you must buy lemons. And naturally there are huge vats of black and green olives in brine. every type of dried bean, rice and other dry goods. And always a small boy in attendance to carry your goods home.

Spices and herbs are both important to Greek cooking. Dill has been used for centuries, and it is recorded that the ancient Greeks would chew dill seeds during the interminable speeches of senators, or throughout long plays to keep themselves awake. These same ancient Greeks felt that herbs improved one's brain power and, therefore, put them in almost all their dishes.

Hippocrates, 'Father of Medicine', used over four hundred different herbs in his cures and, of these, two hundred are still in use today. Tansy was one – the name comes from the Greek word *athansy* which means immortality; while thyme is the symbol of courage. It was thought that chervil, a herb with something of the flavour of caraway, was the cure for hiccups, and parsley was supposed to absorb the fumes of wine and delay intoxication. For this reason the Greeks used to garland their foreheads with wreaths of fresh parsley before embarking on a long drinking bout. Another aid against intoxication was to make wine punches in a bowl made from amethyst – why? I do not know – but the Greek word for intoxication is *methi*.

Much of the best Greek food today is found in the *tavernas* and much of the pleasure of Greek cooking is in the atmosphere. The recipes chosen for this book are the most typical. They represent everyday cooking, of the type anyone can cook. Although at first sight you might think there is not much imagination in Greek cooking, after a while you begin to realize that the Greeks have come to terms with their essential materials and made a fine adjustment with what they have.

Getting Recipes – Acknowledgements

I have collected recipes everywhere – even in aeroplanes. But mainly I prefer to take them from housewives or cooks, in homes and in restaurants.

Some of my recipes have come from *tavernas*. Usually I would eat a dish, like it and then demand its recipe. This involved a miracle of concentration. I remember in one popular *taverna* it seemed as though all the kitchen staff and waiters were bent on making sure nothing was left out. Hands were waved in all directions and other diners must have wondered what on earth had happened.

'Butter fresh', the cook exclaimed. 'Not oil or any other fat', took up a passing waiter. They were describing the making of pastry. 'But, of course, only the best oil from Greece for frying or roasting', insisted another. At the mention of garlic, black eyebrows rose. Of course, plenty of this. Even with beef.

Careful attention was paid to the meat. I needed no translator to tell me what was happening as hands waved and pulled out imaginary sinews and nerves, cutting off odd bits of fat or lesser ends. 'Shrinkage results if all this is left in', it was explained.

And wine – 'Very important'. The whole staff forgot their work.

They almost shouted recipes at me, in that way all nationals do when confronted with a foreigner whose knowledge of their language is weak. Other diners in the restaurant were sympathetic; no one rapped impatiently on their table when their waiter stopped at my table to cry, 'and a very slow oven', before delivering his food.

Books on cooking are never written without a host of willing and interested helpers. I have been singularly fortunate in preparing this one.

I am not a solitary eater – or drinker – and my husband is probably my most willing assistant in any research into food, and, of course, drink. He is prepared to sacrifice himself, he says, to prove to any hard-drinking Greek villager that he can drink for three – and still walk home. He will eat for three as well. So *tavernas* owners look upon us with affection.

Then there are always those people who have lived in countries which we visit and who are willing to give of their longer experience. Such people as John Hare, chief of the British Information Services in Athens, who speaks Greek, knows his Greeks and the country – and where to eat. He almost shut up shop to help me, and got his staff interested too.

There was Harold Byatt, the Press officer, who spent evening after evening taking me to *tavernas*, explaining the ins and outs of them all. And, since he speaks Greek as a Greek, he was able to tell me what was happening all around me, making rapid translations of the many conversations we could listen-in to.

Also in the same office is Mrs M. Brooks-Tsatsopoulou who translated and typed recipes from her mother-in-law's favourite cook book and gave me her own housekeeping experiences. There was Miss C. Politis who also gave me recipes, which were, she declared, special to her family.

Then there were those, like Shan Sedgewick, who took me to such spots as a 'place near Athens' and Robert Liddell, who gave me lots of general advice although, Hellenophil that he is, he is not a lover of the Greek way of eating.

There were so many. Behind it all there was my own ex-

perience with two Greek cooks, Ketty and Valentini, both
now dead but both superb cooks.

Finally there was Penelope Papadakis who so patiently and
with such interest went through the manuscript correcting errors
and making valuable suggestions. And Rosemary White who
gave a final reading to the manuscript. Both did this in New
Delhi while waiting for their daughters to be born.

New Delhi, *November* 1958

Notes

These few notes will help in producing authentic Greek dishes.

Greek cooking is not difficult, neither is it expensive. An added advantage is that much of it is cooked and served in the same casserole. With modern kitchenware this can be done in Britain today without spoiling the table's appearance. For me, Greek cooking also has the advantage that there is much elasticity in the time allowed for cooking most of the dishes. For this reason I have so often written 'about one hour'. It is difficult to be absolutely accurate when there are so many different kinds of cooking stoves. Greek cooking apparatus is not very modern – except in some homes – and ovens are a rarity. 'Little maids', housewives or responsible children trot off in the morning to take the roasts to the baker. When I write *slow* or *cool*, *hot* or *medium*, that is just what I mean. To the average Greek cook 350° means nothing. I also suggest that it is better to read a recipe right through and have all the ingredients ready before starting to cook.

Olive oil varies and all countries producing it insist theirs is the best. It is a matter of local taste. If the olives are of good quality – and Greek olives are considered to be among the world's best – and if they are carefully harvested, collected, stored and properly refined, then the olive oil will be good. However, those who find olive oil too heavy or of too pronounced a flavour, should try peanut oil, much favoured by the Chinese, which has little or no flavour. But, and this is a large but, when cooking dishes which are to be eaten cold and require oil, olive oil is the best, since it does not congeal.

Without the lemon, Greek cooking would undoubtedly collapse, for it is a basic ingredient and is used from the soup to the pudding. Vegetables are soaked or sprinkled with lemon juice, fish is rubbed with it to remove the fishy flavour, meat receives the lemon treatment to bring out its flavour, and lemon is added to sugar-syrup to prevent crystallization. So when cooking Greek dishes, a fair supply of lemons is absolutely essential. Lemon juice should be strained before using.

Like other Mediterranean people, the Greeks adore tomatoes for which they have some basic rules. A small piece of cinnamon is often added to a dish which has plenty of tomatoes. Equally, when tomatoes are used the lemon is ousted. Spinach and tomatoes are not used together. Tomatoes should be peeled for all dishes except for stuffing. It is quite simple to take off the skin. Simply steep the tomatoes in boiling water for about one minute, then take them out and peel them as soon as they can be handled.

Onions and garlic find favour in the Greek kitchen, the first are said to 'cut' the olive oil. When spring onions are called for in a recipe, use as much as possible of the green stalks. This rule also applies to celery, the leaves have an excellent flavour.

Chestnuts are extremely popular with the Greeks in the islands and some of the mainland districts; they are interchangeable with potatoes.

If you see 'tis-Oras' on a menu it means à la minute or 'on-the-spot' cooking.

I have anglicized measurements to make it simpler for British readers. Generally they are given in pounds and ounces, mainly because this is the way I cook. I do use scales, although only when in doubt, since my eye is pretty well used to weights and quantities generally. I use spoons of all kinds in my kitchen and find them often more useful than scales. There are some occasions when I measure in cups; then I use either a regular kitchen measuring cup or an average teacup. All measurements naturally are meant to be taken seriously but this does not mean that one cannot play around with them. The expression 'to taste' is important in all cooking.

The Greeks measure in *oke* and *dram*, and one *oke* is 2⅘ lb.

Appetizers

MEZETHAKIA OR OREKTIKA

The word *mezethakia* is applied to food which is suitable for eating with wine or spirits, and which 'opens the appetite'. While this is more or less equivalent to *hors-d'oeuvre* it is so with a well-seasoned and varied difference. *Mezethakia*, or *mezes*, are eaten at leisure to the accompaniment of ouzo or other drinks before a meal, or with wine during a wine-drinking session. In a restaurant you expect – and get – a continual replenishment to the many rapidly diminishing plates or saucers of food. No Greek would think of drinking without eating.

There are some standard *mezethakia* such as olives, nuts and *feta* cheese, otherwise what you eat depends on the season, the place, the time and the imagination of the cook. Along the seashore, where tables are placed on the sand and the waves gently lap at one's feet, every conceivable variety of fish is served. Sometimes the fish comes out of a large refrigerator belonging to the *taverna* across the road, whose proprietor charges for his fish not by the portion but by the weight. A long session means endless scraps of paper with your final bill. As you nibble at a dish of fried smelts, or pick the bones of some grilled mullet, fish hawkers will come up to your table and offer freshly-gathered sea urchins, clams or cockles. There will always be brown, coarse bread, soft and crumbly bread called *karveli*, very delicious and with the real flavour of bread.

Eating *mezethakia* often consumes an hour or two before dinner, for Greeks eat late, very late, as eating to them is a social occasion. Not for them a quick dinner before the theatre; no, the theatre first, then a long meal in a favourite *taverna* together with a discussion on the play, politics and the affairs of the day. Greeks are never at a loss for conversation. Eating around midnight on a hot summer night is no exception in Athens, so *mezethakia* helps to keep the hunger pangs at bay as well as to provide practical blotting-paper for the drinkers.

Olives

The fruit of the venerable olive tree has always been regarded
by the Greeks as the most valuable and most nourishing of all
foods. Without the olive there would be no Greek cooking. If
a Greek is hungry and the cupboard is bare just give him a
chunk of coarse, brown bread and a dish of olives and he will
thank you and be happy.

The history of the olive is older than the history of Athens
and as old as the mythological history of Greece. The Greek
Goddess, Athene, after whom the city of Athens is named,
owned the olive tree and when she and Poseidon fought for
supremacy over the people of Athens, the gods decided in favour
of Athene because she caused the olive tree to be born and was,
therefore, more important to mankind than poor Poseidon who
had opened up a salt spring with his trident in the rock on which
is the Acropolis. In gratitude Athene was elected the Goddess of
the City of Athens.

The olive symbolizes peace and with the leafy branches of the
olive victory is crowned. From the olive wood the arrows of
Herakles were made, the sceptres of kings and the crooks of
shepherds.

However, despite this charming story I sometimes wonder
who first decided that olives would make good food, for the
olive when it comes from the tree is bitter and horrible. And
yet, from time immemorable, olives have been put into brine
and today the typical Greek olive is always in a tub of brine.
And there are so many olives and so many trees. Sometimes,
driving through the Greek countryside, it seems to be one vast
olive grove; mile upon mile of muted olive green; mile upon
mile of distorted trunks and branches which look like strange
figures from another world; almost a world of Walt Disney.
Travel through the areas where the olive trees grow in the early
evening or through the mists of the early morning, and you will
see what I mean. Some of these trees are so old, I feel they were
part of Athene's first planting.

But if the countryside seems to be devoted to the olive, so
do the streets, for at times they are lined with barrels of olives
in brine, of all sizes and both black and green. Some of the Greek
olives are large as walnuts, and the monks, I am told, stuff
them with caviare. Lucky monks. And the best olives are those

which fall to the ground of their own ripeness, say the Greek connoisseurs.

One of the most enjoyable times in the country is the olive harvest which ends in singing and dancing, feasting and merry-making. And if the harvest is especially good, spirits rise high, for much of Greece's economy depends on the olive.

Nuts

Among these you will find blanched almonds, walnuts, pistachio nuts, peanuts and pine-nuts. Sometimes some honey is poured into a saucer and then heavily garnished with blanched almonds or walnuts – this is considered an excellent accompaniment to wine.

Almonds, incidentally, grow plentifully in Greece and are used in many ways. They are a symbol of happiness and at weddings sugar-coated almonds are offered on silver trays to the guests. Unmarried girls always scramble for them – as we do for the wedding bouquet – and when they are placed under the pillow at night the sleeper must dream of the man she will marry.

Seeds

Usually bought from the *passa tempo* man, and include dried water melon and sunflower seeds. The *passa tempo* man is the nut vendor who rumbles along with a Heath Robinson contraption which looks like a baby carriage. It is fitted with a tray, divided into sections and covered with glass. Inside the sections are the *passa tempo*, or roasted nuts and seeds, which one eats to pass away the time. At one end of the 'carriage' is a charcoal fire with a chimney, the kind of chimney that would delight Emmett.

Chickpeas

These and other smaller peas are roasted and salted.

Fruit

It is not unusual to be served an orange or an apple, usually small, or even dried and peppered figs which are brought in from Corfu. The ripe figs are dried until dark brown, then peppered and encased in bayleaves. Extremely good. From the small island of Poros, not far from Piraeus, come pickled lemons, green and bitter-sweet. And, of course, bowls of grapes.

Fish

A good variety is available at most times of the year. Octopus, dried and grilled or cooked in a wine sauce, will be served. Also grilled mullet, mussels plain or stuffed, clams, cockles, sea urchins and smoked fish, rather salty but excellent for nibbling. There is *lakertha*, usually made either from swordfish or palamid which is a type of pickled fish, or, perhaps better explained, a little like smoked salmon. There are delicious lobster balls, simply pounded lobster meat blended with egg yolk and rolled in ground ginger and fried until brown. Crabs, prawns and shrimps are often served with a mayonnaise sauce. Anchovies reach the table either in long strips or sometimes beaten to a *purée*. As well come fresh sardines and smelts fried crisply like a biscuit and, of course, *taramo salata*, or fish roe salad, as well as dried red caviare, cut into thin slices. Recipes for these, and further descriptions, will be found in the fish section. *Tarama salata* is in the salad section. Snails are not popular but from time to time one comes across them prepared as *mezethakia*. Prickly sea urchins, whose succulent orange-coloured mouthful seems hardly worth the trouble of picking out, prove worth the bother. Squids and cuttle fish covered in their inky brine are quite delicious when properly cooked.

Meat

Meat is usually served in the form of *kebabs* or rissoles. As well come bits of liver, even chicken livers, grilled or fried. Often there will be chunks of grilled lamb, or cold cuts of meat in aspic or brawn.

Salads

These are rather different from our own salads and recipes for them are in the appropriate section. For *mezethakia*, aubergine *purée* is almost always served, so is white bean *purée* (both called salads), sliced tomato salad and taramo salad. Beetroot salad with *skorthalia* is another popular dish. Slices of potato with olive oil constitute a Greek salad, so do whole beans in oil and chopped green peppers, all of which appear in due season on the *mezethakia* list. And I must not forget white cabbage salad, well mixed with olive oil, and pickled cucumbers. Last but not least there is yoghurt and cucumber salad, called *tzatziki* (see salads).

Cheese
All varieties of Greek cheeses are served as *mezethakia* and particularly good are fried squares of *feta* cheese, called *saganaki*. A friend of mine thought he was eating turbot. See cheese section.

Bourekia
These are *phyllo* pastry snacks filled with various mixtures such as cottage cheese, spinach and minced meat. *Bourekia* are sometimes cigarette-shaped, or like tiny envelopes, and almost invariably fried. Extremely good.

Dolmathes
These are stuffed vegetables and are served both hot and cold and more particularly in their season. Vine-leaf *dolmathes* are immensely popular. Depending on how long you are going to drink you will also get (if the drinking is substantial) pepper and aubergine *dolmathes*, although these usually constitute part of the main meal, which, in a *taverna*, is bitty in any case and usually shared by all around the table. However, this pleasant custom of sharing makes for variety and obviates the feeling one so often has that whatever favourite dish one has chosen, the other man's choice always looks much tastier when it arrives. See vegetable section.

Pastourmá
I have eaten this from time to time in Greece but not as often as in Turkey. It is a black, smoked bacon, highly flavoured with garlic and considered by Greek gourmets the bacon of the connoisseur. Generally it is fried until very crisp and sometimes served with eggs.

Brain Salad
This is equally popular in many parts of the Balkans and is usually served cold, doused in olive oil. I try to prevent the dousing if possible for, although I like olive oil in limited quan-

tities in salads, I find brains rich enough without any addition.
But lemon squeezed over is excellent.

Sausages
There is a fairly good array of these, especially of the garlic-
flavoured variety, including *kokoretsi*. They are eaten hot or
cold according to their type.

Vegetables
Radishes, both red and white, are served, also raw and tender
turnips. The latter are served whole but thinly peeled.

A rather special kind of *mezethakia* is *peinirli* but a couple of
these would certainly constitute a meal. They are pieces of yeast
dough, usually pulled into boat-shapes and baked, then packed
with a variety of fillings. Some have eggs and ham, others thick
chunks of *feta* cheese, or simply fried eggs, slices of sausage,
etc. *Peinirlis* are a speciality of one or two *tavernas* on the way
to Phaleron and it is worth asking one's Greek friends to give
exact details.

Others of the larger snacks or appetizers are Cretan cheese
cakes, made of pastry with a filling of fresh cottage cheese
mixed with beaten eggs and honey, like *melopita* (see page 177).
Awfully good when hot and well made and can be bought
throughout the country at road stops and railway stations.

Soups

SOUPA

FISH SOUP
WITH EGG AND LEMON SAUCE
PSAROSOUPA ME AVGOLEMONO

2 *lb white fish*	3 *carrots*
2 *large onions*	*Salt and pepper*
3 *quarts water*	*Egg and lemon sauce*
½ *cup olive oil*	(see page 152)
4 *stalks celery with leaves*	*Juice ½ lemon*

Clean and then cut the fish into pieces, not too small, and each piece more or less the same size. Rub with salt and lemon. Clean the vegetables and cut these into rather chunky pieces but even so not too large. Put the water into a pan and bring it smartly to the boil, then add the oil, stir this well and, when it is blended, add the vegetables; reduce the heat and cook steadily for 40 minutes. Reduce the heat to simmering, add the pieces of fish and cook carefully for 20 minutes. The fish should not break, so cooking must be really slow.

When the fish is tender, take it from the pan, put it aside but keep it hot. Strain the stock and vegetables through a sieve and return to the pan. Re-heat the strained fish stock, add the egg and lemon sauce, stir it well into the soup (not allowing this to boil) and then pour the soup over the fish. Whether you do this in a soup tureen (seldom done, these days, in Britain) or directly into soup plates, depends entirely on the cook.

Some Greek cooks add rice to this type of soup which makes, of course, a more substantial dish. To the above quantity of soup add 3 ounces of long grain rice, after the fish has been removed and the soup strained. Cook it only just long enough to make the rice tender, then add the sauce and continue as above.

FISH SOUP
PSAROSOUPA

A very typical Greek fish soup which provides two courses for
the same meal, fish soup followed by fish.

3 *lb mixed fish*	3–4 *carrots*
4 *pints water*	4 *onions*
12 *potatoes*	*Salt and pepper*
Handful finely chopped parsley	2–3 *oz olive oil*
2–3 *chopped stalks celery*	

Wash and peel the onions and score them but leave them
whole. Coarsely chop the carrots, leave the potatoes whole –
unless they are very large, when you can cut them into halves.
Put these into a large saucepan with the water, olive oil, salt and
pepper. Cook until the vegetables are tender, add the fish and
cook gently for about 10 or 15 minutes, according to the size
of the fish. When the fish is tender, take from the pan, arrange
on a hot platter, surround with the vegetables and put into a
warm oven to keep hot. Strain the stock and serve this as a
clear soup; or bring the stock once more to the boil and add
2 or 3 tablespoonfuls of rice. Also an egg and lemon sauce (see
page 152) may be added.

SOUP MADE FROM SMALL FISH
SOUPA HANOI AVGOLEMONO

Hanoi are small pink fish extremely popular with Greeks and
considered a clean fish as they live near the shore among the
rocks, unlike the red mullet which likes the off-shore mud.

3 *lb small fish*	4 *finely chopped onions*
4 *pints water*	*Egg and lemon sauce*
Handful chopped parsley	(see page 152)
1–2 *stalks chopped celery*	
3 *chopped carrots*	*Lemon juice*
4 *oz olive oil*	*Salt and pepper*

Remove the heads and tails of the hanoi, clean and rub each
fish with salt and lemon juice. Heat the oil, fry the onions and

the parsley, add salt, pepper, the vegetables and water (plus,
if you like, the fish heads to help the flavour) and cook over a
medium heat for 30 minutes. Rub the stock through a sieve,
return it to the pan, add the fish and cook these until tender –
about 10 minutes. Take the fish from the pan with a perforated
spoon, put into a soup tureen or directly into plates, but keep
hot. Strain the stock, bring it to the boil, stir in the egg and
lemon sauce, leave for a minute or so, then pour it over the
fish. Serve at once.

This recipe appears at first glance to be more troublesome
than it really is. It is the second straining which gives a false
impression. Adding some white wine to the stock adds much
to the flavour but it is by no means essential.

GREEK BOUILLABAISSE
KACCAVIA

According to the Greeks, they are the originators of bouilla-
baisse which, they say, is a relic of an ancient fish soup called
kaccavia or *kakavia* and was introduced by the Greeks to the
Marseilla Phocaem Colonies. The name is derived in Greek
from the type of earthenware pot, *kaccavia*, in which the fishermen used to cook their fish and which was placed in the middle
of their fishing boats, around which they would sit and help
themselves. The name was translated into the French bouilla-
baisse from *bouillote*, or pot.

There are several ways to make this soup or stew, some
simple and others elegant. Here is one of the elegant methods.

3 lb mixed fish	4 pints water
2 each of sliced onions, potatoes and carrots	1 bayleaf
	½ cup olive oil
1 chopped celery stalk	Peppercorns and salt
1–2 chopped cloves garlic	Juice 1 small lemon
4 chopped tomatoes	3 tablespoons chopped parsley
1 wineglass dry white wine	Croûtons

Clean and trim the fish and rub it well with salt and lemon.
(You can make 4 pints of fish stock with the trimmings and
use this instead of water). Heat the oil in a large saucepan and

simmer the celery, potatoes, onions, carrots and garlic for about 5 minutes. Add water (or stock), bayleaf, peppercorns (about 3), tomatoes and wine and continue cooking for ½ hour. Strain this mixture and return the liquid to the pan, adding a little more hot water if required. Add salt, parsley and fish – the larger, firmer fish first, and cook this for 5 minutes before adding the smaller fish which may be left whole. Bring once to the boil, then continue cooking until all the fish is tender. Put a tablespoonful of *croûtons* into each soup plate, add the fish and soup, or serve the fish and soup separately, the *croûtons*, of course, with the soup.

Serves 4–5.

A more simple *kaccavia* is prepared by the fishermen in the islands as they haul in their fish along the shore. First they put the small fish into the pot with water to cover, then add olive oil, chopped onions, tomatoes – if available – salt and pepper. When everything is quite soft it is rubbed through a sieve and returned as a thick stock to the pan. Into this they put all kinds of fish, including small lobsters, shrimps – in fact any fish available – then plenty of water and cook over a wood fire until all the fish is tender.

Not all of these fishermen cooks rub the fish through a sieve, some simply put plenty of chopped onions, tomatoes, seasoning, olive oil and water into a pot and bring it quickly to the boil, then add whatever fish they have to hand, putting the tougher fish into the pot first. Then they cook until all the fish is tender. Very good and very simple.

Croûtons are small squares of bread fried until crisp in very hot fat, preferably butter.

BEAN SOUP
FASOLADA

1 *lb dried beans*	2 *large, chopped carrots*
3 *quarts water*	*Handful chopped parsley*
Chopped celery to taste	½ *cup olive oil*
2 *tablespoons tomato purée*	*Salt and pepper to taste*
2 *large onions*	

Soak the beans overnight, then rinse them thoroughly in a colander under running water. Put them into a pan with the 3 quarts of water and bring to the boil. Throw away this water, add the same quantity again, bring once more to the boil, reduce the heat, add the remaining ingredients and continue to cook slowly until the beans are very soft.

Some Greek cooks prefer to rub the soup through a sieve, others are emphatic that this is not necessary. The beans, they insist, should be soft but whole.

Fasolada is the national dish of Greece – it is also considered to be a poor man's dish since beans are very cheap. In the homes of the lesser income groups it is served as often as three times a week.

BEEF AND PASTA SOUP
SOUPA PASTA

Beef stock
Celery and leaves
Chopped parsley } to taste
Salt and pepper

1 cup soup pasta (such as tiny stars, alphabet or other shapes)

Bring as much stock as required to the boil, remove any surplus grease or scum, add the remaining ingredients, except the pasta, and cook slowly until the stock is well-flavoured. Strain, bring again to the boil and add the pasta. Continue cooking until tender, about 10 minutes.

Pasta is a variety of macaroni.

CABBAGE SOUP
SOUPA LAHANA

2 lb finely shredded cabbage
4 pints water
Olive oil for frying
1 lb peeled and chopped tomatoes
1 tablespoon chopped parsley

1 large, finely chopped onion
Croûtons
Salt and pepper to taste
Butter for frying

First make the croûtons. Cut some stale bread into small cubes and fry these in hot butter until brown and crisp. Remove at

once, drain and put aside until required. About 1 tablespoonful
per plate is enough.

Lightly fry the onion in a little oil, add the water, bring this
to the boil, then add the cabbage, tomatoes, salt and pepper.
Bring again to the boil, lower the heat and cook slowly until the
cabbage is tender. Just before serving sprinkle with parsley and
add the *croûtons*.

Finely chopped fresh aniseed can be added to this thick and
nourishing winter soup. Crisp white cabbage is the best for
soup making but other types of cabbage can be used.

EASTER SOUP
MAYIERITSA

The Greek Orthodox Church imposes severe Lenten fasting
upon its communicants, forbidding all animal products, including eggs, butter and cheese. Nowadays fewer Greeks fast
for the whole thirty days but even the most sophisticated fast
during Holy Week. By the time Holy Week arrives there is a
feeling of tension in the air, for the Greeks, intensely emotional,
seem almost to re-live the tragic anniversary of the happenings
in Jerusalem nearly 2,000 years ago. Good Friday is a real day
of mourning and even Athens, probably the noisiest city in the
world, is quiet. Then, almost miraculously, in the evening of
Holy Saturday the city re-awakens to celebrate with bands and
flags, with feasting and ceremony, the '*Proti Anastasis*' (The
Resurrection) at midnight. Everyone, literally everyone, goes
to the churches and cathedrals in villages and towns throughout
the Greek archipelago to hear their priests and archbishops
pronounce in ringing, dramatic tones, '*Christos Anesti*', (Christ
is risen). Everyone takes up the cry '*Christos Anesti*' and breaks
a scarlet egg, which is carried in their pockets or handbags,
bells clang, fireworks explode and rockets soar through the sky,
even factory sirens wail, to announce the glad tidings. Athens'
famed Constitution Square and the Acropolis are floodlit and
thousands of people throng the streets laughing and wishing
all and sundry '*Kalo Pascha*' (Happy Easter). Finally they
slowly wend their ways home, everyone carrying a white candle,
to crack more traditional scarlet-dyed eggs and to eat their

Easter Soup. This is made from the feet, entrails and other odd
bits of the lamb which is to be roasted and eaten on Easter
Sunday.

Here are two recipes to make Easter Soup.

No. 1

The tripe, intestines, heart,	4 oz rice
feet and liver of a lamb	*Juice 2 lemons*
2 oz clarified butter	1 teaspoon flour
Handful finely chopped dill	Salt to taste
Handful finely chopped parsley	Egg and lemon sauce
6 spring onions	(see page 152)

Thoroughly clean all the meat, cut the tripe into 4 or 5 pieces
and turn the intestines inside out. Scald the feet and the tripe,
change the water (you need about 8 pints) and bring this to the
boil; add salt and flour mixed with a little water to a paste.
Cook gently for about 40 minutes.

Meanwhile soak for 30 minutes the remaining intestines,
heart etc, in cold, lemon-flavoured water. Drain and add to the
feet and tripe. Continue cooking. In another pan heat the
butter and fry the herbs and onions until the fat disappears,
then stir this mixture into the soup. Continue to cook, until the
meat is quite tender, strain the soup through a sieve, return it
to the pan and bring once more to the boil. Add the rice, cook
until tender, stir in the egg and lemon sauce, bring once more
slowly to the boil, put aside for 5 minutes, then serve very hot.

No. 2. A somewhat simpler version.

Into a large saucepan with plenty of water put about a pound
of lamb bones with meat attached, a lamb's heart and ½ lb of
lamb's intestines tied in a bundle. Cook slowly until you have a
good stock. Remove the bones, intestines and heart. Strip off
the meat from the bones, slice the heart and return both to the
pan. Add ½ lb of chopped lamb's liver, some chopped spring
onions, plenty of salt, pepper, a little chopped celery, chopped
parsley, dill to flavour and lastly 2 or 3 oz of rice. Cook fairly
rapidly until the rice is soft. Remove the pan from the heat, add
egg and lemon sauce, stir for a few minutes over a low heat,
cover and put aside for 5 minutes before serving.

Both recipes are sufficient for 6 or 8 people.

EGG AND LEMON SOUP
SOUPA AVGOLEMONO

4 *pints strained chicken stock*   *Salt*
3 *oz rice*   *Juice* 1 *large lemon*
3 *eggs*

Bring the stock to the boil, add salt if required. Throw in the
rice and cook this until tender, about 15 minutes.

Whilst the soup is cooking prepare an egg and lemon sauce.
Beat the eggs well, then gradually beat in the lemon juice and,
very slowly, 2 cups of hot broth. Just before serving the soup
add the sauce, stirring all the while. Simmer until the soup is
again hot, cover and let it stand for 5 minutes on the side of the
stove.

This soup has become probably one of the best known of the
Greek soups and is a favourite throughout the Balkans. I have
given the full directions for making the egg and lemon sauce
in this recipe because it is so much part of it.

TRIPE SOUP
PATSA

2-3 *lb tripe*   *Salt and pepper to taste*
2-3 *cloves pounded garlic*   *Egg and lemon sauce*
Rind ½ *lemon*   (see page 152)

Cut open the tripe and wash it thoroughly, scraping the inside
until perfectly clean. Put it into a saucepan, cover with cold
water, add salt and bring slowly to boiling point. Pour away
the water. Cut the tripe into small pieces and with 6 pints of
water, the lemon rind, salt and pepper bring once to the boil,
then simmer until tender, about 2 hours. Skim off the fat.
Take out the tripe and cut it into even smaller pieces, return
these to the stock (which is better if passed swiftly through a
strainer) and bring this once more to the boil. Reduce the heat
and simmer it gently. You may have to add more water or boiling
broth, it depends on how many people are to eat the soup.

Just before serving add the egg and lemon sauce in the usual
way.

Any kind of tripe can be used for this soup, and scraps of

celery, onions and other vegetables are often cooked with it to give additional flavour and strength – or what my mother used to call 'body'.

LENTIL SOUP
FAKASOUPA

1 *lb yellow lentils*
Chopped celery, carrots and
   onion to taste
1–2 *finely chopped cloves garlic*

1 *bayleaf or pinch marjoram*
Salt and pepper to taste
Vinegar

Clean the lentils and cook them for about 1 hour. Strain and return them to the pan with the remaining ingredients, except the vinegar, and at least 3 quarts of fresh water. Bring this to the boil, then simmer until all the vegetables are very soft. Just before serving add a coffee cupful of vinegar and stir this well into the soup. Continue to cook for another 5 minutes.

A bacon bone or some rinds added to the soup (removed, of course, before serving) greatly improves the flavour.

SWEET CORN SOUP
SOUPA APO ARAVOSITO

This is a popular village soup from the island of Crete made from dried sweet corn. The corn is pounded and mixed with dried milk and kept during the winter. When required it is mixed with water and cooked. Its consistency is a matter for each cook to decide.

TOMATO SOUP
DOMATO SOUPA

Generally speaking, in Greece tomato soup is made from the juice of fresh tomatoes, but when these are not in season, from tomato paste. The tomato juice or paste is boiled with water, olive oil is added – to approximately 2 pints of water a $\frac{1}{4}$ cup of olive oil – and plenty of salt and pepper. When the soup has

been boiling for a few minutes 2 tablespoonfuls of rice or noodles
per person is added. Naturally stock may be used instead of
water. The quantity of paste or tomato juice used depends on
individuals, but to 2 pints of water at least 1 good tablespoonful
of paste should be added, or about ½ pint of fresh tomato juice
or even double the quantities.

A tin of tomato soup can be much improved by using it in
this way.

PASTA SOUP
TRAHANA SOUPA

Trahana is not exactly pasta but this is probably the nearest
translation of the word. This soup looks to the average Englishman rather like a dish of porridge and is a speciality of the village
cooks of Asia Minor. The favourite time to prepare *trahana* is
in August when the goat's milk is at its best and the wheat
has been brought in. The *trahana* dough is made by the peasants
from goat's milk and wheat and is thick enough to break off
into small pieces which are then rounded and shaped into balls,
about the size of a hazel nut. These are then dried and rubbed
between the hands until the dough is like a fine oatmeal. This is
dropped into boiling broth, preferably chicken, and slowly
cooked. Sometimes egg and lemon sauce (see page 152) is added.
Those who cannot afford a chicken make their soup simply from
trahana and water.

Both peasants and fisherman like to take a bowl of *trahana*
soup before starting off on their day's work. On their return
in the evening they will take another bowl but, if they can
afford it, they will add a glass or two of red wine to the pot
first.

The Cosro Restaurant in Athens offers this type of soup as
one of its specialities and from time to time so does the White
Tower Restaurant in London; otherwise *trahana* soup is only
prepared in the villages.

VERMICELLI SOUP
FIDES SOUPA

Almost any kind of stock may be used for this kind of soup and it can be either thick or thin. During Lent vermicelli soup should be made with water.

Brown 1 large, finely chopped onion in either butter or oil, then stir in enough tomato paste to flavour. Add 3 pints of stock (or water), salt and pepper. Bring to the boil then add as much vermicelli as you like. Just before the soup is served, add an egg and lemon sauce (see page 152).

A simpler method of making this soup is to boil about 3 pints of stock, add salt, pepper and tomato paste to flavour and bring to a bubbling boil. Add as much vermicelli as you like, cook this until tender and then add the egg and lemon sauce.

All varieties of macaroni may be used in this way as well. There is as much variety of pasta in Greece as there is in Italy. In fact, it is frequently claimed that the Greeks eat more pasta than the Italians and I am inclined to believe this. Stars, rounds, oblongs, lengths, all shapes of pasta are thrown into steaming bowls of broth, plus plenty of tomatoes, onions, garlic and chopped herbs. All this is finished off with the inevitable egg and lemon sauce. Very simple and very good.

Fish

PSARIA

The Greeks have always been fond of fish, it is part of their staple diet, and that there should be plenty of good fish in Greece is not surprising since the mainland is practically surrounded by water and much of the country consists of hundreds of little islands.

In days gone by the arrival of the fresh catch was heralded by the tolling of a bell in all seaport towns. The catch of those days, I think, had more variety than today's, for, with the discovery of dynamite, there has been much indiscriminate fishing in Mediterranean waters. I remember when living in Beirut I could buy imported cold storage fish from Britain far cheaper than I could the local fish, which at times was non-existent. This seemed to me ridiculous, as we had the sea at our doorsteps.

The Greeks eat varieties of shellfish such as sea urchins, sea quinces etc, but although they have oysters they seldom seem to eat them because, they say, the oyster is a dirty eater. But it should be recorded that it is to the Greeks we owe the discovery of the oyster as an edible fish. At least so legendary history tells. One day, many centuries ago, a young Athenian boy was wandering along the beach in search of shells. Suddenly he espied an oyster in the act of yawning. Curious, he picked up the half-open shellfish and put his finger inside the shell. The indignant oyster at once snapped the shell together causing the boy to give a sharp cry of pain and quickly withdraw the injured finger which he at once popped into his mouth. The flavour was delicious, so delicious that he broke open the shell, and swallowed the unfortunate oyster. And, we must suppose, he rushed home to tell his family of his great discovery. Since that fatal day the oyster has been a much harassed shellfish.

The favourite Greek way of cooking fish is to grill it – otherwise

it is mixed with various types of vegetables, especially onions
and tomatoes, and either baked or slowly simmered. I think that
the British housewife would find many of these fish dishes
quite simple and they do have the advantage of usually being
served in the dish in which the fish is cooked.

RED MULLET BAKED IN PARCHMENT
BARBOUNIA STO HARTI

2 lb red mullet   *Slices of lemon*
Olive oil   *Finely chopped parsley*
Lemon juice   *Parchment cooking paper*
Marjoram or thyme to taste   *Salt and pepper*

Clean the fish and rub it with olive oil. Cut the parchment
paper into sizes to fit the fish and brush each piece with oil.
(Remember each fish is to be wrapped separately.) Beat about
4 tablespoonfuls each of the olive oil and lemon juice together,
adding salt and pepper, and one of the herbs – it does not
matter which. Put 1 fish on each piece of the paper and on top
of the fish arrange 1 or 2 slices of lemon. Spoon the oil and
lemon mixture over the fish. Fold the paper carefully so that
none of the flavour of the fish escapes while it is cooking. (The
package can be fastened with paper clips for extra security.)
Place the packages in a baking pan, brush them with oil and
bake in a moderate oven until the fish is tender – about 25 or
30 minutes.
    Larger fish can also be cooked in this manner – allow 15
minutes for each pound of fish.

GRILLED MULLET
BARBOUNIA STI SHARA

Thoroughly clean and wash as many mullet as required. Put
them into a colander, sprinkle with salt and pepper and leave
for 15 minutes. Put half a lemon on the end of a fork and pour
some olive oil into a saucer – this is for basting the fish. Heat
the grill, arrange the fish on a grid above or below the grill,
dip the cut face of the lemon into the olive oil and frequently

baste or rub the mullet with this to prevent the skin from bursting
or becoming dry.

Serve the mullet with a lemon and olive oil dressing.

FRIED MULLET
BARBOUNIA TIYANITA

Thoroughly clean and wash as many mullet as required. Put
them in a colander, sprinkle with salt and lemon juice and
leave for 15 minutes. Lightly coat with flour, then fry in hot
olive oil until brown on both sides.

This is almost the national fish dish of Greece.

SAVOURY MULLET
BARBOUNIA SAVORE

4 *lb red mullet*	*Olive oil for frying*
1 *pint tomato sauce*	1 *oz flour*
(see page 155)	3 *tablespoons wine vinegar or*
Garlic, bayleaves and rosemary	*white wine*

Clean the fish, keeping on the heads and tails. Heat the oil, do
not use too much, and fry the fish until brown on both sides.
Take them from the pan and put into a serving dish deep
enough to take some sauce. Pour off all but about 1 tablespoonful of the oil, re-heat the oil that is left in the pan and stir in
the flour. When this is brown, add the tomato sauce, the vinegar
or wine, finely chopped garlic (to taste), a little rosemary and
1 or 2 bayleaves. Simmer the sauce for 5 minutes, then pour
it over the fish. Serve cold.

FISH ROE RISSOLES
TARAMO KEFTETHES

At one time I met two Greek-American girls who were staying
in the same house with me in Athens and who insisted that
some Greek-American recipes should be in any book of Greek
cooking. The following recipe is one which they gave me. It
can be made with the roe of the grey mullet, or cod's roe.

6 oz fish roe   1 dessertspoon chopped parsley
2 large mashed potatoes   Salt and pepper
1 small scalded grated onion   Flour
1 dessertspoon chopped mint   Olive oil for frying

Steep the roe for 10 minutes in boiling water, then remove and
discard the membranes. Pound the roe in a mortar (or use a
modern rotary beater), add the potato, onion, parsley, mint,
salt and pepper and blend thoroughly with the roe. Shape into
rissoles, roll in flour and fry in deep boiling oil until brown
and crisp on the outside and soft inside.

Extremely popular in Greece, especially during Lent.

MAYONNAISE OF FISH, ATHENS STYLE
PSARI MAYONNAISA

This is simply boiled or steamed white fish, boned and broken
into small pieces, with all the skin removed. It is then remoulded
into its original shape, or as near to it as possible, and thickly
covered with mayonnaise. The usual garnishings are sliced gherkins, green olives and thick slices of fresh cucumber. The quality
of this dish depends entirely on the flavour of the fish and the
mayonnaise (see page 155).

Usually when Greeks boil fish they add to the water 2 or 3
onions, the same quantity of carrots, a stalk or so of celery with
the leaves, and usually 2 or more tomatoes. This stock is strained
and served as a soup, the fish follows surrounded by the vegetables. To give variety the stock is sometimes flavoured with an
egg and lemon sauce (see page 152) but if you do not care for
fish soup followed by fish, then the stock can be utilized the
following day. In any case it should not be thrown away nor
should the fish be cooked in plain salted water.

BAKED FRESH SARDINES
WITH LEMON AND MARJORAM
PSARI RIYANATO

3–4 lb fresh sardines   Marjoram
Juice 2–3 lemons   Salt
1 cup olive oil

Clean the sardines and arrange them in a fairly large baking
dish. Beat the oil and lemon juice together until well blended
and pour over the fish. Add salt and marjoram to taste and bake
in a moderate oven until tender, not more than 15 minutes.

If fresh sardines are not available, other small fish can be
cooked in the same manner but *not* tinned sardines.

FISH AS PREPARED IN THE
ISLAND OF SPETSAI
PSARI FOURNOU SPETSIOTIKO

4 *lb of any firm white fish*	1–2 *cloves chopped garlic*
1½ *cups olive oil*	*Salt and pepper to taste*
2 *tablespoons tomato purée*	*Breadcrumbs*
Handful chopped parsley	*Lemon juice*

Clean the fish, rub it well with salt and lemon juice, then arrange
it in a baking dish. Put the oil and the remaining ingredients
(except breadcrumbs) into a bowl and blend as for a sauce.

Pour most of the sauce over the fish and cover with half of
the breadcrumbs. Take the remainder of the sauce and pour
this over the breadcrumbs. Add the remaining breadcrumbs to
make a top layer (this is done to produce a thick crust). Bake
for about 1 hour in a moderate oven, basting the fish from time
to time in its own sauce. If the fish should seem too dry, add
some hot water, or, better still, white wine, but only a little
sauce should be left by the time the fish is ready.

BAKED FISH WITH TOMATOES
PSARI FOURNOU

4 *lb white fish*	*Finely chopped parsley*
3 *lb finely chopped tomatoes*	¼ *pint olive oil*

This is a simple dish. Clean the fish, arrange it in a baking dish,
add the olive oil and cover with the tomatoes. Sprinkle with
parsley and bake in a medium oven until tender.

Slices of potatoes can be added and the fish may be either
all of one kind or well and truly mixed. If you let the fish remain covered by the tomatoes for an hour or two before cooking
there is a considerable improvement in the flavour.

In Crete, where I lunched one day with the peasant caretaker
of a girls' school, I was offered an extremely pleasant but simple
dish of baked mixed fish of the cheapest kind. It had been prepared as above except that plenty of sliced onion had been added
and also small potatoes surrounded the dish. It had been cooked
in the local baker's oven, for ovens are rare in Cretan homes.

PALAMIDA COOKED WITH TOMATOES
PALAMITHA PLAKI

Plaki is an all-embracing term and means any fish which is
baked or braised with vegetables. Palamida is a large silver
fish, very fat with a rich and heavy flesh, much of which is not
quite white and often streaked with brown. It comes from
Africa to the Black Sea where it lays its eggs before returning
to Africa again. It swims the surface of the ocean and returns
to Greek waters via the Dardanelles in shoals of billions from
November to December. It is not generally considered an elegant
fish but many discerning eaters (including myself), like it very
much, especially when pickled and served as a *mezé*, as in
Istanbul. In this recipe, if palamida is not available use any
similar fish – cod, whiting or fresh haddock.

2–3 *lb fish*	3 *large sliced tomatoes*
¼ *cup olive oil*	2 *cloves garlic*
2 *finely chopped onions*	*Juice of* 1 *lemon*
2–3 *thickly sliced potatoes*	*Handful finely chopped parsley*
2–3 *chopped stalks celery*	2 *pints water*
2–3 *sliced carrots*	*Salt and black pepper*

Heat the olive oil in a shallow pan and fry the onions until they
are brown. Boil the water and slowly add this to the onions and
simmer until these are soft. Pound the garlic and add this with
the prepared vegetables to the pan. Season with salt and pepper
and cook for about 10 minutes. Clean the fish and cut it into
pieces, any size you like. Arrange these on top of the vegetables.
Add the parsley and sprinkle generously with lemon juice.
Continue to cook for about 15 minutes or until the fish is tender.
Arrange the fish in the centre of a platter and surround it with
the vegetables.

FISH BAKED WITH TOMATOES, ONIONS AND BLACK OLIVES
PSARI PLAKI TOU FOURNOU

4 *large fish – about 4 lb*   1 *sliced lemon*
1 *large sliced tomato*   1 *cup olive oil*
2 *large sliced onions*   *Salt and pepper*
12 *stoned black olives*   *Chopped parsley to taste*
1 *glass white wine*

Wash and thoroughly clean the fish, remove the heads and tails (the last is an optional operation), and rub the fish with salt, pepper and lemon. Brush a baking tin with olive oil, cover with a layer of onion and tomato then add the fish, the remaining onion and tomato, the parsley and the olives. Pour in remaining olive oil and wine and arrange remaining slices of lemon down the length of the fish. Bake in a moderate oven for about 40 minutes – longer cooking will not hurt the fish unless it becomes too dry.

BRAISED MACKEREL
SCOUBRI PLAKI

Clean and fillet 4 mackerel, then cook them in boiling water for 2 or 3 minutes. Leave until cold, then remove the bones. Do not discard the liquid.

Heat about 4 oz of olive oil and fry 4 sliced onions in this until brown. Lay half the onions at the bottom of a saucepan, add a handful of chopped parsley and the oil from the pan. On top place the filleted mackerel, cover with the remaining onions and chopped parsley to taste. Add half a cupful of white wine or wine vinegar and about a pint and a half of the liquid in which the mackerel was pre-cooked. Add salt and pepper to taste, cover and cook over a moderate heat for about 15 minutes. Quite often peeled and sliced tomatoes are added, or a tablespoonful of tomato *purée*.

BAKED FISH WITH BLACK OLIVES
PSARI PLAKI ME ELIES

2 *lb fish*	1–2 *cloves garlic*
4 *chopped tomatoes*	*Salt and pepper*
4 *finely chopped large onions*	$\frac{1}{4}$–$\frac{1}{2}$ *cup olive oil*
8 *black olives*	

If using large fish, cut it into rather thick steaks. Smaller fish, such as red mullet, can be used whole.

Clean the fish and place it in an oiled baking dish. Heat remaining oil in a frying pan, add the onions and garlic and fry until a light brown. Add tomatoes and continue cooking until these are fairly soft. Cover the fish with this mixture, add salt and pepper, about a quarter of a cup of water and cook in a medium oven for 30 minutes. Stone the olives and add these about 5 minutes before the fish is ready.

More olives may be used – up to a dozen or so – and white wine instead of water.

FISH COOKED IN PAPER
PALAMITHA STO HARTI

Chop off the head, clean and wash the fish, then rub it in salt and lemon juice. Rub a fairly large piece of parchment paper with olive oil, place the fish on this, wrap it securely, and put the package into a baking dish. Rub the paper again with olive oil, and bake the fish in a moderate oven for about 30 minutes or according to its size, remembering 10 minutes' baking to every pound of fish.

Remove the paper, or better still undo the package, slide the fish on to a plate and then fillet it. Put the fillets on to a serving platter and cover with an oil and lemon dressing. Serve hot or cold.

For palamida see page 39.

FISH BAKED IN ONION SAUCE
PSARI ME SALTSA KREMITHIA

1 *fish about 3 lb*	*Olive oil*
2 *large onions*	*Handful finely chopped parsley*
3 *large peeled and sliced*	*Salt and pepper*
tomatoes	*Capers to taste* (optional)
1 *tablespoon lemon juice*	1 *quart boiling water*

Peel the onions and cut them into thick slices. Put these into a
pan with the boiling water, salt and pepper to taste and the
lemon juice. Cook until the onion is quite tender.

Clean the fish and cut it into thick slices; remove as many
bones as possible without actually filleting it. Cook for 10
minutes with the onions. Take the fish from the pan and arrange
it in a casserole, cover with tomatoes, parsley, capers and the
olive oil. Add all the onion and enough of the onion liquid
to just cover, then bake in a moderate oven until the fish is
tender. Serve hot. Enough for 6 people, if allowing half a pound
of fish per person.

Almost any kind of white fish is suitable for this method of
cooking fish, especially cod or haddock.

BAKED FISH
(WITH ONIONS AND GARLIC)
PSARI STO FOURNO

1 *large fish*	$\frac{1}{2}$ *cup hot water*
Juice 1 lemon	2 *tablespoons finely chopped*
2 *large finely chopped onions*	*parsley*
3 *cloves pounded garlic*	*Marjoram to taste* (optional)
$\frac{1}{2}$ *cup olive oil*	*Salt and pepper*
1 *lemon sliced*	

Clean the fish and split it down the centre. Rub inside with salt,
pepper and lemon and leave for half an hour, then drain. Place
it in a baking dish and add the water. Fill the inside with parsley
and marjoram. Heat the olive oil and lightly fry the onions
and garlic until the onions begin to soften but not brown.
Pour this mixture over the fish, oil as well, arrange the slices
of lemon down the length of the fish and bake in a moderate

oven until the fish is tender, about 1 hour, but the time varies according to the size of the fish. Basting from time to time is necessary.

This recipe is unusual as Greeks generally do not stuff their fish.

BAKED FISH IN A WINE SAUCE
PSARI FOURNOU ME KRASSI

1 *large fish*	2 *cups tepid water*
Salt and pepper	2 *cups white wine*
Olive oil	2 *teaspoons mustard*

Make a slit in the fish large enough to clean it inside and out but do not remove the head and tail. Rub inside and out with salt and pepper and place it in an oiled baking pan. Add the water and the wine, and the mustard mixed with a little water or wine to a thin paste.

Bake in a moderate oven until the fish is tender, basting from time to time. If the sauce is reduced too much before the fish is cooked, add a little more wine. Allow 10 minutes' cooking for each pound of fish and if it is lean, gash the skin in 2 or 3 places to keep it from bursting.

GRILLED FISH
PSITO PSARI

Despite the Greek preference for cooking fish with olive oil and tomatoes they are also very fond of all kinds of grilled fish, particularly when grilled over charcoal. In the *tavernas* cooks are often apt to lay the fish directly on top of their huge wood-burning stoves, a method which produces a rather dried-out result. This is then gleefully counteracted by a basin-full of olive oil poured over the fish. This is not one of my favourite methods of cooking fish but I do like charcoal-grilled fish.

Clean (but leave the heads and tails on) as many fish as required and sprinkle each inside and out with lemon juice, salt and pepper. Leave for about 30 minutes – the Greek house-wife usually leaves the fish in a colander. Put one half of a lemon on the end of a fork and some olive oil into a saucer. Place the

fish on a grid over glowing charcoal and brush it from time to
time with the lemon dipped in oil. Carefully turn it when brown
and repeat the operation. Serve the fish straight from the grill.

Many Greek cooks – especially *taverna* cooks – prefer to
make a dressing from olive oil and pour this over the fish as
soon as it is grilled, then leave it for 10 minutes or more. This
means that the fish is served lukewarm, a fact which does not
disturb the Greeks one iota but which causes tremendous stir
among most foreigners. I prefer my fish either hot or cold but
I did find after a while, as I became more used to the pattern
of *taverna* life, that I did not mind lukewarm fish so much.
However, I admit it took quite a while to get me to this state of
grace.

Grilled fish is always served with small wedges of lemon.

MACKEREL
SCOUBRI

Cut off the heads and clean as many mackerel as required.
Sprinkle with plenty of salt and leave for 1 hour. Rub a gridiron well with olive oil, lay the mackerel on top of this and grill
gently over a charcoal fire. Turn to brown the other side.
When the fish are cooked right through (unless it is a large fish
they are usually cooked through when browned on both sides)
garnish with chopped parsley and sliced raw onion rings and
generously sprinkle with lemon juice. Serve hot.

FISH STEAKS
FILLETA PSARIOU

Rub the fish steaks or slices with salt. Cover a gridiron with
fresh bayleaves, and lay the fish on it. Grill over a moderate
charcoal fire. Turn with care and when browned on both sides
sprinkle with lemon juice, or serve with an almond and garlic
sauce (see page 153). The fish is done when it flakes easily with
a fork.

COD STEAKS
FILLETA BAKALIAROS

Rub the fish steaks with salt and sprinkle with flour. Rub a
gridiron with olive oil and lay the fish on top. Grill in the usual
manner, turning the fish to brown on both sides. Cover the
bottom of a platter with finely chopped parsley and sliced raw
onions and place the grilled slices of fish on top. Garnish with
wedges of lemon.

SNAPPER
TSIPOURA

This fish is considered one of the best in Greece – it resembles
snapper, has a white flesh and not too many bones. It is often
grilled, first being rubbed with oil and lemon and then very
slowly cooked on both sides.

I remember the first time I ate *tsipoura*. My hostess pointed
at the choicest portions then, from time to time, to make quite
sure I missed nothing, she would dig out bits of the flesh for
me and almost push this into my mouth – and with each piece
I ate came an oration on the especial merit of this or that minute
section of what I must agree was an excellent grilled fish.

GRILLED FISH WITH MARJORAM
PSARI ME RIYANI

Fish   *Salt and pepper*
Lemon juice   *Marjoram*
Olive oil

The fish can be either whole or in fillets. Rub well with salt and
pepper, brush with oil, sprinkle with lemon juice and marjoram
to taste. If whole, retain heads and tails but clean thoroughly.

Grill the fish by whatever means you have until it begins to
brown, baste with lemon juice, brush with oil, turn and repeat
this on the other side, and turn again once or twice, until the
fish is cooked through. If fillets are used you need only to turn

once. Serve hot, sprinkled with a little freshly chopped marjoram and wedges of lemon.

A rather bitter type of salad, sometimes made with spinach,
is often served with grilled fish in Greece. Otherwise a lettuce
or watercress salad is the best.

Even nicer, according to Greek taste, is a salad of wild *radikia*,
which is a type of wild radish found in the mountains. They
have a bitter flavour, far removed in taste from the cultivated
variety, and are 3 or 4 inches long with curly leaves.

FRIED FISH WITH SAUCE
PSARI ME SALTSA

3–4 *lb fish*	*Olive oil for frying*
Flour	*Salt and pepper*

The fish for this type of preparation can either be cut into
thick slices or steaks or, if small, kept whole. Heads and tails
of whole fish are usually left on. Clean the fish, rub with salt
and pepper, then roll in seasoned flour. Fry in boiling oil.
When brown on one side, turn and brown the other. Take from
the pan and keep hot while you make the sauce.

Saltsa

1 *tablespoon tomato purée*	1 *oz flour*
2–4 *cloves garlic*	½ *cup white wine*
1 *bayleaf*	*Pinch fresh rosemary* (if liked)
½ *cup hot water*	*Salt and pepper*
Handful chopped parsley (optional)	

First pound the garlic. Pour off most of the oil from the pan in
which you have fried the fish, leaving just enough to fry the flour
for a full 5 minutes, stirring all the while.

Dilute the tomato *purée* with the hot water, stir this into the
flour, add salt, pepper, bayleaf, garlic, parsley and rosemary
and cook gently for 10 minutes, stirring continuously. Add the
wine, stir this into the sauce and simmer for a further 15 minutes.
Pour the sauce over the fish and serve hot.

FRIED SMELTS
MARIDES TIGANATES

Wash as many smelts as required and pat them dry, then lightly
coat with flour. The easiest way is to put the fish into a bag
with some flour and shake the bag. Heat some olive oil and fry
the smelts until they are as crisp as a biscuit.

If the smelts are very small you throw a number of them into
the oil together. If large, press 4 or 5 of them together by their
tails and shape them like a fan before frying.

DRIED FISH SALAD
TSIROS SALATA

Tsiros is a 6-inch long silver fish – not unlike, I think, the Bombay
duck before it is dried. Like Bombay duck it is dried and salted
but then held over burning paper until the outer skin blisters
and breaks. The fish is then filleted and broken into pieces. These
are mixed with oil and vinegar and left marinading for 30
minutes. It is drained before serving as an appetizer.

My Greek friends told me that when their cooks are burning,
or rather blistering, the *tsiros* they are banished to the kitchen
balconies as the smell is quite impossible.

FRIED SALT COD
WITH GARLIC SAUCE
BAKALIAROS SKORTHALIA

A recipe for those with a palate for strong flavours.

2–3 *lb dried salt cod*   *Batter*
Olive oil for frying   *Skorthalia sauce* (see page
                              152).

This is one of the few occasions when the Greeks use a batter
coating. The batter can be any kind you prefer.

Soak the fish in cold water for 12 hours, changing the water
twice. Wash very thoroughly in cold water and remove the bones
and skin. Dry and dip in batter and fry in hot deep olive oil
until browned on both sides. Serve hot with a Skorthalia sauce.

BOILED SALT CODFISH
BAKALIAROS VRASTOS

2 *lb salt codfish* $\frac{1}{4}-\frac{1}{2}$ *cup olive oil*
10–12 *small peeled onions*   *Juice half small lemon*
2 *lb small peeled potatoes*   *Pepper*
3–4 *chopped stalks celery*

Cut the fish into serving pieces and soak for 12 hours in cold
water, changing it twice. Wash it and remove the skin. Drain
and put into a pan with the onions, celery and potatoes. Cover
with cold water. Whip the olive oil, lemon juice and pepper
together and stir into the water. Cook very gently until the fish
is tender, about 30 or 40 minutes.

Serve with the vegetables and an oil and lemon dressing.

LOBSTER WITH MAYONNAISE
ASTAKOS VRASTOS ME MAYONNAISA

1 *small lobster per person* $\frac{1}{2}$ *cup vinegar*
Salt and fresh parsley   *Mayonnaise* (see page 155)

Plunge the live lobsters head first into a large pot filled with
boiling, salted water flavoured with vinegar. Cook rapidly for
five minutes, then lower the heat and cook for another 10
minutes. Cool them in water for 15 minutes. Dry with a cloth,
break off the claws and carefully cut the lobster lengthwise.
Remove the dark vein along the back, and the small sac behind
the head, lift the meat from the tail and cut this into thick
pieces and arrange on a platter. Crack the claws and take out
the meat – put this with the tail meat. Take out the coral and
the green liver and mix with the mayonnaise.

Serve the lobster with a coating of mayonnaise – or even a
simple oil and lemon dressing.

BRAISED SHRIMPS (OR PRAWNS)
YARIDES ME SALTSA

2 lb unshelled shrimps (or prawns)	2–3 tablespoons chopped parsley
2 medium finely chopped onions	1 tablespoon tomato purée
4 chopped tomatoes	Salt and pepper
	$\frac{1}{4}$ – $\frac{1}{2}$ cup olive oil

Wash the shrimps (or prawns) thoroughly and drain. Heat the oil in a large saucepan and fry the onions for about 5 minutes, add the *purée* and the chopped tomatoes and cook over a moderate heat for about 5 minutes. Add the parsley, salt, pepper and finally the shrimps. Cover and cook for 15 minutes or until the shells are a bright pink and easily removed. Take the shrimps from the pan (keep the sauce simmering) and when cool enough to handle, quickly peel them and remove the black vein that runs down the back. Drop the shrimps back into the sauce. As soon as all the shrimps are back and just re-heated, serve.

OCTOPUS IN RED WINE
HTAPODI KRASSATO

Octopus is not often available in the average British city but even so I think it is important to give a recipe for its preparation as it is a popular item of Greek cooking. Also, as so many Britons travel to Greece for holidays these days, some might want to try this local delicacy and know how it is prepared. I suggest that perhaps visitors to Athens might like to try it for the first time at Zonars, a restaurant which, for the beginner in unusual eating, provides an international and consequently more 'at home' atmosphere, then he can switch to the coastal *tavernas* for his octopus.

Octopus, when it is good, has something of the flavour of lobster and can be much more tender. It all depends on the method of killing the creature, the usual way being a systematic slow beating against a rock or something equally hard and handy. I remember once, when staying in a small hotel along the coast just outside Athens, I heard every morning a slow thump, thump. Curious, I went down to the shore and saw men slapping grey

masses of octopus against the flat rock. The octopus, I was told,
dies hard and must be killed in this manner; the flesh can be
very tough and it needs at least forty hearty slaps to make it
tender. It is always the fisherman and not the housewife who does
all this beating or slapping and it is usual to kill the octopus as
soon as the boats land. By the time they reach the shops or market
they are ready for cooking, although a little more hammering
with a kitchen mallet does them no harm.

1 *octopus weighing 2 lb*	½ *teaspoon pepper*
2 *finely chopped onions*	1–2 *stalks celery – chopped*
¼ *cup olive oil*	1 *bayleaf*
2 *cups dry red wine*	

Carefully clean the octopus, extract and discard the inkbag.
Put the octopus into a pan without adding any liquid and cook
it over a moderate heat until it becomes red. Remove the tentacles and cut these into pieces. Cut the remaining flesh into
chunks, and peel off the skin (this peeling is optional, some
Greeks do, some don't). Heat the olive oil and lightly fry the
chopped onion until it changes colour, then add the remaining
ingredients and the octopus pieces. Simmer gently for about
3 hours. Stir occasionally and serve hot.

OCTOPUS STEWED IN ONIONS
HTAPODI STIFADO ME KREMITHIA

2 *lb small octopus*	¼ *cup olive oil*
1 *lb sliced onions*	*Salt and pepper*
½ *cup good quality vinegar*	1–2 *crushed cloves garlic*
½ *cup white wine*	
¼ *pint tomato purée diluted with water*	

Clean the octopus and remove the inkbag (some cooks keep
the inkbag intact but this makes not only a very dark sauce
but also gives a pretty strong flavour). Cook in a pan without
adding any liquid until the octopus becomes red. Chop off the
tentacles and cut the body into strips of more or less equal size.
Heat the oil and simmer the onions until they begin to soften
but do not let them change colour. Add the garlic and the
octopus and continue simmering for 5 minutes before adding

the vinegar, wine, salt, pepper and tomato *purée*. Cover the pan and cook slowly for 3 hours or until the octopus is really tender.

SQUIDS
KALAMARIA YEMISTA

These can be delicious when really small and tender and one of the side pleasures of drinking ouzo on the seashore is to eat these tiny squids which have been fried in deep oil, some times *au naturel*, sometimes dipped in egg and breadcrumbs. The important point is to get them served piping hot for, as I have already remarked, the Greeks are never troubled when their food is served lukewarm.

Larger squids are somewhat tougher and are better when they are stuffed.

1 *dozen squids*	¼–½ *cup olive oil*
Salt and pepper	½ *cup thick tomato juice*

Filling
½ *cup olive oil*	2 *tablespoons chopped dill or*
3 *large finely chopped onions*	*mint*
4 *oz Patna-type rice*	1 *heaped tablespoon pine-nuts*
4 *tablespoons chopped parsley*	½ *cup red wine*

Wash the squids thoroughly, remove the inkbag, head and entrails. Cut off the feelers from the head and put these aside for later use. Season the bodies with salt and pepper. Mix the oil and tomato juice, drop the squids into this and leave them until required.

Filling. Heat the olive oil and lightly brown the onions. Cut the feelers into small pieces and add them to the pan, simmer until they change colour. Add the rice, parsley, dill (or mint) and nuts and cook for 5 minutes, stirring the mixture from time to time, preferably with a wooden spoon.

Partially fill the squids with the stuffing, not too full, for the rice has to swell. Close the openings either by rough sewing or with tooth-picks. Arrange the squids in an oiled baking dish

and then carefully pour a little of the wine into each. Pour over
them the olive oil and tomato juice in which they have been
marinating and enough boiling water to just cover. Bake in a
medium oven for about 1 hour, or until the squids are tender and
the sauce is thick. Preferably, according to the Greeks, served
cold.

STUFFED MUSSELS
MITHIA YEMISTA

3 *dozen mussels*	½ *cup dry white wine*
3 *cups boiling fish stock or water*	*Salt and pepper*
4 *tablespoons tomato purée*	

Filling

½ *cup olive oil*	2 *oz currants*
4 *oz uncooked rice*	*Salt and black pepper*
4 *large chopped onions*	2 *tablespoons chopped parsley*
1–2 *oz pine-nuts*	

Scrub the shells with a stiff brush and wash them well. Open the
mussels carefully without breaking or separating the shells.
Remove and discard the beard and the black parts of the mussels,
wash in several waters and then leave in cold water until required.
  Filling. Heat the olive oil and fry the onions until a golden
colour, add rice, cover and continue cooking for 20 minutes. Add
the remaining ingredients and continue to cook for another 20
minutes, by which time all the liquid should be absorbed. Leave
to cool. Fill each of the mussel shells with some of the stuffing,
close the shells firmly and tie each one with thread. Pack the
mussels tightly into a saucepan, pour in three cupfuls of water,
the tomato *purée* (diluted with the wine), salt and pepper and
cook slowly for 30 minutes. Leave to cool in the pan, drain off
any remaining liquid, there will not be much. Remove the thread
and serve the mussels cold with wedges of lemon. If preferred you
can serve them hot. Either way they are extremely good.

SEA URCHINS
AHINOI

Sea urchins or, as some people call them, 'pin-cushions of the sea' have long been a Mediterranean favourite. Recently in England they have suddenly had a vogue and gourmets compare them with, say, caviare or *pâté de foie gras*.

Sea urchins are usually served as appetizers. The shell must be prised open – as one does with an oyster – and they are laid out on a plate, again in the manner of arranged oysters. The top half of the shell is discarded, the yellow roe (or edible ovaries) nestling inside the lower half of the shell is then sprinkled with a little lemon juice and olive oil. Served with buttered brown bread and white wine, they make a good beginning to any meal. In Greece pedlars wander around the beaches with baskets of sea-urchins and *kydonias*, which are sea quinces, another small shellfish, and perfectly delicious.

Meat

KREATA

While the modern Greek means lamb when he talks of meat, and then goat and pork, the ancients talked much of beef. Homer sang of the delights of roast beef on which his men feasted. And one wonders whether Charles Lamb was right with his story of the first roast pig, for Aeschylus wrote long before Lamb, of sucking pig:

> But I will place this carefully fed pig
> Within the crackling oven; and, I pray,
> What nicer dish can e'er be given to man?

I wonder whether those carefully-fed pigs were peach-fed like those of Hungary?

Although the Greeks still have their roasts baked in the oven, most of the best meat cooking of Greece is done on a spit, much the same kind of spit their ancestors used. With the introduction of the electric rotary spit, culinary art has been brought full circle. We started with the spit and we have come back to it. In days gone by small dogs and manpower rotated the mighty spits; today in Greece manpower still operates.

Looking into the history of spit-cooking there is one story I like very much. It concerns the spit of the noble and opulent Count de Castel (not a Greek, I know) who had a spit which turned 130 different roasts at the same time. It also played twenty-four different tunes. For example, the fifth tune might announce that the chickens were ready, and at the tenth it was time to look at the turkey. The twelfth, perhaps, announced the sucking pig was done to a turn and so on. The cook, it is said, knew the exact note on which to grasp the roast as it turned slowly round and round.

Many of the meat recipes in this section are for spit roasting, and the vast majority can be used rather well with mutton, although the recipes call for lamb.

Meat in Greece is not butchered as in England and when Greeks go shopping they like to see carcasses hanging up bright and dripping, waiting for the butcher to hack off just the piece they want. This can be disconcerting for the housewife used to simply asking for the cuts which the cookery book calls for – but it does help one's knowledge of animal anatomy.

LAMB ROAST ON A SPIT
ARNI

When a Greek talks of meat he usually means lamb. Following closely in his mind is milk-fed kid which, if killed before it is three weeks old or before it has been out to pasture, has a flesh as white and as delicate as a spring chicken. Mutton for the Greeks does not exist. It is old, it has an odour – it is in fact mutton. Just how the Greeks maintain their supplies of lamb for their four main seasonal and traditional lamb-eating ceremonies I am not at all sure. Certainly, during the troubled times just after the last war, they even went to the extreme of importing lamb from their neighbour, Turkey, with whom they are so rarely on speaking terms.

Greeks, it is claimed, are either feasting or fasting. After they have fasted they like to make up for lost time. They try to eat lamb four times a year: at Christmas, when it is in the stage known as 'yearling lamb', quite large but still tender and juicy; in the first two weeks of carnival, when it is young and melting; on St. George's Day, April 23rd; and, most important, at Easter. At Eastertide the whole country, including all the hundreds of surrounding islands, is covered by a cloud of lamb-impregnated smoke. Starting in the early morning, from every nook and cranny you see the thin spirals of smoke rising from charcoal fires. In the country men sit gazing almost entranced beside the roasting pits, which are filled with charcoal, expertly turning the Easter roasting lamb on its spit. Often the charcoal is made from pine wood which gives a slight flavour of resin to the meat as it sputters and spits and the fat drops from the slowly revolving lamb into the smouldering charcoal.

A lamb is prepared the day before roasting. Its entrails are spiced and made into a soup, the Easter *Mayieritsa* (see page

28), so that nothing is wasted. Although the lamb can be roasted in the home, Greeks in the country prefer their lamb to be cooked on a spit out of doors. In the towns, instead of tunnelling charcoal pits in the earth, special charcoal stoves of tin or other similar metal are made. The principle is the same: the bottom is filled with charcoal and a spit is built above on which the lamb is stretched. One end of the spit is made into a handle which can be turned like the cranking handle of a car, but with less effort.

First prepare the lamb. On no account must it be cut up. Its entrails are removed through the stomach by cutting a slit in it; the kidneys are taken out through two small openings made in the back. The inside must be well salted and generously rubbed with lemons. The stomach opening must then be laced up and the spit pushed through the lamb, along the spinal column and coming out through the centre of its head. Then secure the lamb to the spit by using a packing needle and thick string; this should keep it firmly in place. Press the ends of the hind legs towards the spit so that they can be crossed above it and the stumps folded below, and tied firmly with string. Rub the outside of the carcass with lemon, salt and pepper and make small slits in the flesh to ensure that the salt and pepper is properly rubbed in. The lamb is now ready for roasting.

Two things are important with the roasting of lamb. First, the fire must be regulated to give a uniform heat, and secondly, the lamb must be placed sufficiently far from the fire to prevent it from scorching. This distance is decreased as the roasting continues. The dripping pan below must contain a sufficient quantity of butter, flavoured with thyme and lemon juice. The spit is turned slowly and patiently for three hours and the lamb continually basted. The spit is then brought nearer and nearer to the fire as the lamb begins to turn a golden brown, so the heat is concentrated on the legs and shoulders. Less heat is required for the belly and head parts. Both these latter parts burn easily and if cooked at the same heat as the fleshy parts will become dry while the rest will only be half cooked. The juice from the lamb is caught in the dripping pan.

Let me admit that roasting the Greek Easter Lamb does require an experienced hand for it to become the delicacy it should be. Perfection has been achieved by the shepherds in

the Greek mountains who know how to roast meat on a spit
better than most people. And it is easy to see why. After St.
George's Day the shepherds must move with their flocks of
sheep and goats to new pastures. They will be away from home
and good food for a long while, during which time they live a
frugal and meatless existence. So, before they leave, they are
determined to have one last meat fling. It is no uncommon sight in
the country, in April, to see the shepherds, man and boy, patiently
roasting a lamb on a spit (savouring every smell) for a meal
which in memory will last them for a period when their main
items of diet will be rather hard, black bread, strongly flavoured
goat's cheese and curds.

Those shepherds who do not stick to the mountains but
yearn for the bright city lights have discovered a good source of
income. They have opened up simple but appetizing lamb-
roasting restaurants in the heart of Athens. These can be found
off Ommonia Square where anyone who is not foolishly fastidious about his surroundings can enjoy at almost any time of
the day and night hot, juicy lamb, or other spit specialities
such as the 'turning-*kebab*' and the Greek *kokoretsi* and young
pig. Here you can drink a glass of ouzo or *retsina* wine for almost
next to nothing.

But it is not only in the mountains and in the heart of Athens
that you can get a meal of lamb or other meat roasted on a spit.
There are many *tavernas* throughout the country which prepare
such food. I remember, in particular, driving along the coastal
road below the dark hills of Delphi where I spotted a whole
succulent yearling lamb being tenderly roasted. We decided that
since it was lunch time we would eat then and there. The car
was stopped and we stepped out under the pines to sit at a table
set on the beach. The proprietor rushed up to John Hare, our
host, and greeted him with an almost violent effusion of Greek
which turned out to be a friendly welcome to an old friend.
He quickly brought us ouzo and black olives, for this is the area
of some of the finest and largest olive groves in Greece, and some
white *feta* cheese, all this 'on the house'. We followed this with
soft brown bread, tomato salad and finally tender chunks from
the yearling lamb which the proprietor's wife was turning very
slowly over glowing charcoal. By this time we had changed our
drink to the local *retsina* wine which matched the scent of the

pine trees. Soon our table was covered with plates of lamb, for
we were four, and although we protested that we simply could
not eat another morsel we managed to deplete that lamb con-
siderably. One or two other tables were taken up by gay, excited
Greeks who also took their toll of the meat. Another lamb, I
was assured, would take its place for the evening customers,
for our small *taverna* had a high local reputation. It was a very
genuine *taverna*, its kitchen also the restaurant, although for
most of the year clients could eat to their stomach's content
under the pines on the seashore.

EASTER LAMB
(for the town)
ARNAKI STI SOUVLA

Although the country people can prepare a whole Easter lamb
in their front or back gardens, most people in Athens and the
larger towns find this more difficult. This recipe is one which the
townswoman can manage in any country where milk-lamb is
available. If you use older lamb, or even mutton, the results will
be good but it will *not* be Easter Lamb.

Cut the milk-lamb into serving pieces (or a leg of lamb if a
milk-lamb is not available) and put them into a baking tin in
a very hot oven to quickly sear. Baste generously with butter,
reduce the heat and roast until the meat is about half tender.
Add some half-cooked butter beans, or fresh broad beans, a
fair quantity of small onions, and cover with stock. Add salt,
pepper, and garlic to taste. Continue roasting for another 35
minutes, adding more hot stock if required.

Easter lamb can be cooked just as easily on top of the stove
in a braising pan.

In Athens potatoes are often added when the meat is about
half-cooked. In the days before home ovens were popular,
every week-end during the lamb season, baker's ovens, after
the bread baking, used to be filled with tins of meat prepared
in the above fashion.

STUFFED EASTER LAMB
(Dodecanese style)
ARNAKI YEMISTO

1 *very young lamb or kid*
1 *lb minced meat*
Offal (heart, liver, lungs, etc.)
¾ *lb rice*
6 *oz salt butter*
2 *large grated onions*

3 *large lemons*
2 *tablespoons finely chopped mint*
Salt and pepper
Small piece cinnamon

Wash and dry the lamb or kid. Rub inside and out with salt and pepper, 2 ounces of butter and the juice from the lemons. Trim the offal and chop this into very small pieces. Mix this with the minced meat, put into a dry pan and *sauté* for about 10 minutes, stirring to avoid burning. Add remaining butter, stir this until it is melted and very hot, then add the onions, rice, salt and pepper and the piece of cinnamon. Stir and cook slowly for 5 minutes, then add the mint, stir again and continue cooking for 10 minutes.

Get the lamb ready for stuffing by partially sewing up its neck aperture, then push the rice mixture through the remaining aperture and completely sew up. Place in a large roasting pan, add 2 or 3 cups of boiling water and roast in a moderate oven for about 2½ hours, or until the meat is very tender.

LAMB ROAST IN PAPER
ARNI EXOTICA

Food cooked in a paper wrapping is called *klephtes* in most parts of Greece and had its origin, so one hears, in the days of the Turkish occupation. The *klephtes*, or guerrilla bands, which roamed the mountains harassing the Turks, wrapped their food in this way in order that the aroma of food being cooked should not reach the nostrils of the Turkish guards. In the mountains the meat was heavily seasoned with mountain herbs (such herbs still reach the sophisticated shops of Athens today), wrapped in oiled paper, pushed into earthenware containers and cooked for hours among the smouldering embers of pine logs and twigs. This recipe is for the urban version of *klephtes* cooking.

2–3 *lb shoulder of lamb or a small leg*
Salt, pepper and marjoram to taste
Plenty of garlic cut into slivers
Roughly 4 tablespoons olive oil

Juice 1 large lemon
About 2 oz Kasseri (or Gruyére) cheese cut into cubes
4–6 pieces parchment cooking paper large enough to hold individual portions

Wipe the meat clean then cut it into serving portions. Rub well with salt, pepper and marjoram (another similar herb will do as well), olive oil and lemon juice. Cut incisions into the meat and insert the garlic into these. Lightly oil the sheets of paper and arrange some of the meat on each piece. Top with cheese. Wrap carefully and fold the paper securely, twisting the ends tightly so that none of the juice escapes. Rub the packages with oil, place in a roasting pan and bake in a moderate oven for about 3 to 4 hours. Serve in the paper.

This method of cooking lamb is popular in many of the Greek *tavernas* and the recipe varies according to the ideas of the Greek owner.

There are one or two points about this kind of cooking which it is as well to know. The oven should really be moderate and when the packages are placed in the baking pan they should all just touch, that is, there should be no space left in between each package. No water, no oil, may be added; don't cover the pan and don't turn the packages. The cheese must always be on top of the meat and care must be taken that the paper does not scorch. So do not hurry the cooking. Serve piping hot in the paper to retain the piquant flavour of the meat.

For variety you can use less lamb and make up with chopped vegetables, such as squares of onion, egg-plant, potatoes, a few peas and strips of green pepper.

Two pounds of meat is sufficient for 4 people.

BRAISED LAMB
ARNI KOKKINISTO

3–3 *lb lamb*
3 *oz butter*
1 *large finely chopped onion*
1 *bayleaf*

Garlic to taste
Salt and pepper
Stock or water
½ *glass white wine*

Wipe the meat with a damp cloth and cut it into serving pieces, not too small for the meat will shrink. Heat the butter, either in a saucepan or a braising pan, add the meat, then when it is brown (or as the Greeks say, red) add the onion and continue frying until this is a light golden colour. Add the wine, rather gradually, then enough stock to just cover the bottom of the pan. Flavour with salt, pepper, garlic and the bayleaf. Cook over a medium heat until the meat is so tender that it will break easily with a fork.

Serve with any green vegetables, cauliflower or rice, or small new potatoes which can be put in with the meat 30 minutes or so before it is ready. The garlic can be rubbed into the meat if preferred and a handful of chopped parsley may be added with the bayleaf.

Arni Kokkinisto really means 'red' lamb.

LAMB WITH TOMATOES
ARNI ME DOMATES

3 lb lamb	Small piece cinnamon
6 large peeled and chopped tomatoes	3 oz butter
	Salt and pepper
½ pint hot water	

Clean the meat and chop it into serving pieces. Rub liberally with salt and pepper. Leave for 30 minutes. Heat the butter in a frying pan, add the pieces of meat and let them brown. Transfer to a saucepan. Put the tomatoes into the frying pan, bring once to the boil, then cook until soft. Add the tomatoes to the meat, add salt, pepper and cinnamon and cook slowly until the meat is very tender. From time to time peer into the pan and if the meat shows signs of becoming too dry, gradually add boiling water. The meat should be neither dry nor swimming in sauce. Remove cinnamon before serving.

Can be served with rice, potatoes or any of the pasta family, such as noodles or spaghetti. Enough for 4–6 people.

LAMB COOKED WITH BEANS
ARNI ME FASSOLIA

A typical and simple dish. White beans are soaked overnight and next day cooked with cubes of lamb flavoured with chopped onions (sometimes first browned). When the meat and beans are almost cooked, some peeled and chopped tomatoes are added and slow cooking continued until the meat and beans are tender. Garlic is sometimes added.

The Greeks have a word for the type of white beans used in this recipe – it is 'giant'.

LAMB WITH SPINACH
AND EGG AND LEMON SAUCE
ARNI ME SPANAKI AVGOLEMONO

3 *lb lamb*	*Salt and pepper*
3 *lb spinach*	1 *cup stock or water*
2 *medium finely chopped onions*	*Egg and lemon sauce*
3 *oz butter*	(see page 152)

Wipe the meat with a damp cloth and cut it into stewing pieces. Heat the butter; when this is hot, add the onions and fry these until a light brown. Add the meat (stirring as you do so), salt and pepper and cook over a fairly high flame for just 5 minutes which will bring everything to the boil. Add the liquid, reduce the heat to almost simmering point and continue to cook until the meat is tender.

In the meantime clean and pick over the spinach, discarding any coarse leaves and the stems. Put into a saucepan over a medium heat and cook without water until the spinach is tender. Drain and remove the strong greenish liquid. Now put the drained spinach on top of the meat, cover and cook slowly for 15 minutes, moving the pan from time to time to prevent sticking. You may find that a little more liquid is required; if this is added it should be hot stock or water, but any extra liquid must be added with caution as this is meant to be a fairly dry dish. On the other hand, there must be just enough liquid left to add to the sauce. Five minutes before serving add the egg and lemon sauce and serve hot.

The Greeks usually cook dishes of this type in fireproof two-handled casseroles, which can be brought to the table and are easy to handle, especially when shaking the pan is required.

BAKED LAMB WITH TOMATOES
PSITO ARNI ME DOMATES

Put 2 pounds of lamb into a baking pan with butter, salt and pepper. Cover with peeled and sliced tomatoes. Sprinkle with oil and melted butter and bake in a slow oven until tender, about 2½ hours if lamb is used, longer for mutton.

LAMB WITH LETTUCE HEARTS
ARNI ME MAROULIA

A Greek philosopher, Aristoxenus, called lettuce 'the green cakes that the earth has prepared'. It is said that he loved lettuces so much that he used to water them with the sweet wine of Chios.

Cut 2 pounds of leg or shoulder of lamb into pieces about the size of an egg. Put these into a pan with 2 or 3 tablespoonfuls of olive oil or butter, add 4 finely chopped onions and simmer everything until most of the fat has been absorbed but neither the meat nor the onions have become brown. Add 1 ounce of flour, stir this into the meat and onions, then, still stirring, add hot stock or water to cover.

In the meantime, while the meat is simmering, steep 3 or 4 very small lettuce hearts in boiling water (dark or coarse leaves should be discarded) and add them to the meat, pressing them down slightly. Add some finely chopped dill, salt and pepper and cook for another 15 minutes.

This dish can be served as it is or with an egg and lemon sauce (see page 152). If a sauce is added, take the pan from the heat, gently stir in the sauce and leave it to settle for a few minutes before serving, remembering, of course, to take a little of the liquid from the pan to put in the sauce.

LAMB WITH ARTICHOKES
AND EGG AND LEMON SAUCE
ARNI ME ANGINARES AVGOLEMONO

2 lb leg of lamb   Lemon juice
1–2 chopped onions   Handful chopped parsley
12 small globe artichokes   Egg and lemon sauce
2–3 oz butter   (see page 152)
1 oz flour   Salt and pepper

Wash and dry the lamb and chop it into small pieces. Snip off
the stems of the artichokes and cut the heads into two, remove
the choke and any coarse leaves. Trim each artichoke round the
base, rub it with lemon juice and drop into cold water until
required.

Heat the butter, lightly fry the onions, add the meat and
simmer without browning either the meat or onions until all
the butter has been absorbed. Add flour, stir this well into the
meat and onions, then pour in enough water to a little more
than cover. Bring to the boil, put the artichokes on top of the
meat, add parsley, salt, pepper and 1 tablespoonful of lemon
juice. Cover and cook until the meat and artichokes are quite
tender. Avoid stirring, for the artichokes might break and this
spoils the appearance of the dish. When the meat is tender,
add egg and lemon sauce (taking some of the broth from the
pan to make the sauce), simmer for 5 minutes, then leave covered
but without heat for 5 minutes. Serve hot.

Tinned artichokes can be used in this recipe but they need
very little cooking so add them to the meat when it is quite
tender.

To serve this dish, first take out the artichokes and arrange
them on a plate so that they surround the meat.

LAMB WITH CELERIAC AND LEMON SAUCE
ARNI ME SELINO AVGOLEMONO

2–3 lb lamb   Salt and pepper
3 oz olive oil   Egg and lemon sauce
1 large finely chopped onion
1 lb celeriac   (see page 152)

The type of celery used in this recipe is not celery as we know it in Britain. It is the variety known as celeriac or celery root. If this is not available use ordinary celery, for it is the celery flavour with the lamb which is important.

If using celeriac, this must be peeled and trimmed and cut into wedges; if using ordinary celery, clean and cut it into substantial pieces. Clean and cut the meat into cubes the size usual for a stew.

Heat the oil, lightly brown the meat, add the onion and cook over a medium heat for 5 minutes. Reduce the heat, add salt and pepper and hot water to cover. Continue to cook fairly slowly until the meat becomes tender, then add the celery and cook this until it is soft. Take the pan from the heat, stir in the sauce and do this carefully, otherwise the celery becomes too mashed, return the pan to the heat for 3 minutes, then leave covered for 5 minutes by the side of the stove. Serve hot.

Garlic may be added to this dish, for it adds flavour both to the meat and the celery. If using celeriac it must be added to the pan fairly soon after the meat for it takes some time to cook – at least 1 hour. Lamb with celery or celeriac is not frequent in Greece for the flavour of this vegetable is considered to go better with pork, a richer and fatter meat.

LAMB WITH COURGETTES
ARNI ME KOLOKITHIA

The difference in size and flavour between the British marrow and the Continental *courgette* is one which many cooks are willing to discuss at some length. Ever since the enormous and rather tasteless harvest-festival marrow was pronounced perfect and prizeworthy, marrows have been ruined in Britain. Why the British cook, when faced with an already watery vegetable, should decide to add more water and not simply cook her harvest-festival horror *au naturel* is a mystery to most Continentals. Its fantastic proportions are, however, an even greater mystery. The *courgette* is a baby marrow, of a kind which could quite easily come from English gardens but so seldom does.

3 lb leg lamb   1–2 crushed cloves garlic
2 chopped onions   Handful finely chopped parsley
6–8 courgettes   4–6 small tomatoes
4 oz oil or butter   Salt and pepper

Wipe the meat with a damp cloth and cut it into egg-sized
pieces. Heat 3 ounces of oil or butter and gently fry the meat
until just brown. Add the onions, fry these for a few minutes,
then add the tomatoes, garlic, parsley, salt and pepper. Cook
over a low heat for 1 hour or until tender. While the meat is
cooking, very lightly scrape the skin off the *courgettes* and cut
them into halves, or better still leave whole if small enough.
Heat the remaining oil or butter, slightly brown the *courgettes*,
then add them to the simmering stew. Continue to cook gently
for another 20 or 30 minutes or until the lamb is quite tender.

If a slightly less rich dish is preferred add the *courgettes*
without first browning them. Other vegetables such as peas,
cauliflower and small new potatoes can be cooked with lamb in
this fashion.

LAMB AND LADIES' FINGER STEW
ARNI KOKKINISTO ME BAMIES

Ladies' fingers is the name given to a green vegetable grown in
the tropics and in the pleasant climate of the Mediterranean.
In shape a ladies' finger looks like – a lady's finger; and it has
a rather gooey texture. It is seldom found in Britain in its
fresh form but it is usually available in tins in specialist shops,
imported from Greece, Cyprus and Turkey. It is also popular in
America, especially in the deep south, and there it is called okra.

3 lb leg lamb, cut into serving   ¼ pint vinegar
    pieces   3 oz butter
1½ lb ladies' fingers or 1 large tin   Salt and pepper
1 pint tomato sauce or juice or soup

If using fresh ladies' fingers, they must be washed and the
stem ends cut off, but care should be taken not to cut into the
flesh, otherwise they ooze a slightly sticky substance. Mix the
vinegar with 1 pint of cold water and in this soak the ladies'

fingers for 30 minutes, turning them from time to time. Strain
before using.

Heat the butter in a large saucepan, fry the pieces of meat
until brown, turning them frequently. Add the tomato sauce
(juice or soup), salt and pepper to taste and simmer for 1 hour.
Add the ladies' fingers and arrange these so that the meat remains in the centre of the saucepan. Continue cooking over a
low heat until the meat is really tender and the ladies' fingers
soft. Turn out to serve but try to keep the meat in the middle
of the dish and the ladies' fingers surrounding it.

If using tinned ladies' fingers it is not necessary to soak
them in vinegar, but add just a little vinegar to the stew. Tinned
ladies' fingers should be put into a strainer and washed under the
tap to remove the slightly acid flavour of the preservative.

LAMB WITH FRENCH BEANS
ARNI ME FASSOLIA FRESCA

3 *lb lamb*	1–2 *cloves garlic*
2 *lb French beans*	3 *oz oil or butter*
4 *chopped tomatoes*	*Salt and pepper*
1 *large finely chopped onion*	½ *pint boiling water*

Top and tail the beans, then break each one into 2 or 3 pieces.
Wash and dry the meat and cut into large cubes or serving pieces.
Sauté these quickly in the oil or butter and fry until brown.
Transfer the meat to a saucepan and in the same fat fry the onion
until a light brown. Add the tomatoes, garlic, salt and pepper
and cook until the mixture is like a sauce. Pour this mixture
over the meat, cover it and cook slowly until the meat is quite
tender. Add the boiling water, then the beans, shake the pan and
continue cooking for another 30 minutes. By this time the beans
will not be the bright green dear to British taste but a rather
darker green than we usually like, but of an extremely good
flavour and coated with tomato sauce.

Instead of leg of lamb, this dish can be prepared with lamb
chops, veal, pork chops, or with beef.

LAMB WITH SPAGHETTI
ARNI ME SPAGETO

Meat with any of the pasta products is tremendously popular
in all parts of Greece.

3 *lb leg of lamb*	2 *pints hot water*
1 *large finely chopped onion*	1–2 *tablespoons tomato purée*
1 *lb broken spaghetti*	*Salt and pepper*
4 *chopped tomatoes*	*Grated cheese* (optional)
1–2 *cloves garlic*	

Clean the meat, cut it into cubes and put into a large baking
tin. Add the tomatoes, tomato *purée*, onion, garlic, seasonings
and half a pint of hot water. Bake in a moderate oven until the
meat is tender, add the remaining water and bring this to the
boil. Add the spaghetti and continue to cook until this is tender,
about 20 minutes. Stir the spaghetti and the meat together.
Serve hot and, if liked, sprinkle with grated cheese.
    This can be cooked equally well on top of the stove.
    Cutlets may be used instead of leg of lamb.

ROAST LAMB WITH NOODLES
YIOUVETSI

This is a speciality of several Athenian *tavernas* as well as of
Greek housewives. In the Athenian winter, which can be very
cold, the warm smell of the kitchens penetrates the eating section
of the *tavernas* and the stomach takes kindly to a plate of *yiouvetsi*. Some *tavernas* prepare this in small individual earthenware
dishes and bring it piping hot from the oven to the table. Then
the waiter turns it out with one swift movement. This recipe is
for a family *yiouvetsi* and is made in one large casserole or pot.
It can be served from the casserole or turned out on to a large
platter.

2 *lb leg or shoulder of lamb cut*	*About* 1 *pint thick tomato*
into cubes	*sauce or soup*
3 *oz butter or oil*	*Cheese* (see below)
4 *pints hot meat stock or water*	*Salt and pepper*
1 *lb noodles or broken macaroni*	

Put the lamb into a roasting tin or shallow casserole, sprinkle with salt and pepper and add either butter or oil. Put into a moderate oven to brown. Turn the pieces from time to time. Add the tomato sauce or soup and 1 pint of the meat stock or water. Continue baking until the meat is tender, stirring frequently. When the meat is really tender, take it from the pan and keep hot. Add the remaining stock to the pan, season to taste, then bring the liquid to the boil. Add the noodles or macaroni, cook these until they are tender and have absorbed all the liquid. Arrange the hot meat on a platter and smother it with the noodles. Or return the meat to the noodles and serve the *yiouvetsi* in the casserole. Garnish with some small squares of cheese. The Greeks use *Kasseri* cheese but if this is not available use a Gruyère or Cheddar.

Any type of pasta or rice can be cooked in this manner but actually macaroni is preferable, as the sauce fills the cavity of the macaroni and adds to its flavour.

LAMB FRICASSEE
WITH EGG AND LEMON SAUCE
ARNI FRICASSE AVGOLEMONO

The Greeks have many kinds of fricassee dishes which are made with veal, lamb or beef. Lamb fricassee is their favourite. This recipe results in a rather refined kind of lamb stew.

Cut 2 pounds of lamb into stew-sized cubes. Place in a saucepan with 3 large sliced onions, 3 or 4 spring onions, with most of the green stems being used as well, 1 or 2 lettuces, broken as for a salad, some finely chopped parsley or dill, or both. Add sufficient water or stock to cover completely, salt and pepper to taste, and simmer until the meat is quite tender.

Add an egg and lemon sauce (see page 152) very slowly. Stir until the sauce has had a chance to thicken. Serve hot with peas or, if you like, rice or mashed potatoes.

Generally Greeks prefer to steep lettuces in boiling water before putting them into meat dishes. It is considered that this removes their slightly bitter flavour.

ROAST LAMB
ARNI PSITO

In every *taverna*, or almost every large *taverna*, you will see
several small roasts of lamb, at first glance looking rather dried.
But on tasting you will find them tender and garlic-flavoured.

1 *leg of lamb*	4 *cloves garlic*
Juice 1 lemon	2 *oz oil or butter*
1 *cup hot water*	*Salt and pepper*

Peel the garlic and cut it into thin slivers. Wipe the meat clean
and cut small incisions in it. Into these insert the garlic. Rub well
with salt, pepper and lemon juice. Heat the olive oil or butter,
add the meat and gently roast it for one hour, then add the hot
water and continue roasting until the meat is very tender. Baste
fairly frequently. Quite often small potatoes are added during the
last 45 minutes of cooking – they will become brown and soft
but not crisp as the English style of roast potatoes for there is too
much water in the pan. However, their taste is very good for they
have absorbed much of the garlic-flavoured gravy.

BAKED LAMB, PEASANT STYLE
ARNI STO FOURNO HORIATIKO

2 *lb lamb, breast or shoulder*	2 *tablespoons oil*
1 *lb feta cheese* (see page 196)	*Salt and pepper to taste*
2 *lb peeled and sliced tomatoes*	

Wipe the meat with a damp cloth and cut it into large cubes. Put
these into a baking pan. Cut the cheese into smaller cubes and
arrange these on top of the meat. Cover with tomatoes and
sprinkle with salt and pepper. Sprinkle with oil and bake in a
moderate oven until the meat is very tender, basting carefully
from time to time.

MINCED LAMB AND NOODLES
HILOPITES ME KIMA

No exact measurements are required for this simple dish but if
you use about 2 pounds of minced meat you should use 1 pound
of broken noodles.

Fry the minced lamb in olive oil or butter, flavouring it with
as much finely chopped onion, crushed garlic, peeled and chopped
tomatoes, salt and pepper as taste dictates. Simmer until these
ingredients have the appearance of a really thick sauce. Heat a
pan of water until it is boiling, add salt and the noodles. Cook
rapidly for 10 minutes, drain, and if by this time the meat is tender
and you have a thick sauce, stir in the drained noodles and continue cooking very slowly for another 10 minutes.

LAMB CUTLETS IN PAPER
ARNISSIA PAITHAKIA STO HARTI

Half-fry as many lamb cutlets as required, using either olive oil
or butter or a mixture of both. Remove the cutlets from the pan
and keep hot. Into the same fat put some chopped onion, tomato
paste or *purée*, salt, pepper, chopped parsley to taste and enough
white wine to bring this to a sauce consistency. Simmer until the
sauce is reduced and quite thick. Place each cutlet on a separate
piece of oiled kitchen paper, and pour one tablespoonful of
sauce over each. Wrap the cutlets, arrange in a baking tin, each
package close to the other, and bake in a moderate oven for
about 30 to 40 minutes, the time depending largely on the size
and quality of the cutlets. As long as the oven is not too hot,
long cooking will do the cutlets no harm, for they are well
protected.

LAMB CUTLETS IN MARJORAM SAUCE
ARNISSIA PAITHAKIA RIYANATA

Allow 2 or 3 (or more) cutlets per person; rub them with salt,
pepper and lemon juice and arrange them in a shallow fireproof
casserole. Brown them quickly in butter (or any other preferred

fat), cover with the marjoram sauce and bake in a moderate oven (or cook on top of the stove) until tender.

Sauce. Mix in a basin 3 tablespoonfuls of olive oil, salt, pepper and 1 heaped teaspoonful of dried marjoram. Add the juice of 2 large lemons and ½ cup of stock or water. Stir and when the mixture is blended pour it over the chops. A little white wine may be added.

Sauce enough for about 9 cutlets. Serve in the casserole.

LAMB GRILLED ON SKEWERS
(*Kebabs*)
ARNI SOUVLAKIA

This is one of the simplest and best dishes of the Balkans, for no one can pretend that grilled lamb belongs to any one Balkan country, or for that matter any Arab or Asian country. I could almost write a book on *kebabs*. From Yugoslavia to Persia and on to Pakistan and Malaya meat is spiced, skewered and grilled over charcoal.

Cut the meat from a leg of lamb into cubes about 1 inch square. Rub with salt, pepper, lemon juice, olive oil and marjoram. Impale the meat on skewers and grill them over charcoal, turning the skewer from time to time to avoid burning the meat. Serve still on the skewers on a bed of parsley or watercress and with thick wedges of lemon.

You will also find grilled and skewered lamb with each piece interspersed with thick wedges of tomato, or onion, or a bayleaf – it is really a matter of taste. The really long skewers look the most effective for any type of *kebab*.

LAMB-ON-A-SPIT
(Turning *Kebab*)
DONNER KEBAB

This form of *kebab* is not made at home although in the Balkans you can always organize a cook to come and prepare these *kebabs* in your garden for a special occasion. The meat, always lamb, highly flavoured with garlic, herbs and spices, is cut from the rump into long strips and then wound round the spit (or skewer). This is fixed in a vertical position a few inches from a vertical charcoal fire with its opening in front instead of at the top. The spit revolves all the time the lamb is cooking – hence its name. The meat is carved off vertically in thin slices with a very sharp knife and as it is carved it drops into a small tin pan with a handle. An exact portion is carved, leaving the raw under layer of meat now exposed to the fire and it in turn is nicely grilled. The *kebab* which started in the morning the shape of an enormous carrot – the usual spit is about three feet high, the width of the meat across the top ten inches and at the base about three inches – gets smaller and smaller. In the evening, as a general rule, there is nothing left but the spit and the dying embers of the fire. But by this time it is very late indeed.

Each portion of the *kebab* is laid on a 'bed' of finely sliced onion, chopped parsley and lightly sprinkled with red pepper.

LAMB'S HEAD WITH MARJORAM
ARNISSIO KEFALAKI RIYANATO

Nothing of the Greek lamb goes to waste, not even the head. Get your butcher to split a lamb's head in half and tie it together again to keep the brains intact. Soak the head for a while and clean it until all the blood has gone. Rub it generously with lemon juice, salt and pepper.

Remove the strings and place the head in a baking pan with the cut side uppermost. In another pan make a sauce with chopped garlic, 2 or 3 leaves of fresh marjoram, salt and pepper and some tomato sauce diluted with water. Pour this over the head, and bake in a fairly hot oven until the meat is tender and will easily leave the bones. Baste frequently.

You can either serve the head intact – which is not always popular since it looks vaguely cannibalistic – or remove the meat neatly from the bones with a sharp knife and serve it on a heated platter, garnished with watercress.

Failing fresh marjoram leaves use about half a teaspoonful of dried marjoram.

It is essential for this recipe that the lamb's heads are really small – if too fat or too large they are not tasty.

SPICED 'SAUSAGE' GRILLED ON A SPIT
(Lamb's Offal)
KOKORETSI

Another method of Greek cooking which is left to the expert and can be found in the more humble eating houses around Ommonia Square or at Zonars, the fashionable restaurant which serves *kokoretsi* in the evening as an accompaniment to drinks. It is made from the offal, the heart, liver, kidneys and sweetbreads of a lamb as well as its intestines, and is highly seasoned with salt and pepper, flavoured with marjoram and plenty of lemon juice.

The meat is coarsely chopped and around it is wound the intestines; it is then moulded into a fairly thick and long 'sausage', which is skewered or impaled on a spit, grilled slowly for several hours and basted with olive oil and lemon juice. When served it is cut into slices. *Kokoretsi*, which I think is in the salami class, is not to everyone's taste and I must confess that some of my Greek friends will not eat it, or say they don't. But my taste is varied and catholic and when *kokoretsi* is properly made and not over-spiced I like it very much.

Trayodia – Goat Song

For a great many people in this world – including gourmets – goat and sheep are interchangeable. Most British people turn pale if asked to eat goat, although many of us have eaten and enjoyed goat and kid under the impression we were eating lamb.

The Greeks, however, appreciate young goat and kid as much as they do yearling lamb and the milk-lamb. They refuse to eat 'lamb' when it has reached the age of mutton. It has, they say, a peculiar odour, and they grimace as they curl their tongues inside their mouths to show the effect this muttony flavour has on their palates. They feel as strongly about mutton as the Briton does about goat.

For the Greeks the goat has long been a symbol in mythology. When the shepherds in the mountains saw the light, gambolling mountain goat, fleet of foot, daring and apparently full of the pleasure of life, they created Pan in the image of the goat, symbolizing the joy of living.

The goat has also been the subject of songs from the ancient playwrights and poets such as Sophocles, Euripides and Aeschylus. In the theatre of Dionysus the dramas celebrating the God of Spring, of Corn and Wine, had actors clothed in goat-skins who danced a chorus to the sound of flutes and drums. One day a man named Thespis suddenly broke the ranks of the chorus and started to argue with the leader of the chorus. This was the first dialogue in the theatre and Thespis the first actor who spoke on the stage. From that time on the Greeks called the spoken stage-show 'Trayodia', which means goat-song. And the goat was also an animal considered fit for sacrifice to the great gods of Greek mythology.

There is a charming story told of Noah and his animals after the Flood when his ark had come to rest. According to this it was the goat which led Noah to the discovery of wine. Noah, it was said, loved the goats best of all the animals in his ark and would watch over them most carefully. One day he noticed that one of the billy-goats did not stay with the other animals once the ark was on dry land but went his own mysterious way. Noah watched him and discovered that the goat in the evening would go skipping and jumping down the hill, obviously intent on something important. Noah, curious, followed the goat and saw it nibbling contentedly at a great vine 'bearing luscious and heavy fruit'. Noah also picked a bunch of grapes intending to take it back to show his family, but on his way back he absent-mindedly nibbled at the grapes. Finding them quite delicious he went back to the vine and ate some more. The goat was still with him. Noah and the goat meandered down the hill together and Noah noticed the gaily prancing goat was uncertain on his legs; Noah too found his legs were heavy although his head felt light. He had no cares and by the time they reached the bottom of the hill he too was prancing and dancing as merrily as the goat. However, back at the door of the ark he collapsed and his unhappy children, taking him for dead, laid him out on his bed and wept. But the next morning the old patriarch awoke hale and hearty and told the story of the vine. He took his family along to try the grapes as well. Since that day man has known the pleasures of wine and owes it all to the gay-spirited billy-goat. Not the biblical version.

Muslims also eat goat and the Prophet Mohammed pro-

nounced: 'There is no house possessing a goat but that blessing
abideth therein.' Solomon of the Jews sang: 'Thy hair is as a
flock of goats.' So the goat has a history of its own – and one of
which it can be proud.

The Italian peasants eat kid or young goat at Easter, the
Mexicans, the Californians – even the Texans – eat kid and goat.
It is as at home in the modern world as it was in the ancient. The
goat can thrive on almost nothing. The rocky and barren Greek
and Middle Eastern soil where there are waterless hills and only
the grey asphodel grows, is the home of the nimble goat. A goat
will climb to heights that sheep or other domestic animals would
fear: his is a free spirit, a gay spirit and he will venture far. He is
as much at home in the towns as in the country, in the Eastern
world as in the Western. In the high mountain ranges of India
goats mean more to goat-herds than do their wives – and perhaps
this is to be understood, for the goat has long hair which can be
used in making valuable wool for blankets, and the mountain
goat has no objection to being used as a pack-animal.

Goat's milk has more vitamin B and albumen than cow's milk,
while butter made from it, although white, has a higher propor-
tion of vitamin A than cow's milk butter. In goat's milk too
there is a softer curd and less fat. The goat milkman is a familiar
sight in the streets of Athens (and Madrid) and the Greeks have
been drinking goat's milk since before there was an England.
Aristotle wrote that the milk of the goat is the best of all milk
and most easily acceptable to the stomach of man.

Because Greeks like kid they breed their goats to have their
kids in the spring and when they are ready for eating they have
a feast. Here then is the Greek recipe for dealing with kid – a
recipe that can be used for lamb or even mutton.

ROAST KID
KATSIKAKI PSITO

Rub a whole kid with lemon juice, salt and pepper, and insert
slivers of garlic into its skin; score it lightly. Arrange it in a baking
pan and quickly sear in a hot oven, then add olive oil or butter,
some mountain herbs, if available, otherwise herbs of your own
choice such as parsley or a *bouquet garni*, and roast the meat in

a moderate oven until it is almost tender. Add a cup of water
to the pan, baste with this frequently and continue roasting until
the meat is very tender – almost dropping off the bones. Serve
with peas and tomatoes – if you like, even with mint sauce or
cranberry jelly.

Sometimes the kid is served with a spiced and fragrant wine
sauce. This is simply made by adding red wine to the gravy,
bringing it once to the boil and straining it. This addition, however, is an Italian influence.

BRAISED VEAL
MOSCARI KAPAMA

This is an extremely popular dish despite the Greek preference
for lamb. Quantities vary according to taste and there is no
exact recipe.

Wipe clean some 3 pounds of veal and cut it into serving
portions. Brown this in butter or oil in a baking tin, put on top
of the stove. Add a fair amount of chopped onion and also some
crushed garlic. Let this brown, then stir 1 ounce of flour into the
pan, add red wine to cover, salt, pepper, and cinnamon to taste.
Gently simmer, until the meat is tender. Slow, very slow, simmering gives the veal something of the flavour of game. Chopped
and peeled tomatoes may be added, as well as chopped parsley
and other herbs.

Can be served with fried or mashed potatoes, or any of the
pastas, or cauliflower, it really does not matter which.

VEAL WITH MACARONI, CORFU STYLE
PASTITSADA KERKIREÏKÏA

Cut as much veal as required into chunky pieces. Chop very
finely a good quantity of onions. Heat enough oil to fry the
onions until they begin to change colour. In the meantime drop
the meat into boiling water to remove any odour. (This advice
can be ignored if the meat is both fresh and odourless.) Drain,
dry and brown the meat lightly with the onions. Add either a
large quantity of peeled and chopped tomatoes or some thick

tomato sauce and enough water and white wine to cover. Add
salt, pepper and herbs to taste. Remember that the veal is to be
eaten with either macaroni or spaghetti so that plenty of sauce
is required.

Cook the macaroni (or spaghetti) in the usual manner, drain
and stir into it some melted butter. Take most of the sauce from
the pan and stir this into the macaroni. Serve with the meat on a
platter.

Garlic may be added to taste.

VEAL RAGOUT
MOSCARI RAGOUT

2 lb veal
2 lb small onions
Crushed garlic to taste
1 bayleaf
1 glass red wine

3 oz butter
Salt and pepper
Egg and lemon sauce
                    (see page 152)

Cut the meat into cubes. Heat the butter in a saucepan, brown
the meat, add the onions and when these are brown – but only
just – add the wine, garlic, salt, pepper, bayleaf and enough
water to cover. Cover and simmer until the gravy is thick and
the meat quite tender. If more liquid is required it can be added,
either more red wine but not too much, or more hot water, or a
mixture of both. Add the egg and lemon sauce 5 minutes before
serving.

An exceedingly good winter dish which goes well with boiled
rice or creamed potatoes.

MINCED VEAL WITH NOODLES
MACARONI ME KREAS
(Youvetsi)

1 lb cooked noodles
1 lb minced veal
2–3 oz butter
¼ pint dark red wine
3 finely chopped onions

¼ pint tomato sauce
                    (see page 155)
1 tablespoon finely chopped
    parsley
Salt and pepper

Put the meat into a pan with a little water and cook until the
liquid is absorbed. Add the butter, onions, parsley, wine and
seasoning and cook very slowly until the meat and the onions
are tender. Put half the noodles into a baking dish, cover with
all the meat and onion mixture, add the remaining noodles and
the tomato sauce and bake in a moderate oven for about 20
minutes.

Macaroni is a general term for all pasta in Greece. When a
Greek housewife wants macaroni she goes into a vivid panto-
mime description of her needs until the proprietor produces
noodles, long or short, wide or narrow, or any of the 'drain pipe'
pastas. Spaghetti, however, keeps its own name.

VEAL RAGOUT (DODECANESE STYLE)
MOSCARI STIFATHO

2 *lb veal*   1 *bayleaf*
20 *small onions*   2–3 *oz olive oil or butter*
2 *cloves crushed garlic*   *Salt and pepper*
½ *cup wine – or vinegar*
4–6 *large, peeled and coarsely*
   chopped tomatoes

Wipe the veal with a damp cloth and cut it into large cubes.
Heat the oil or butter and brown the meat. Transfer the meat
from the pan to a saucepan and brown the onions and garlic
in the same fat. Add 1 pint of water, wine and tomatoes and
stir all this together, season generously and pour this mixture
over the meat. Stir, cover the pan and cook over a very slow
heat for at least 2 hours; if you can, simmer it for even longer.
The pot should remain covered all the time. If you feel that
perhaps the meat is sticking to the bottom of the pan, shake it
from time to time, but if the heat is really low there should be
no danger of either burning or sticking. This type of stew is
extremely rich and for those who enjoy onions very palatable
indeed. Enough for 4 or 5 people.

ROAST PIG
HIRINO PSITO

One of the nicest meals I had in Athens on my last holiday there
was with Shan Sedgewick, an American newspaperman and his
Greek wife; Rex Warner, who was writing yet another book on
Greece, and his wife; also Elizabeth Ayrton and her husband.
I had talked with Shan on the subject of Greek cooking and he
had declared that Greek food is truly the food of the gods and
to prove it he would arrange a supper party 'in a wood near
Athens', at Halendre, the legendary spot of Shakespeare's
Midsummer Night's Dream. The meal was eaten in the garden
of a simple *taverna* where we sat at a large trestle-type table,
drank *retsina* wine and ate roast pork cut from a whole pig
which was turning and roasting just a few feet away from us.
As always before eating any of these roast-on-a-spit dishes we ate
kokoretsi and other spiced sausages, coarse brown bread and
skorthalia, a superb garlic sauce for which I have given four
recipes on pages 152–4. We ate well, we drank well, and we all
decided that we had talked well.

I do not know how many people can today manage to find
sucking pig in Britain, or have the facilities to roast it on a spit
if they have the piglet. But here are the directions for roasting
sucking pig on a spit in the open air or in a large enough oven.

ROAST SUCKING PIG

1 *sucking pig, about 4–6 weeks old*
Salt, pepper and marjoram (or rosemary)

1 *breakfast cup olive oil, mixed with half the quantity of lemon juice*

Assuming that you have acquired a nice piglet and that it has
been cleaned and made ready for roasting, wash it inside and
out with cold water and thoroughly dry it. Then rub inside and
out with salt and pepper and whichever herb you prefer. Pull the
front legs forward and tie these together. Wedge the mouth open
with a small piece of wood (or anything handy in the kitchen)
and insert the spit through the body from the tail to the head.
Now rub the piglet generously with the oil and lemon juice mix-

ture and roast over a slow charcoal fire for about 4 hours or until the meat is quite cooked through and tender. Serve with a *skorthalia* sauce and coarse wine.

You can be elegant and eat the piglet with a knife and fork but it is much better to use one's fingers, pulling the flesh from the bones and dipping the bits into the sauce.

Failing a spit in the garden or 'in a wood near Athens', or one of the new spit-roasting ovens, you can roast the piglet quite easily in a moderately hot oven. The piglet should lie on a rack in the roasting pan. It requires the same treatment as when being roasted on a spit and 20 minutes or so should be allowed for each pound of meat, plus extra time if you want to have the dropping-off-the-bone tenderness of the Greek pork.

SUCKING PIG STUFFED WITH *FETA*
GOUROUNAKI YEMISTO ME FETA

1 *sucking pig ready for roasting*   *Pepper, salt and parsley*
2 *lb feta cheese*   *Olive oil*
Marjoram

The piglet should be rubbed inside and out with salt and pepper and just an 'idea' of marjoram. The outside only is then rubbed with a suspicion of olive oil and the piglet stuffed with the cheese. Roast in a hot oven until tender.

Feta cheese varies. If it is the hard variety it must be crumbled; if soft, chopped.

Duck, game or lamb may be stuffed and treated in a similar manner.

PORK WITH CELERY
AND EGG AND LEMON SAUCE
HIRINO ME SELINORIZES

An excellent dish and the speciality of more than one of the Athenian *tavernas*, including the Pindaron Taverna known locally as *Yero Phinika* (The Old Palm) because its *décor* is bamboo and palm.

If using ordinary white celery, use a large head and all of the stalks plus as much as possible of the leaves. If celeriac, peel it first and cut into cubes. About 1 pound of the latter should be sufficient.

2–3 *lb lean pork*	1 *oz flour*
2–3 *oz butter*	*Salt and pepper*
2 *medium chopped onions*	*Egg and lemon sauce*
Handful of chopped parsley	
Small glass red or white wine	(see page 152)
1 *lb celeriac or 1 large head*	
and leaves of celery	

Wipe the meat clean and cut it into serving portions. Heat the butter and quickly brown the meat, add the onions, and as they begin to brown, stir in the flour, blend, then add the wine and the parsley. Pour in enough hot water to cover, add salt and pepper, and simmer over a slow heat for at least 2 hours.

If you are using celeriac, it must be put with the meat about 30 minutes after it has been simmering, or even with the wine and parsley. Celeriac is a root vegetable and requires long cooking. Ordinary celery can be added to the meat about three-quarters of an hour before it is ready.

Add the egg and lemon sauce just before serving, stir it well into the liquid, simmer for 5 minutes, then stand on the side of the stove, covered, for 5 minutes more.

PORK CHOPS IN RED WINE
HIRINES BRIZOLES KRASSATES

This seems to me almost straight Italian, but the Greeks shrug their expressive shoulders and say, 'Well, maybe, but we eat it regularly all the same.'

Trim and simmer in boiling water as many pork chops as required. When they are partially cooked, drain off the water and add enough butter or other fat to brown the meat. When browned on both sides, add red wine to cover and simmer gently until the meat is quite tender.

The chops will have a far nicer flavour if they are rubbed with salt, pepper and lemon juice half an hour before using.

PORK BRAWN
PIHTI HIRINO

Brawn is quite popular in Greece so I feel I must give a recipe for its preparation, although I do not think many urban housewives in Britain will be rushing out to buy a pig's head and start making their own brawn. But one never knows.

Put a pig's head into plenty of cold water and soak it for at least 3 hours, then clean it really thoroughly, removing every one of the little hairs – the long soaking helps this operation. Put the head into a saucepan with fresh water and bring it to the boil. Remove the scum from the top of the water, add 2 or 3 cloves, a few peppercorns, 1 bayleaf, salt and pepper, and cook until the meat is tender. Take the head from the pan, strain the stock and put it over a low heat to simmer and reduce until there is just enough liquid to cover the meat when it is stripped off the head, adding 3 tablespoons of vinegar. When the head is cool enough, strip off the lean meat, the tongue and some of the skin and cut this into small pieces. Mix with a few chopped, pickled gherkins, 2 or 3 sliced hard-boiled eggs, a sliced, cooked carrot, and add plenty of salt and pepper. Arrange all this in a mould. Add the liquid, which should be enough to fill up the spaces in the mould, and put into a cool place for several hours. Turn out to serve.

Frequently served in Greece with a *Sauce Tartare* or *Vinaigrette Sauce*.

BEEF COOKED WITH VEGETABLES
VOTHINÓ ME LAHANIKÁ

2 lb beef	4 sliced potatoes
2 oz butter	2–3 chopped stalks celery
12 small onions	2 coarsely chopped leeks
3 sliced carrots	Salt and pepper

This is a simple but most appetizing dish. Cut the beef into pieces the size of a walnut and brown them in butter. Add the onions, carrots, potatoes, celery and leeks – from the last two ingredients use as much of the green as possible. Cover with water, add salt and pepper, and cook until the meat and vege-

tables are tender. At this point you can remove the meat and rub
the vegetables through a sieve and then return the *purée* to the
meat, or you can serve the meat with the vegetables left as they
are. Garlic may also be added.

BEEF STEW
VOTHINÓ STIFATHO

3 *lb beef*	1 *large clove garlic*
3 *lb small onions*	¼ *pint fresh tomato juice*
1 *large onion finely chopped*	1 *bayleaf*
3 *oz olive oil or butter*	*Salt and pepper to taste*
2 *tablespoons vinegar*	1 *pint hot water*
Small glass of white wine	

Wipe the beef and cut it into stew-sized pieces. Heat 2 ounces
of oil or butter and lightly brown the chopped onion and the
meat. Add tomato juice, vinegar, wine, about half the hot water,
bayleaf, garlic, salt and pepper and cook over a medium heat
until the meat is tender. In the meantime peel the small onions
and brown these separately in another pan with the remaining
oil or butter. Add them to the beef and at the same time pour in
the remaining hot water, or enough to cover. Continue to cook
slowly until the small onions are soft.

Some Greeks remove the onions before serving the stew but
this is not usual.

BEEF LOAF
ROULÓ

2 *lb minced beef*	1 *beaten raw egg*
1 *cup soft breadcrumbs*	1 *cup red wine*
2–3 *hard-boiled eggs*	1 *cup tomato juice*
1 *large minced onion*	*Salt and pepper*
2 *tablespoons finely chopped*	3 *oz olive oil or butter*
parsley	

Mix the beef, breadcrumbs, onions, parsley, salt and pepper and
knead to a paste. Spread out on to a pastry board. Put the hard-
boiled eggs in the centre, then roll up the meat. Brush with

beaten egg. Heat the oil or butter in a baking or braising pan and carefully lift the meat roll into the pan. Fry to a golden brown, first on one side, then on the other. Add the wine, cover the pan and simmer for a few minutes; add the tomato juice, just a little water, and continue to cook slowly for about 45 minutes.

Rouló is usually served surrounded with noodles, but peas, potatoes or other vegetables may be used instead.

Cut the loaf into thick slices, arrange down the centre of a hot platter and pour the sauce over the meat and noodles, or vegetables.

ROLLED BEEF WITH NOODLES
ROULÓ ME MAKARÓNIA
A Macedonian dish but available in most Greek towns.

3 *lb lean beef*	1 *bayleaf*
1 *clove garlic*	*Salt and pepper*
½ *pint thick tomato juice*	1 *pint boiling water or stock*
3 *oz butter*	

Wipe the meat with a damp cloth, roll it and tie firmly. Rub with salt and pepper. Finely chop the garlic and insert the pieces into the meat. Heat the butter in a baking pan and brown the meat, then bake it in a medium oven until tender. Add the liquid and leave the meat in the oven until this re-boils. Take the rolled meat from the pan, and thickly slice it. Put the pan on the top of the stove, add the bayleaf and tomato juice. Stir this well into the gravy, return the meat to the pan and continue to cook slowly until the sauce thickens.

Noodles. These are cooked separately and for this particular dish square noodles are recommended. The quantity depends on appetites but, however much you cook, the noodles should be boiled in plenty of boiling, salted water until tender. Drain and stir into the noodles a generous lump of butter. Serve with the meat on the same platter.

MARJORAM BEEF STEAKS
VOTHINÓ FILLÉTO RIYANÁTO

Beef steaks, but very tender   *Butter*
Lemon juice   *Salt and pepper*
Marjoram

Wipe the meat with a damp cloth and arrange on a grill trivet.
Spread lightly with butter, sprinkle generously with lemon juice,
add salt and pepper, and flavour to taste with marjoram, either
fresh or dried. Grill the meat until brown on one side, turn it
over and repeat the process. Baste with the juice which falls from
the meat and serve the steaks as hot as possible, lightly sprinkled
with lemon juice and garnished with a knob of butter flavoured
with marjoram.

STEAK IN A GARLIC SAUCE
SOFRITO

This is a recipe from the island of Corfu where the cooking is
much influenced by both the Italians and the British. The steak
used in this recipe need not be of the finest quality, although
obviously if you want to prepare a really tender steak in this
manner there is nothing to prevent you. Living most of my life
in what some people call 'foreign parts', I have become used to
steaks of dubious origins and I find this recipe covers a multitude
of sins.

The recipe I have comes from the owner of the Corfu Restaurant in Athens, which serves Corfu specialities. The proprietor
declared that all his produce was flown in by plane from Corfu
to Athens, including fish. As we talked the restaurant was beginning to fill up with hungry mainland Greeks and others, but
each waiter, as he passed the table where I was busy learning
about Corfu cooking from the proprietor, would throw in his
contribution and his special bit of knowledge. Afterwards I was
taken into the kitchen where a practical demonstration was given.
Later, much later, that evening, I returned to the restaurant to
eat *sofrito* – and enjoy it. Now we eat it often, utilizing our dubious
steaks.

Cut as much rump steak as required into fairly large pieces,

beat it for a while and make slits all over the surface of the flesh –
this is to prevent shrinking. Remove all sinews. Rub with salt
and pepper and coat it quite thickly with flour. Heat butter (yes,
it was insisted, butter, not olive oil) and fry the pieces of meat
until browned. Sprinkle again with flour. Now add a really
generous quantity of finely chopped garlic (a whole head if you
like and can take it), plenty of salt and pepper, and when the
garlic begins to change colour add enough wine mixed with a
little vinegar to make a thick sauce. Put all this into a casserole,
add some water and bring to the boil. Reduce the heat and
continue cooking slowly until the meat is really tender and the
sauce thick. Serve with creamed potatoes and as hot as possible.

As you will see, this is a recipe which can be made to require-
ments and for which one does not need exact measurements.
The main point is that the sauce should be thick and taste of garlic.
If you use a dark wine the sauce will be dark, whereas using a
white wine produces a lighter sauce.

BEEF AND MIXED VEGETABLE CASSEROLE
KREAS KE LAHANIKA STI CATSAROLA

This recipe comes from a Macedonian Greek friend and has much
of the Bosnian flavour.

2 lb beef	3 large onions
1 small white cabbage	1 small red cabbage
4–5 large potatoes	½ lb white dried beans
4 large tomatoes	1 bottle white wine
2 large green peppers	Salt and black pepper

Cut the beef into slices. Soak the beans overnight and cook next
day until almost soft. Peel and slice the potatoes and tomatoes,
cut the white and red cabbage into strips and mix. The onions
can be sliced or chopped according to fancy. The core and pips
of the peppers should be discarded.

At the bottom of a casserole arrange one layer of meat, then
add a layer of all the vegetables in turn. Continue in this way
until all the ingredients are used up – the top layer should be
either of tomatoes or potatoes. Sprinkle each layer generously
with salt and pepper. Add the white wine, cover and gently

simmer either in the oven or on top of the stove for at least 3
hours. The result is a thoroughly delicious dish, rich and aromatic. You can also add a layer of peeled and sliced aubergine
and marrow, even peas and carrots, it really does not matter.

Serve in the casserole in which it is cooked.

MEAT AND POTATO PIE
MOUSAKAS I

1 lb minced meat
2 lb peeled and sliced potatoes
2 large sliced onions
Handful finely chopped parsley
2 oz butter

3–4 peeled and sliced tomatoes
2 oz grated cheese
Salt and pepper
½ pint béchamel sauce
                                (see page 151)

Put the meat, onions, and parsley into a pan with a little water
and simmer until all the water is absorbed. Add the butter and
cook slowly for about 20 minutes, then add the tomatoes, salt
and pepper. Continue to cook for another 15 minutes or until
the tomatoes are soft. Grease a round casserole and arrange a
layer of potatoes at the bottom, overlapping the slices, then
add a layer of the meat and tomato mixture, another of potatoes
and continue until these ingredients are finished. The top layer
should be of potatoes. Add the cheese to the sauce and pour this
over the potatoes. Bake in a moderate oven for about 1 hour.

Some Greeks prefer to fry the potatoes very lightly first.

MOUSAKA – SALONICA STYLE
MOUSAKAS II

8 medium-sized aubergines
1½ lb minced meat
3 minced onions
Handful finely chopped parsley
¼ lb breadcrumbs
1–2 tablespoons tomato juice
Salt and pepper

Olive oil for frying
1 pint béchamel sauce
                                (see page 151)
2 egg yolks
Grated cheese
Butter

First peel and slice the aubergines, sprinkle with salt and leave
between two large plates until all the water is drained from

them. Wipe dry. Heat plenty of olive oil in a deep pan and fry the
aubergine slices until brown on both sides. Put these on a large
platter to drain.

Pour off almost all of the oil from the pan and lightly fry the
minced meat and the onions until brown, then add the parsley,
tomato juice, salt and pepper. Simmer for about ½ hour then
add the breadcrumbs and stir everything in the pan together.

Grease a large, square baking tin with oil and cover the bottom
with fried aubergine. Spread this with half the meat and onion
mixture; add another layer of aubergine and spread this with the
remaining meat and onion.

Beat the egg yolks into the *béchamel* sauce and pour this over
the meat. Sprinkle generously with breadcrumbs and grated
cheese, add a few slivers of butter and bake in a moderate oven
for 30 minutes. The top should be brown and like a crust. Serve
hot. The correct shape for this type of *mousaka* is either square
or oblong and the texture should be firm enough to cut it like a
cake.

MEAT AND AUBERGINE PIE
(Greek-American style)
MOUSAKAS III

4 *large aubergines*	3 *oz grated cheese*
1½ *lb minced meat*	½ *cup dark red wine*
3 *large coarsely chopped onions*	*Salt and pepper to taste*
6 *medium-sized tomatoes – or*	¾ *pint béchamel sauce*
1 *large tin*	(see page 151)
3 *oz olive oil (or butter)*	*Oil for deep frying*
Handful finely chopped parsley	8 *oz very fine breadcrumbs*
2–3 *beaten eggs*	

Peel and thickly slice the aubergines, sprinkle with salt and place
between two large plates. Heat 2 ounces of oil or butter, add and
brown the meat, then add the onions and brown these. Add the
tomatoes, wine, parsley, salt and pepper and simmer until the
liquid is absorbed. Cool, add the eggs, cheese, and half the breadcrumbs.

Heat plenty of oil in a deep pan, wipe the slices of aubergine
and brown each piece on both sides. Sprinkle the bottom of a

casserole with the remaining breadcrumbs, cover with a layer
of fried aubergine, cover this with a layer of the meat mixture,
another of aubergine, then of meat and continue until all the ingredients are used up, finishing with aubergine. Cover thickly with
the *béchamel* sauce and bake in a moderate oven for about 1 hour.

This *mousaka* is rich but it can be made less so by not frying
the aubergine before putting it into the casserole. If this is done,
bake more slowly and for 30 minutes longer.

MINCED MEAT CASSEROLE
(Rhodes)
SFOGATO

1½ *lb minced meat – any kind*	2 *large minced onions*
1 *lb courgettes, peeled and*	*Salt and pepper*
cubed	½ *pint stock or water*
4 *eggs*	2–3 *oz olive oil or butter*
Handful chopped parsley	

Heat the oil or butter, add the onions and when they change
colour add the meat. Add the *courgettes*, liquid, salt, pepper and
parsley and cook over a low heat until the meat is tender and the
sauce fairly thick.

Beat the eggs until light and quite fluffy; let the meat mixture
cool slightly, then fold the beaten eggs into it. Pour into a casserole and bake in a moderate oven until firm.

Failing *courgettes* use a small vegetable marrow. If you put
the casserole into a pan with boiling water (and in the oven) the
eggs will cook more slowly and set better.

This is an excellent way of dealing with not so tender meat.
Serve with a tomato sauce and green vegetables or salad.

Sfogato is a kind of meat and vegetable custard.

CEPHALONIAN PIE
KREATOPITA

The chief feature in the preparation of this pie is that it is made
with three kinds of meat, usually lamb, goat or kid, and chicken.
The goat flesh must be from the female goat and the chicken meat
the dark portion of the legs, etc.

Filling

4 lb mixed meats, coarsely minced	Pinch salt and sugar
¾ lb chopped onions	Handful chopped parsley
8 oz butter	(optional)
1 lb peeled, chopped tomatoes	1 teaspoon sugar
4 oz rice	1 oz stoned raisins (or sultanas)
4 oz grated Kasseri cheese or Parmesan	6 well-beaten eggs
	White wine
1–2 bayleaves	8 finely chopped cloves garlic
	Salt and pepper to taste

Short crust

1¼ lb sifted flour	Warm water or milk for mixing
¾ lb butter	Ground cinnamon
2 eggs	Olive oil

Wipe the meat and cut it into small pieces, then put it into a pan with warm water to cover. Bring this to the boil, scoop off any scum which may form.

Cook the onions in water until they are soft, then drain. Heat the butter and fry the onions until they begin to change colour. Add about half a pint of white wine, the tomatoes, rice, meat, raisins, salt, pepper, garlic, sugar and bayleaves and simmer gently for about 20 minutes or until the meat is tender. Add the grated cheese and the eggs. Stir as you add the eggs to prevent them from curdling. When the ingredients are all blended remove the pan from the fire and leave until cooled.

Make the pie crust. Put the flour into a large bowl, add sugar and salt and then add the butter, rubbing it in with the fingers until the mixture becomes crumbly. Add the eggs and gradually the warm milk or water. Knead for 10 minutes until the dough is very soft, and then chill.

Divide the dough into two portions, one slightly larger than the other, and roll these out on a floured board. The bottom layer should be fairly thick and large enough to line a baking pan. Fill this with the filling, spreading it evenly, and cover with the remaining pastry. Brush this lightly with olive oil, score the top and crimp the edges slightly. Prick with a fork and sprinkle with ground cinnamon. Bake in a moderate oven for about 1 hour or until the surface is lightly browned. If it becomes brown too quickly place a wet sheet of paper on the top until the pie is

baked. Let it "settle" for a few minutes after taking it from the
oven and then cut into squares to serve.

This is a popular Carnival and Ascension Day dish with the
inhabitants of the Island of Cephos. It is very rich. This recipe
makes a really large pie, for at least 10 to 12 persons, and could
be served as a party-piece. The meats can be varied. Try mutton,
lamb and veal mixed, or pork, chicken and veal, it really does not
matter. As it is a dry pie, with no gravy at all, it is ideal for a
buffet party.

MEAT WITH QUINCES
KREAS ME KYTHONIA

3 *lb meat (lamb, veal or beef)*	*Salt and pepper*
4 *lb quinces*	1 *teaspoon sugar*
1–2 *onions*	1 *pint hot water*
2–3 *oz butter*	

Wipe the meat clean and cut into cubes. Finely chop the onion(s).
Peel the quinces and cut into thick slices. Heat the butter and
fry the onion(s) and the meat until brown. Add the hot water
and cook slowly until the meat is tender. Add the quinces – a
little more water if required – salt, pepper and sugar and cook
until soft.

No other vegetables are required.

MINCED MEAT WITH BÉCHAMEL SAUCE
PASTITSIO

One thing is quite certain; that even the most unobservant
foreigner in any part of Greece will discover that *pastitsio* is a
popular and very frequent Greek dish. Sometimes it will be
very good and at other times incredibly stodgy. At its best it is
simply minced meat cooked slowly in a shallow pan with macaroni and covered with *béchamel* sauce (see page 151) and usually
generously sprinkled with grated cheese. Sometimes bits of
chopped ham are included which, although it adds quite a
flavour, is deplored by the more traditionally minded. When
it is stodgy it is a mixture of solid noodles and very little meat.

MEAT WITH CHESTNUTS
KREAS ME KASTANA

2 lb chestnuts   2–3 oz butter
4 lb veal or beef   Salt and pepper
1–2 onions

Wipe the meat with a damp cloth and cut into pieces about the
size of an egg. Finely chop the onions. Boil the chestnuts until
it is easy to peel off the brown skins.

Heat the butter and fry the onions until just brown, then
add the meat. When this is brown, add 1 pint of water, salt and
pepper and cook slowly until the meat is tender. Add the chestnuts and continue to cook slowly until the chestnuts are soft.

In many Greek homes chestnuts and potatoes are interchangeable.

GREEK RISSOLES
KEFTETHES

This type of small rissole or meat ball is popular throughout
the Balkans, the Middle and Far East. The Greeks serve them
on almost all of their festive occasions, for weddings, christen-
ings, picnics, etc.

1½ lb minced meat   1 tablespoon grated cheese
4 oz soft breadcrumbs   Salt and pepper
        (moistened in milk)   Flour
3 small minced onions   Olive oil or butter for frying
2 well-beaten eggs   Enough ouzo to moisten
Handful chopped parsley   (see page 213)
1 teaspoon chopped mint

The ouzo is optional and is not used by all Greek cooks. It
adds just a little something unusual in flavour to the meat balls.

Put the minced onions into a strainer and pour boiling water
over them. Mince the meat twice or even thrice. Squeeze the
breadcrumbs, mint, ouzo, cheese and eggs to a paste and leave
for 30 minutes. Shape into balls, dust lightly in flour and fry
in hot oil or butter until brown. Serve hot.

These meatballs should not be large – about the size of a walnut. If you are not going to use ouzo, add instead some lemon juice, about 2 tablespoonfuls is enough of either.

An Australian-Greek told me her mother covers her *keftethes* with lemon leaves for a while if they are going to eat them cold but warned me they must not be left too long thus covered otherwise they will become very bitter.

MEAT BALLS IN EGG AND LEMON SAUCE
YOUVARLAKIA

2 *lb minced lamb, veal or beef*   3 *oz butter*
1 *large finely chopped onion*   1 *egg white slightly beaten*
3 *tablespoons uncooked rice*   *Egg and lemon sauce*
2 *tablespoons chopped parsley*   (see page 152)
Salt and pepper

Mix together the meat, parsley, rice, onion, egg white, salt and pepper and knead to a smooth paste. Break off pieces the size of a walnut, roll lightly into balls and leave for 1 hour.

Put 2 pints of water and the butter into a saucepan, bring it to the boil, add the meat balls carefully to avoid breaking them and simmer over a low heat for 30 minutes. Take the pan from the stove.

Take some of the liquid and mix with the egg and lemon sauce, and pour this over the meat balls. Return the pan to the stove and cook the meat balls in the sauce over a very low heat until the sauce just begins to thicken. Serve the meat balls with the sauce.

Youvarlakia are usually served without any addition, even of potatoes. Instead of water, strained meat stock may be used, in which case use less butter.

MEAT WITH GREEN OLIVES
KREAS ME ELIES

For this recipe olives in brine are required and these are usually available in stores dealing with foreign produce.

3 *lb veal or beef*	4 *oz butter*
2 *lb green olives*	1 *teaspoon sugar*
2 *pints tomato sauce*	Pepper

First deal with the olives. Carefully remove the stones, then drop them all into boiling water. Leave for 30 minutes. Wash 2 or 3 times in cold water.

Ask the butcher to slice the meat thinly. Heat the butter and brown the slices of meat on both sides. Add the tomato sauce, plenty of pepper, sugar and the olives. Simmer gently until the meat is tender. You may require salt but not much since the brine from the olives will be salty enough.

This is a speciality in one of the many Greek monastries.

SMYRNA SAUSAGES OR MEAT BALLS I
SOUDZOUKAKIA I

Sausages

2 *lb minced veal or pork*	Olive oil *for frying – or* butter
Handful finely chopped parsley	1 *wineglass dry vermouth*
2 *crushed cloves garlic*	(optional)
2 *slices white bread*	Flour
1 *wineglass wine – red or white*	Salt and pepper
2 *beaten eggs*	

Soak the bread in the wine until the latter is completely absorbed. Mix the meat with the parsley, garlic, salt, pepper and bread, and knead to a paste. Bind with the eggs and leave for half an hour. Make the tomato sauce. Shape the meat into small fat sausages and lightly roll in flour. Heat either oil or butter and fry the sausages until brown. Pour the vermouth into the pan and let this entirely evaporate. Add the tomato sauce and continue cooking for about 15 minutes, do not stir but shake the pan from time to time to avoid sticking. Serve with rice or mashed potatoes.

Tomato Sauce

1 *small tin tomato purée or paste*	Salt and pepper
1 *teaspoon sugar*	1 *pint water*
	2 *oz butter*

Heat the butter, add the tomato paste diluted with some of the
water, stir until blended, then add sugar, salt, pepper and the
remaining water. Simmer for 15 minutes until the sauce begins
to thicken.

SMYRNA SAUSAGES OR MEAT BALLS II
SOUDZOUKAKIA II

1½ lb twice-minced meat	*Salt and pepper*
1 cup soft breadcrumbs	*Pinch cumin (see page 205)*
Red wine – about 1 small wine-	*Olive oil or butter for frying*
glass	*½ pint tomato juice or sauce*

Stir the crumbs and the wine together until the crumbs are
moistened. Combine with the meat, salt, pepper and cumin
until smooth. Shape into sausages and leave for 30 minutes.
Heat about 2 ounces of oil or butter and fry the rissoles until
brown, then add the tomato juice and simmer gently until the
meat is quite cooked – about 30 minutes. Serve with rice or
potatoes, or with a green salad.

LIVER IN A SAUCE
SIKOTAKIA ME SALTSA

A recipe from Rhodes, a charming island which has taken some
of its cooking as well as its wine from the Italians.

Marinate about half a pound of chopped calves' liver in red
wine for an hour or more. Heat about 4 tablespoonfuls of olive
oil in a pan and lightly brown 2 small sliced onions. Take the
liver from the wine, pat it dry and lightly coat in well-seasoned
flour. Brown the liver – you may have to add a little more oil
if the onions have absorbed too much – stir in a little marjoram
or rosemary, the red wine in which you marinated the liver,
and cook slowly until the sauce has thickened and the liver is
tender. Serve hot with creamed potatoes.

I first ate liver cooked in this way on the wide seafront of the
main town of Rhodes and asked the proprietor for the recipe.
I rather wondered at the time whether the liver had really been

marinated in wine as the cook had told me, but I discovered later that wine is very cheap, cheaper probably than vinegar, and certainly the sauce had the flavour of wine.

Kidneys can be cooked in exactly the same way.

Poultry and Game

POULERIKA KE KYNIYI

In all the following recipes I am assuming that the housewife or cook knows how to clean and prepare a fowl or game bird for cooking. Usually those sufficiently interested in cooking to buy books giving international recipes also have on their bookshelves those equally important basic cooking books which give accurate and graphic descriptions for the more complicated operations needed with birds. So I assume, when explaining the following recipes for cooking feathered creatures in the Greek manner, that they are already cleaned and prepared for pots of various kinds.

There is one tip I would like to pass on, although it is not strictly Greek but came from the French wife of a Greek friend. When her chickens are ready for cooking, whether she is going to steam, boil, roast or fry them, she puts them in the kitchen sink and pours over them a kettle of boiling water. This causes them to plump out and whiten and it makes it easier for any type of cooking. She also insisted that the flavour is much improved by this method of hers – but there I am not sure. Other improvements I can vouch for and, in fact, I have always acted on her advice since.

As far as chickens in Britain are concerned, only young and plump birds should be used for roasting, frying, steaming or boiling chickens. The older, skinnier ones are best left for soup making or, at the very most, used minced.

In the matter of game, the Greeks do not hang their birds as long as we do and they usually do not care for the condition we so enjoy in Britain, and call 'high'. So whether the following game recipes are made with birds which have been hung or with fresh ones, depends entirely on the taste of the individual cook. Rabbits can also be given the boiled kettle treatment and are most certainly improved by being rubbed with lemon.

COLD STEAMED CHICKEN
KOTOPOULO

This is more a tip than a recipe. Steam (or boil) a chicken in
any manner you prefer. When it is cold rub it thoroughly with
cut lemon and leave it for at least ½ an hour before serving.
This adds to the flavour and makes the flesh whiter.

GRILLED CHICKEN AND SAUCE
KOTOPOULO TIS SKARAS ME SALSA

2 grilling chickens   Olive oil or butter
Salt and pepper   Garlic
½ lemon

Sauce
1 tablespoon olive oil   1 teaspoon chopped or dried
1 tablespoon lemon juice   thyme
½ teaspoon dry mustard   Salt and pepper to taste

Split the chickens down the centre and rub each piece with salt,
pepper and one cut clove of garlic, then finally with a little oil
or butter. Place in a shallow pan, not too near the grill, turn
from time to time and baste frequently with the sauce until they
are nicely browned and tender.

To make the sauce, mix the oil and lemon until well blended,
then add salt, pepper, dry mustard and thyme. Cook for about
3 minutes, stirring all the while.

ROAST CHICKEN WITH MARJORAM
KOTOPOULO RIYANATO

1 large roasting chicken   Salt and pepper
2 oz melted butter   2 cups hot water
2 oz olive oil   ¼ teaspoon marjoram
Juice ½ lemon

Rub the chicken well with salt, pepper and lemon juice. Leave
for 1 hour. Put the olive oil, butter and water into a pan and
then the chicken, lying it on its back. Sprinkle the chicken with

marjoram, put the pan into a moderate oven and baste the
chicken frequently until it is very tender. Lift it from time to
time to prevent the skin from sticking to the pan.

CHICKEN STEW
KOTOPOULO KAPAMA

1 good-sized chicken	3 oz butter
6 peeled and chopped tomatoes	Juice 1 lemon
2 tablespoons tomato purée	Salt and pepper
½ teaspoon ground cinnamon	1 pint hot water
3 oz olive oil	Ground cloves

Thoroughly clean and joint the chicken. Mix with the lemon
juice, the cloves, cinnamon, salt and pepper and rub each piece
of the chicken well with this mixture. Heat the butter and oil
together and brown the pieces of chicken, take them from the
pan and keep hot. Add the tomatoes and purée, stir this well
into the hot butter-oil, then add the water. Cook over a gentle
heat until the tomatoes are very soft – like a sauce – then return
the chicken to the pan. See that each piece is well coated with
the tomato sauce, cover and continue to cook until the chicken
meat is so tender that it almost falls off the bone.

CHICKEN ON THE SPIT
KOTOPOULO TIS SKARAS

One of the best of Athenian dishes. This recipe is adapted for
the meal in the garden or what the Americans might call the
barbecue.

Wash the chickens – they should be very young and plump
– and dry them inside and out. Rub them well with salt, pepper,
garlic and lemon and leave for 1 hour before grilling. Push
each chicken on to a revolving spit, turn it frequently until it
browns and is cooked through. If you are in doubt about its
being cooked, twist the leg of one of the chickens. If it breaks
easily then the chicken is ready. Delicious when served with a
garlic sauce (see page 152) and, when in season, watercress.

The heat, whether charcoal or electricity, must be very low, otherwise the chickens are burned on the outside and not sufficiently cooked inside.

CHICKEN-IN-THE-POT
KOTOPOULO STO STAMNI

This is a speciality of one or two of the *tavernas* just outside Athens – and elsewhere in Greece – but more particularly of the Becami Taverna in Rafina Road, in the direction of Parnetha.

Definitely there are no specific directions. A tender chicken, first having been rubbed with lemon juice, is gently squeezed into an earthenware pot, aad wine, tomato juice, herbs, salt, pepper and some butter is added. The pot is then firmly sealed and shaken so that all the ingredients are properly mixed. It is then baked in a slow oven and the pot brought to the table for serving. The waiter, with considerable skill born of long practice, breaks the pot in front of you and the whole steaming, aromatic contents are poured out. A splendid dish.

Other meats are sometimes prepared in the same manner.

CHICKEN WITH NOODLES
KOTOPOULO HILOPITES
This chicken dish comes from the Peloponnese.

1–2 *young chickens*	3–4 *stalks chopped celery*
3 *oz butter*	2–3 *tablespoons finely chopped*
2 *medium, finely chopped onions*	*parsley*
1 *cup dry white wine*	*Pinch cinnamon*
1–2 *cloves pounded garlic*	1 *lb noodles*
6 *peeled and chopped tomatoes*	*Salt and pepper*
½ *pint thick tomato sauce – or*	*Freshly grated cheese*
soup	*Hot water*

The Greeks use a grating cheese called *kasseri*, or sometimes they use *kefalotyri*. If neither is available, Parmesan can be substituted.

Clean the chickens and joint them into serving pieces. Rub generously with pepper and salt. Heat the butter in a thick-

bottomed pan and brown the chicken pieces. Take them from
the pan and keep hot. Put the onions and garlic in the same fat
and when they begin to change colour, return the chicken, add
the wine and simmer for 15 minutes. Add the tomatoes and
the sauce, then the celery, parsley, salt and pepper and enough
hot water to cover. Simmer, tightly covered, until the chicken
is quite tender. About 20 minutes before the chicken is ready,
start to cook the noodles in another pan in rapidly boiling,
salt water. Fifteen minutes before it is ready add the cinnamon
to the chicken – if you put the cinnamon in too soon it will lose
its flavour. Drain the noodles when tender. Take the pieces of
chicken from the pan and keep hot. Add the sauce and the
cheese to the noodles alternately. Arrange the noodles and the
chicken on a large platter and serve hot. You can use a little
more grated cheese if required as a garnish.

CHICKEN PIE
KOTOPITA

This is a pie for a party or those with a large family, made
with *phyllo* pastry. Failing *phyllo* pastry the pie can be made
with flaky pastry in the usual British way, using, however, the
Greek type of filling.

2 *chickens*	½ *pint milk*
3 *lb sliced onions*	Salt and pepper
4–6 *eggs*	Nutmeg
3 *tablespoons grated cheese*	18 *sheets phyllo pastry*
About 4 oz butter	(see page 162)

Clean the chickens and cook them in plenty of water. Remove
any scum which arises on the stock before adding the onions
and salt. When the meat of the chickens is so tender that it
comes away easily from the carcass, take them out of the pan
and put aside. Continue to cook the onions, stirring from time
to time until the mixture forms a thick *purée*. Bone the fowls
and shred the meat. If you want to use the skin, cut it finely.
When the onions have become like a sauce, add the milk and
the chicken meat, stirring continuously until the mixture boils.
Take from the heat. Leave until cool, then add the cheese,

eggs (breaking these directly into the mixture), salt, pepper and a good-ish pinch of nutmeg. Line a baking dish with about 6 sheets of *phyllo* pastry, buttering each sheet before putting it in the dish. Add the mixture, spreading it well over the pastry, then cover with the remaining sheets, buttering each one. Brush the top sheet with butter and score this into squares so that when it is cooked it is marked out into serving pieces, but do not actually cut through the sheets of pastry. The top layers of the covering sheets should overlap so that the mixture can be enclosed. Bake for 1 hour in a moderate oven. Usually served hot.

This same mixture served between 2 layers of ordinary puff pastry is excellent and makes a very special kind of chicken pie. When I make Greek chicken pie using flaky pastry I always bake it in a fairly shallow pan because the filling is a fairly solid one, without much gravy.

CHICKEN LIVERS IN MADEIRA SAUCE
SIKOTAKIA TIS KOTTAS ME SALTSA

This is a recipe from Corfu – with a strong Italian influence or flavour.

18 *chicken livers*	*A little chopped parsley*
6 *lamb kidneys*	1–2 *cloves garlic*
3–4 *oz butter*	*Salt and pepper*
½ *pint chicken consommé*	*Small glass Madeira wine*
Grated onion to taste	*Creamed potatoes*
1 *oz flour*	

Remove the white centre and skin from the lambs' kidneys and cut them into pieces in size to match the chicken livers. Heat the butter in a shallow saucepan and quickly fry the liver over a fast heat for 4 minutes, shaking the pan frequently to prevent burning or browning. Sprinkle in the flour and cook over a fast flame to let the flour just brown. Mix it well into the butter to form the basis of the sauce.

Heat the *consommé* and gradually stir it into the butter and flour *roux*, add the onion – not too much of this otherwise the liver flavour becomes lost – the garlic and parsley and cook

over a low flame, stirring all the while until this mixture begins
to bubble and boil. Add salt and pepper, take the pan from the
heat, remove the livers, quickly strain the sauce, return it to
the pan, add the Madeira, stir it well into the thick sauce,
return the livers, carefully re-heat and serve the livers and sauce
with creamed potatoes.

GOOSE WITH APPLE AND CHESTNUT STUFFING
HINA YEMISTI

1 *goose – weighing about* 10 *lb*	2 *teaspoons sugar*
4 *large apples*	*Salt and pepper*
1 *lb boiled, chopped chestnuts*	

Goose is usually very fat so it should first be pricked all over
with a sharp fork. Peel, core and chop the apples and simmer
gently in just enough water until they are soft, but not too soft.
Add sugar, salt and pepper and the chestnuts (which I hope
you have shelled and skinned). Fill the goose with this mixture,
then place it on a rack in a baking pan and roast in a moderate
oven until the flesh is tender and a golden brown. As the fat
accumulates, pour it off. A goose weighing 10 pounds will take
about 3½ hours to cook.

Personally, I prefer to use whole apples. I peel and core them
and stuff the cavities with chopped chestnuts. Then I push the
apples and the remaining chestnuts into the goose, secure the
openings with a toothpick and roast it in the usual manner. The
apples are sufficiently cooked and the flavour is the same.

Some Greek cooks also like to add pine-nuts and some chopped
fried onion, but I do not think this is at all necessary.

'HYDRA' CHICKEN
(Chicken cooked in brandy and cream)
KOTOPOULO TIS HYDRAS

1 *young chicken*	*Butter*
Cocktail glass brandy	*Lemon*
Same quantity thick, fresh cream	*Salt and pepper*

Another recipe, which, in all honesty, I cannot categorically
claim as Greek, nor for that matter as really belonging to the

Island of Hydra, a charming island where artists and writers holiday – and work. It was given to me by a distinguished Greek artist whom I met when crossing from Piraeus to Hydra with some friends.

This is his special recipe, made with Greek brandy, but he agreed any other brandy could be used. The chicken is jointed according to its size and tenderness, lightly fried in butter until a golden brown (no flour, no egg, no breadcrumbs) and then the brandy is poured over it and it is simmered until the brandy is absorbed. Then the cream is poured over the chicken pieces and, when this is just hot, the chicken is served. Quite delicious, although when one considers the matter, how could such a recipe fail, providing the chicken is young and tender? If potatoes are creamed to perfection, this is all that is needed to go with it – and this simply so that you can savour the sauce longer and wipe up every single drop.

HARE IN WALNUT SAUCE
LAYOS ME SALTSA KARITHIA

This rather unusual Greek dish is really delicious. I do not think any of the ingredients should be omitted or substituted since they all add to the general flavour.

1 *hare – prepared and cut into serving pieces*	*Handful chopped celery*
	4 slices lemon
Vinegar and water in equal proportions	*A little fresh marjoram*

Put the hare either into a bowl or jug, cover with a mixture of water and vinegar and the remaining ingredients. Leave in a cool place for 1 or 2 days. Drain and wipe dry before using.

2 *oz butter*	$\frac{1}{2}$ *teaspoon cinnamon*
2 *oz olive oil*	12–15 *good-sized walnuts*
Juice $\frac{1}{2}$ *large lemon*	1*Salt and pepper*
1 *liqueur glass brandy*	1 *oz flour*
2 *cups meat stock* (*or water*)	6 *slices fried bread*
1 *bayleaf*	

Shell, peel and crush the walnuts. Heat the butter and olive oil together, then add the hare and lightly brown it. Add the lemon juice and the brandy, stirring carefully all the while and, when all this has been absorbed, add the stock (or water), bayleaf, cinnamon, salt and pepper. Cover and cook very gently until the meat is really tender. Hares should have long, slow cooking. Just before it is ready, add the crushed walnuts and the flour and continue cooking until the hare sauce has become quite thick. Have ready a slice of fried bread on each plate, spread this with some of the sauce, put a piece of the hare on each slice, then add remaining sauce. If watercress is available, this makes an excellent garnish.

HARE IN WHITE WINE SAUCE
LAYOS ME SALTSA

1 *good-sized hare*

From some celery, onion, carrot, leeks, parsley and equal parts of water and vinegar make a marinade, enough to cover the hare

Flour

Olive oil for frying

Salt and pepper

1¼ *pints white wine*

2–3 *slices bacon*

6–8 *small, whole onions*

6 *tablespoons tomato purée*

1 *bayleaf*

Small glass brandy

1 *clove garlic* (optional)

Joint the hare after thoroughly washing and cleaning it. Put it into the marinade and leave overnight. Next day remove it from the marinade, wipe the pieces dry, roll in seasoned flour and fry in deep, very hot fat until brown. Take from the frying pan and put into a large saucepan. Pour off most of the fat from the pan and leave just enough to fry 1 ounce of flour until it is brown but not scorched. Gradually pour in the white wine, stirring all the time, let it come to the boil, then pour it through a strainer over the hare pieces. Add the bacon, onions (peeled and left whole), garlic (if used), tomato *purée*, bayleaf, salt and pepper. Cover the pan and cook over a medium heat until the hare is tender. (Or all of this can be put into a casserole and baked in the oven.) Before serving discard the bayleaf, cut the bacon in small pieces and stir in a small glass of brandy.

The Greeks produce their own brandy, most of which is

very good. So, although adding brandy may be expensive for some of us, for the Greeks it is not so. Therefore, brandy may be optional – but it does add to the flavour. If you cannot get Greek brandy try Cyprus brandy.

HARE STEW
LAYOS STIFATHO

1 *medium sized hare*	1–2 *cloves garlic*
12 *small onions (whole)*	*Few currants or seedless raisins*
2 *cups tomato sauce (or juice)*	1 *bayleaf*
2 *cloves*	*Salt and pepper*
1 *pint water*	*A little sugar*
¼ *cup olive oil*	

You can dispense with the garlic if you prefer or add more small onions, there is no hard and fast rule. In Athens, instead of cloves they use a round black seed with a clove flavour, but the two are interchangeable.

Wash the hare and cut it into serving pieces. Arrange in a baking dish, add remaining ingredients, blending them well together. Cover tightly and cook in a slow oven for several hours, the longer the better. Give an occasional stir, being careful not to break the meat. Preferably serve with mashed potato – although a famous Greek general told me mashed potato is a very 'sissy' kind of food, 'fit only for the aged and toothless'.

This recipe can be used with tongue and rabbit.

ROAST RABBIT WITH MARJORAM SAUCE
KOUNELI RIYANATO

1 *rabbit*	1 *dessertspoon chopped marjoram*
Juice 2 large lemons	1–2 *crushed cloves garlic*
½ *cup olive oil*	*Salt and pepper*

Prepare the rabbit and soak it in salt and water for 1 hour to remove all the blood. Drain it thoroughly and wipe it dry with a cloth. Put the rabbit in a baking tin into a really hot oven and

quickly brown it, then reduce the oven heat to slow. Beat the
olive oil and lemon juice together until thoroughly blended,
then add the chopped marjoram, crushed garlic, salt and pepper.
Pour this mixture over the rabbit and continue to bake until
the rabbit is tender. Baste from time to time with the sauce
from the pan. Take the rabbit from the pan, mix the drippings with
the remaining sauce, add a little flour to thicken and just a little
stock or water. Stir this into a gravy on top of the stove and serve
with the rabbit.

Failing marjoram, parsley goes extremely well with rabbit
and, I think, plenty of parsley can be used.

RAGOUT OF RABBIT
KOUNELI STIFATHO

There is a legend concerning this kind of cooking, bound up, as
Greek legends so often are, with mountains and bandits. The
story is that some bandits were in hiding near a mountain village
and sniffed the delicious aroma coming from a nearby cottage,
where a rabbit or two were simmering in a pot on the usual
outdoor stove. The bandit chief commanded his men to go and
fetch that pot of stew and, according to the legend, the leader
ate the whole lot himself while his fellow bandits looked enviously
on. But, the legend also adds, the leader, in gratitude for such
a fine meal, spared the village from plundering – which must
have been grand for all but the housewife who was left without
a meal to serve her hungry family.

The main distinction of the *stifatho* is that the meat is always
literally smothered with small onions and well-seasoned with
garlic and spices. It is cooked without any other vegetable,
it requires no accompaniment and is served with Greek brown
bread and always a bottle or so of red wine (preferably *retsina*).
Even children must drink wine with *stifatho* as it helps the
digestion. There are some Greeks who insist that only rabbit
should be used for a *stifatho* but I have had *stifatho* of all kinds
served to me, made with beef, hare or even lamb chops.

There are no absolute quantities one can give for this recipe,
it is all a matter of taste. Essential details only are important.

Clean and joint one good-sized rabbit. Heat about 4 ounces

of either olive oil or butter and lightly brown the pieces. Take from the pan and keep hot. In the same pan fry and brown 2 or 3 pounds of small, peeled but whole onions and 3 or 4 crushed cloves of garlic. Return the rabbit pieces to the pan, add about ½ a pint of thick, fresh tomato sauce (or tinned tomato soup) and ½ a pint of either white wine or white vinegar. Stir all this thoroughly, add a clove or so, a piece of cinnamon stick, some fresh, chopped parsley, salt, pepper, 1–2 bayleaves and enough water to cover. Simmer over a low heat, tightly covered, for at least 3 hours – peek from time to time to see if there is still enough liquid and if not, stir in enough to keep the sauce thick but not like a gravy. Cover again and continue simmering. The sauce when served with the rabbit and onions should be as thick as a *purée*. This kind of dish improves if prepared in advance, left to stand for sometime and then re-heated.

I find that if plenty of finely chopped parsley is sprinkled over the fried rabbit when it is taken out of the pan, the flavour is better.

RABBIT WITH CREAM
KOUNELI ME KAÏMAKI

A recipe from Salonika

1 *rabbit*	1 *pint vinegar*
1 *pint fresh cream*	1 *bayleaf*
3–4 *oz butter*	3 *cloves*
Salt and pepper	

Clean the rabbit and joint into serving pieces. Leave it for 2 hours marinating in the vinegar. Heat the butter, wipe the pieces of rabbit dry and fry them until brown in the hot butter. Sprinkle with salt and pepper and pour the vinegar over them. Continue cooking until the rabbit is quite tender. Add the cream, bayleaf and cloves and simmer gently for another 20 minutes. Just before serving, remove the bayleaf and cloves.

For people who think they do not like rabbit because of its appearance, it can be boned or cut to disguise its look and no announcement made.

Greek cream or *kaïmaki* is thick, so thick it can be sliced. The nearest British equivalent is Devonshire cream.

PARTRIDGE WITH OLIVES AND CELERY
PERTHIKES ME ELIES KE SELINO

Small birds, partridge, snipe etc, are fairly easily available in
most parts of the Mediterranean.

2–3 *partridges*	4 *peeled and chopped tomatoes*
2 *heads celery*	*Butter or olive oil for frying*
3 *oz stoned, green Greek olives*	*Salt*

First simmer the olives for 10 minutes in their own juice. Clean
the celery and chop it into small pieces. Heat enough butter to
fry the partridges until brown, then add the celery and the olives,
the tomatoes and enough water to just cover. Add salt and cook
until tender. Cut the birds into halves, arrange on a platter and
pour the sauce over them.

STUFFED TURKEY
YEMISTES YALLOPOULES

Many Athenians assured me they like to eat turkey at Christmas
and although the actual method of cooking does not vary much
from the British, some of the Greek stuffings are rather more
enterprising. In this recipe I shall also explain how one should
prepare and roast the turkey because it is simpler if trying out
a new stuffing recipe to have the whole process of roasting to
hand.

1 *turkey* – between 12–14 *lb*	*Salt and pepper*
1 *lemon*	*Butter*

First the turkey should be 'dressed' for roasting and it is usually
bought from the poulterer in this condition. If, when you get
it home, you find there are some pin feathers, remove them and
singe off any remaining hairs. Pull out remaining lungs or stringy
odds and ends (if any). Cut out the oil sac on top of the tail.
Wash in cold water, pat dry inside and out, rub with salt, pepper,
lemon and a little melted butter. Leave for 30 minutes while you
cook your stuffing.

Meat Stuffing I:

6 oz minced lamb	2–3 oz butter
Heart and liver of turkey – minced	1 talbespoon pine-nuts
1 minced lamb's liver	1 pint turkey broth (made from neck and gizzards)
1 lb boiled, peeled and broken chestnuts	1 cup soft breadcrumbs
4 oz rice	2 sour apples
2 finely chopped onions	Salt and pepper
	Melted butter

Peel the apples and chop them into small pieces. Heat the butter and fry the onions until they begin to change colour, then add the minced meat and simmer gently for 15 minutes. Add the minced heart and liver, the chestnuts and pine-nuts and simmer for another 5 minutes. Add the broth and bring this to the boil. Add the rice and cook quickly for 10 minutes, then add the lamb's liver, breadcrumbs and apples. Stir well.

To stuff the turkey slit the skin at the back of the neck and cut off the neck down to the turkey's shoulders. Lightly fill the breast cavity, remembering the stuffing always swells and too much swelling might cause the neck skin of the turkey to burst. Sew (or pin with a skewer) the neck flap to the back of the turkey. Just as lightly, fill the body cavity and sew or skewer this together.

Tie the legs to the tail and fix the wings snugly to the body – do not bring the cord across the breast for it marks the skin. Rub the turkey with salt, pepper and melted butter, place it in a large shallow pan and roast in a moderate oven for about 4½ hours. Weigh the turkey when stuffed and roast it according to this weight, i.e., 25 to 30 minutes for every pound.

If you have made too much stuffing for your turkey it can be roasted in the tin and served with the turkey. Or it can be made into rissoles, dipped into beaten egg and breadcrumbs and served as a garnish. Greeks prefer to have plenty of stuffing so that it can be cooked separately and served with the turkey.

Meat Stuffing II:

1 *turkey liver, minced*
1–2 *medium-sized onions finely chopped*
2–3 *cups toasted breadcrumbs*
1 *lb roasted, peeled and broken chestnuts*
3 *oz sultanas or seedless raisins*

6–8 *stoned black olives*
2–3 *chopped sticks celery*
Butter for frying
Salt and pepper
Turkey stock from gizzards and neck, or water, or milk

Heat about 3 ounces of butter and just brown the onions. Add the liver, simmer for a few minutes, then stir in the breadcrumbs. Add the remaining dry ingredients, then the stock. Stir this all together with some care, let it come to the boil but cool it before stuffing the turkey. About ½ a pint of stock should be sufficient. If this does not seem enough, cautiously add some more, but the stuffing must be neither too moist nor too dry. Exact measurements are rather difficult to give. Some shelled, peeled and crushed walnuts may also be added.

Meat Stuffing III: This is very straightforward.

2 *lb chestnuts*
2 *large, chopped onions*
1–2 *oz butter*
2 *tablespoons tomato purée*
½ *pint turkey stock*

1 *lb moist breadcrumbs*
Handful chopped parsley or mint
Salt and pepper

Roast the chestnuts until they are easy to peel, then cook them in water until the inner skin comes off easily. Crush them. Heat the butter and fry the onions until they begin to change colour. Add the tomato *purée*, stock, salt, pepper and parsley (or mint) and simmer gently for 15 minutes. Add the breadcrumbs and the chestnuts and mix thoroughly. Cook for another 5 minutes, then stuff the turkey.

Meat Stuffing IV:

1 *lb minced lamb*
8 *oz long grain rice*
3 *large, finely chopped onions*
4 *oz butter*
1 *teaspoon ground cinnamon*
2 *tablespoons tomato purée*

1½ *pints turkey stock*
Turkey liver and heart, finely chopped
Salt and pepper
Finely chopped mint to taste

Heat the butter and fry the onions and when they begin to change colour add the meat, heart and liver. Simmer for 10 minutes. Add the tomato *purée* (diluted with some of the stock), stock, mint, cinnamon, salt and pepper. Bring to the boil, add the rice and cook over a moderate heat for 10 minutes. The rice will continue cooking while inside the roasting turkey so that 10 minutes is ample time.

Vegetables

LAHANIKA

Vegetables have always held an important position in Greek cooking and generally they are used with intelligence and variety.

The Greeks make a main dish from a mixture of vegetables, in much the same way as the French do, although their methods of cooking vegetables are very un-French. Even in the days of ancient Greece, of Achilles and Ulysses, we read that often the most conspicuous dishes at state banquets were those consisting of vegetables.

Alexander must have been extremely fond of vegetables for he was for ever finding new ones and bringing them back to Greece and trying them out on his troops. Onions he found in Egypt, tried them, and decided they might be good to inspire martial ardour among his fighting men. (Indians are convinced that the onion arouses other ardours, and many of them ban it from their kitchens.) It was Alexander who discovered for Europe the haricot bean. Busily conquering bits of India he came across it, tried it out, found it good and brought back samples to grow in Greece. The Greeks have cultivated its various uses to far greater effect than the Indians, who seem to have pretty well forgotten all about their ancient haricot. In return for the haricot, Alexander, who must have been as interested in food as he was in warring, gave the Indians their first vines. But the Indians have neglected these even more than the haricot bean.

Oddly enough the cabbage has a long history and a proud one. In ancient times it was not the much maligned and neglected thing it often is today. The ancient Egyptians rated it so highly they raised altars to it. Both the Greeks and the Romans thought it a sovereign remedy against drunkenness. Athenaeus quoted Eubulus as crying:

> Wife, quick! some cabbage boil, of virtues healing,
> That I may rid me of this seedy feeling.

And it had other virtues. Erasistratus considered it a positive cure for paralysis and even in those far-off days it was never cooked in plain salted water, but with a number of spices including cumin, caraway, pepper and fresh coriander.

Leeks were also popular, considered as a cure-all for many diseases, often cooked with cabbage, olives, beetroot, beans and other vegetables. And talking of beetroot, they have long been served in Greece with a simple dressing of oil and lemon or garlic sauce.

So many of the vegetables in vogue today had their origin in Greece and the Mediterranean generally. The cardoon – which is seldom seen in England, but can be grown there and looks a little like celery – is one; the artichoke has its roots, we are told, in Greece (although there are rival stories about Sicily); turnips and radishes, all these were known to the ancient Greeks, and naturally still are to the modern.

But Greeks are almost as fond of wild vegetables as they are of the cultivated kind and it is still a feature of Greek family life to go from time to time in due season to the mountains to collect the wild herbs and vegetables. Among these was the wild artichoke (still available), wild chicory and a type of wild spinach. There are dandelions, much used for stomach troubles among the country people, and, of course, there was, and still is, every kind of wild herb. These the industrious Greek housewife arranges and dries or uses as long as she can while fresh. And while searching for vegetables and herbs the Greeks may look for snails and put them into a sack in which flour has been generously sprinkled – to take away the ooziness of the snails. These sacks of snails, even today, are often carried for long distances to be turned later into succulent island meals – for snails are more popular in the islands than on the mainland.

STUFFED VINE LEAVES
DOLMATHES

In Greece, fresh vine leaves are available from spring to the end of autumn. After that they are kept, pliable and ready for use, preserved in brine in large tubs, and are sold in all the delicatessen stores. In Britain tinned vine leaves can now be bought in many specialist shops but, when not available, I would recommend using the leaves of the beet or very large spinach leaves. Lettuce leaves can be used but I do not think they are as good as either those of the beet or spinach for they are inclined to disintegrate easily.

Stuffed vine leaves may be eaten hot or cold but the method of preparation for the cold and hot stuffings is different. If using cold, you must use olive oil, otherwise there will be the flavour of congealed butter or fat. Also, it is better to prepare the *dolmathes* the day before they are required and keep them in a cool place – but not in the refrigerator.

Dolmathes are really not difficult to prepare and their flavour is delicious. They are usually served as an appetizer with drinks – at a table and sitting down. They are rather difficult to cope with as a cocktail snack, even though one usually eats *dolmathes* with one's fingers. In Britain they would make an excellent and unusual *hors-d'œuvre*.

50 *or* 60 *vine leaves, or one tin*	1 *pint stock or water*
Hot or cold rice stuffing	*Juice* ½ *lemon*
(see page 117)	1 *tablespoon tomato purée*

Take the leaves, whether from a tub of brine or from a tin, and drop them quickly into hot water. Then spread them out on a table and select all the best ones. On to each put a teaspoonful of rice stuffing. Roll the leaf into a neat little roll, roughly 2 inches long and about an inch across, to look like a small fat sausage. Tuck in the edges of the leaf as you roll.

Cover the bottom of a thick-bottomed pan with vine leaves – any torn leaves can be used for this – then arrange a layer of *dolmathes*, packing them tightly to prevent movement while cooking. Between each layer of *dolmathes* arrange another layer of leaves. When all are in the pan, add the stock or water mixed with the tomato *purée* and the lemon juice, cover with a plate – this also is to prevent the *dolmathes* from moving – then cover the pan with its lid. Cook very slowly for about 2 hours.

A tin of vine leaves usually contains about 50 leaves and the quantity of rice stuffing given in the recipe is for about 40 *dolmathes*. My own experience is that most people can eat from 4 to 6, for they are very small.

If serving the *dolmathes* hot, remove them from the pan and put into a warm oven while you make a sauce from the liquid in which they have been cooked. This consists of merely straining it and removing any bits of leaf. Some cooks stir a little yoghourt into the sauce, adding a flavour I heartily recommend.

If serving the *dolmathes* cold, leave them in the pan until they are quite cold. Then remove them carefully on to a platter and leave them until next day, or until really cold. Serve without sauce.

The secret of making successful *dolmathes* is to make them as small as possible and with not too much wrapping.

RICE AND MEAT STUFFING FOR HOT *DOLMATHES* ONLY
YEMISSIS ME KREAS KE RIZI

1 *lb minced lamb*
1 *breakfastcup rice*
2 *medium finely chopped onions*
2 *breakfastcups boiling stock (or water)*
1 *tablespoon chopped parsley*
A little sage
Salt and pepper
4 *tablespoons olive oil*

Heat the oil in a large saucepan and lightly fry the onions, meat and parsley, then add the rice. Fry for another 5 minutes. Add the stock, the seasonings and the sage. (You can also add chopped mint). Cook over the lowest possible heat for 15 minutes, by which time the rice should have absorbed all the liquid.

If olive oil is not available use either butter or good quality cooking fat. As soon as the stuffing is cool enough to handle, it is ready for use.

RICE STUFFING FOR COLD *DOLMATHES*
YEMISSIS ME RIZI

For this stuffing you *must* use olive oil. It is, I think, the only cooking oil which, when served cold, does not become thick, cloying and unpleasant.

8 oz rice
¼ pint olive oil
½ pint boiling water
1 tablespoon tomato purée
2 chopped onions
1 tablespoon pine-nuts

1 tablespoon currants
1 tablespoon chopped mint
1 teaspoon chopped sage
1 dessertspoon sugar
Salt and pepper

Heat the olive oil and lightly fry the onions. Add the rice and cook over a low heat for 20 minutes, stirring almost all the time. Add the water, the tomato *purée*, currants, pine-nuts, sage, mint, salt and pepper. Stir well, cover and continue cooking over a low heat for yet another 20 minutes. Stir in the sugar. By this time all the liquid should be absorbed but if not, pour away any which remains. Leave to cool in the pan before using.

I must apologize for repeating two recipes which have been already published in my books, *A Sultan's Pleasure* and *Cooking from the Commonwealth*. But these two recipes for stuffings are classical and they cannot fail to give the authentic flavour. They are typical of the Balkans from Yugoslavia to Istanbul and throughout the Middle East.

MEAT AND CELERY STUFFING
YEMISSIS ME KREAS KE SELINO

¾ lb minced meat – lamb or beef
3 oz rice
1 large finely chopped onion
2 stalks finely chopped celery
Handful finely chopped parsley

4 tablespoons olive oil
½ teaspoon cinnamon
Salt and pepper
Breadcrumbs

Enough to fill 6–8 large tomatoes, small aubergines, *courgettes* or peppers.

Scoop out the pulp from the vegetables which you propose to stuff. Chop this finely. Mix the meat, rice, onion, pulp, salt, pepper, 3 tablespoonfuls olive oil, cinnamon, parsley and celery.

As this is a stuffing using both uncooked rice and meat, at least an hour of slow baking should be allowed. It must also be remembered that rice swells in cooking and that the vegetables you are stuffing should never be more than three-quarters filled.

See stuffed peppers and stuffed tomatoes for further directions.

STUFFING FOR VEGETABLES
(Without Meat)
YEMISSIS HORIS KREAS

2 *finely chopped onions*	1 *tablespoon finely chopped dill*
4 *oz rice*	1 *cup olive oil*
3 *tablespoons pine-nuts*	*Salt and pepper*
Handful finely chopped parsley	

The above quantity is sufficient to fill 12 tomatoes, or about 10 large aubergines or *courgettes*. It is hard to give exact quantities in such recipes.

First scoop out the pulp from the vegetables you are wanting to stuff, and chop it finely. Heat the olive oil, then lightly fry the onions. When they begin to change colour add the vegetable pulp. Stir this for 5 minutes, add the rice, nuts, parsley, dill, salt and pepper and cook gently for 10 minutes. The stuffing is then ready to be filled into the empty vegetable cases. Only three-quarters fill the cases as the rice will continue to swell. See Stuffed Tomatoes.

ARTICHOKES
ANGINARES

When the Greeks talk of artichokes they mean what we call globe artichokes – and botanically they are correct. There are two other so-called artichokes, the Jerusalem and the Chinese, but these, botanists declare, are not true artichokes at all. The Jerusalem belongs to the sunflower or *helianthus* species, and the Chinese is a *stachys*. This information I find far less interesting than the legendary origin of the true artichoke, said to come from one of the Aegean Islands called Zinari where lived a beautiful girl named Cynara. She was so beautiful that a jealous God (or Goddess) turned her into a globe artichoke, which is of the species *cynara*.

However, botanists have another, unhappily more prosaic story which states that the artichoke is the result of the study and skill of botanists who worked on the cardoon and the common thistle, creating a hybrid.

A very long time ago Theophrastus, a Greek writer, wrote

of the artichoke, insisting that it was first grown in Sicily and
not in the Aegean Islands, which does, I fear, knock my legend
for six. He stated, 'they are edible when picked, are slightly
bitter and men preserve them in brine'. And he had the reputation of being a reliable reporter.

The Romans also liked artichokes and at one time they were
one of the most expensive items of their diet. At a much later
period Catharine de Medici took artichokes with her to France.
It was about then that the artichoke lost its reputation – like the
onion and garlic – and became a by-word for its 'heating' or
aphrodisiacal qualities, perhaps because of the Medicis.

By the seventeenth century the artichoke had won its way,
however, into English cooking and artichoke pie was considered a famous delicacy. Ben Jonson in his book, *Every Man
in His Humour*, mentions the 'artichoke that has pepper and
salt in and needs no more'.

There are several varieties of globe artichokes, at least a
dozen and possibly more. They grow extremely well in England.
Apparently our foggy, damp climate with not too much sun
suits the artichoke well. One gardener told me the reward for
his gardening efforts in artichokes was fresh, young artichokes
crisp to the tooth with the delicate sweet-bitter flavour un-
impaired.

BOILED GLOBE ARTICHOKES
ANGINARES VRASTES

Rinse as many artichokes as required in cold, salted water, pull
off any discoloured leaves, then trim the remaining leaves of
each artichoke with a pair of scissors, cutting off about half an
inch from the top. Trim round the base with a knife. Tie the
leaves together with cotton, bring this down under the artichoke
and affix quite firmly a thin slice of lemon to the base. (This is
to keep the base white, or as near as possible white, for it is
really a soft shade of green.) Have ready a large pan of boiling,
salted water and drop the artichokes into this. Cook steadily
for 45 minutes, or longer if they are still not tender. To test
for tenderness pull away a leaf. If it comes off easily the artichokes
are cooked.

Remove the cotton and the lemon and turn the artichokes upside down to drain. Serve with hot butter or a lemon and mustard sauce (see page 154).

Most people who like them can eat 2 medium-sized artichokes – or for that matter 2 large ones.

Try adding 1 whole clove of garlic, 1 tablespoonful of olive oil and 2 tablespoonfuls of vinegar to the pan when cooking artichokes. It may not be strictly Greek but it adds a certain piquancy to the flavour of the artichokes.

ARTICHOKES – CONSTANTINOPLE STYLE
ANGINARES À LA POLITA

A very popular dish among Greeks when the artichokes are first in season.

12 *medium-sized artichokes*
2–3 *thickly sliced carrots*
12 *small onions*
1 *lb small potatoes, preferably new*
1 *cup olive oil*

1 *tablespoon finely chopped dill*
4 *finely chopped spring onions, green stalks as well*
Juice 4 *lemons*
1 *tablespoon flour*
Salt *and pepper*

Thoroughly wash the artichokes, cut off the stems to about 1 inch of the globe, remove the coarser outer leaves and cut off ¼ inch from the tips of the remaining leaves. Cut each artichoke in half and scrape away the fuzz or choke. Leave the artichokes for about 15 minutes in salt water flavoured with the juice of 1 lemon. Drain well.

Put the artichokes, the carrots, potatoes (peeled or scraped), onions, dill, spring onions, salt and pepper into a pan and just cover with water. Beat the olive oil with the remaining lemon juice, add the flour, and when this mixture is well blended add it to the pan. Cover and cook very slowly for 1 hour, or until the artichokes are very tender. Serve them in the sauce in which they are cooked, garnished with the vegetables.

Many Greeks prefer to cook the artichokes whole but then they must be very young, too young for the fuzzy choke to have become coarse. Baby artichokes are quite delicious.

ARTICHOKES À LA GRÈQUE
(Greek-American Style)
ANGINARES HELLENIKES

1 *dozen small artichokes*
6 *very small peeled onions*
1 *clove garlic*
½ *cup white wine*

Juice 1 *lemon*
¼ *cup olive oil*
Salt and pepper to taste

Prepare the artichokes as in preceding recipe, then let them stand for 10 minutes in a bowl of boiling water. Drain. Put into a pan the onions, garlic, wine, lemon juice, olive oil, salt, pepper and finally the artichokes. Add boiling water to cover and cook them for 25 to 30 minutes, or until you can pull off the leaves easily. Take out the artichokes, turn them upside down to drain, then arrange on a dish. Reduce the liquid in which they have been cooked to about half or just a little less, add, if required, a little more salt and pepper and pour this, while still hot, over the artichokes. Leave until cold before serving.

This is the Greek-American version of *Anginares à la Polita*.

ARTICHOKE BOTTOMS AND BROAD BEANS
ANGINARES ME KOYKIA

For this recipe you can use tinned artichoke bottoms.

Cook in the usual manner about 2 pounds of broad beans, strain them and keep a little of the water in which they were cooked.

Heat 3 tablespoonfuls of olive oil in a pan and stir into it about 1 tablespoonful of flour or cornflour. Add a pint of the liquid from the beans, the strained juice of 1 lemon, a handful of finely chopped parsley, and blend this mixture thoroughly. Add the artichoke bottoms and the beans and simmer until the artichokes are hot.

Serve the vegetables in the sauce. It is a good idea to make the sauce in a fireproof dish which can also be used as a serving dish as this obviates the business of removing the artichoke bottoms and possibly breaking them.

STUFFED ARTICHOKES
ANGINARES YEMISTES

A popular dish with Greeks during the week preceding Easter.

8–10 *artichokes*
Juice 1 *large lemon*
¼ *pint olive oil*

1 *lb broad beans, these can be*
   fresh or frozen

Stuffing
1 *medium, finely chopped onion*
2 *cloves crushed garlic*
3 *finely chopped stalks celery*
Bunch *finely chopped parsley*

Handful *finely chopped dill*
1 *teaspoonful finely chopped*
   mint
Salt *and pepper*

Thoroughly wash the artichokes and cut off enough of the stems to make them 'sit' firmly when served. With a sharp pair of scissors, cut off about ½ inch of the tips of the leaves and sprinkle the artichokes well with lemon juice. Cook until almost tender. Drain, cool and then remove enough of the centre to be able to scrape away at the fuzzy heart or choke.

Make the Stuffing. Heat a tablespoonful of olive oil and lightly fry the onion and the garlic. Add the chopped herbs, celery, salt and pepper. Take from the pan and mix in a bowl with half the remaining oil. Insert this mixture into the leaves of the artichokes. Put the artichokes into a saucepan, add water almost to cover, and the remaining oil, and cook slowly for ½ hour. Add the beans (if using fresh) and continue to cook for another 25 minutes or until they are tender.

If using frozen beans cook them only for the length of time indicated on the packet. Stuffed artichokes may be served hot or cold.

FRIED ARTICHOKES
ANGINARES TIYANITES

6–8 *medium globe artichokes*
2 *eggs*
Juice 1 *lemon*

4 *oz breadcrumbs*
Salt *and pepper to taste*

Strip off the outer, tougher leaves of the artichokes, then cut each one lengthwise into halves and scrape out the choke.

Cover with water and lemon juice and leave them for about 2 hours to remove all the tiny insects which harbour within the leaves. Boil for about 30 minutes or steam for about 40 minutes, longer if the heads are large. Drain thoroughly.

Beat the eggs until light, adding one tablespoonful of warm (not hot) water. Dip the drained artichoke halves first into beaten egg, then breadcrumbs, again in egg, and then fry them in deep very hot oil until a golden brown. Can be served as a main dish or with fowl or meat. Many Greek cooks mix grated cheese with the breadcrumbs.

As my recipes are from varying sources there may appear certain inconsistencies. For example, this is the only recipe with artichokes which suggests soaking them in order to remove possible insects. Other Greek cooks prefer to remove all the leaves after washing the artichokes, boiling only the bottoms until just tender and then, with great care, drying these on a clean towel before they are fried. This method, remarked one Greek housewife to me, produces the flavour of the most exquisite brains, although why she should want her artichokes to taste of anything but artichoke is a puzzle to me.

AUBERGINES
MELITZANES

Aubergine, or egg plant, as the Americans call it, has a large and enthusiastic following in many parts of the world. The Italians, French, Greeks and all the Balkan peoples use it extensively. So do the Indians, who call it *brinjal*.

There are several varieties, ranging from almost black to ivory white, and in shape, from tiny balls to long sausage shapes. They were introduced into England in the nineteenth century but as this was before the days of greenhouses gardeners found them almost impossible to grow; they do require some warmth. The name aubergine is supposed to have been derived from an Arabic word meaning 'peach'.

There are some general rules for cooking aubergines. First, they contain a large percentage of water, a fact which can cause trouble to the unwary cook, for when an aubergine is peeled or cut the watery content is not apparent at all. Before frying aubergine I usually sprinkle the slices generously with salt then pile them on to a platter and cover with a plate. If left for an hour or so, much of the water disappears. Before using, the slices should be dried and then fried in deep boiling oil, otherwise they will not be crisp. Properly fried thick slices of aubergine are soft inside and delightfully crisp on the outside.

AUBERGINES WITH ONIONS AND TOMATOES
MELITZANES YAHNI

Slice 2 or 3 medium-sized aubergines, sprinkle with salt and press between 2 plates. Leave for an hour or so, then wipe dry.

Heat plenty of olive oil in a pan and quickly brown the aubergine slices. When these are ready, take them from the pan, pour off most of the oil, then brown one sliced onion. Return the aubergine slices plus plenty of chopped parsley, peeled and thinly sliced tomatoes, a bayleaf and some slivers of garlic. Cook very slowly for 45 minutes. Serve hot.

This is not unlike the Provençale dish of *ratatouille*. Some Greek housewives prefer not to fry the aubergine slices before putting them on to the browned onions. It is less rich this way.

Enough for 3 or 4 people, depending on the size of the aubergines.

STUFFED AUBERGINES
MELITZANES YEMISTES

4 *medium-sized aubergines*	*Handful finely chopped parsley*
2 *large chopped tomatoes*	3 *tablespoons olive oil*
1–2 *crushed cloves garlic*	*Salt and pepper*
1–2 *chopped onions*	

Put the aubergines into a large pan, cover with water and bring to the boil. Cook for 5 minutes, drain and pat dry. Cut 3 or 4 slits, lengthwise, into each aubergine. Mix the tomatoes, garlic, onions, parsley, salt and pepper and push as much of the mixture as will go, into the slits. Rub the aubergines with olive oil and place them in a baking tin. Add ½ pint of hot water and bake in a moderate oven for 1½ hours, or until tender.

Failing an oven, cover the pan and cook on top of the stove.

Sufficient for 2 or 4 people, according to the size of the aubergines.

STUFFED AUBERGINE IMAM BAYILDI
IMAM BAYILDI

Strictly speaking this is a Turkish recipe but the Greeks have taken it into their kitchens. Some Greeks even claim it as a Moorish dish. An amusing story is connected with it; in fact, there are many versions of the same story. Once there was a famous Turkish *Imam* (a priest) who was particularly fond of aubergine. Naturally his wife tried to give him aubergine as often as she could, always thinking up new ways of cooking it. One day she prepared some in the manner of this recipe and her delighted *Imam* found them so good that he swooned in ecstasy. Since then both her recipe and the story have become legendary, hence the name, which means 'fainting *Imam*'.

Two other reasons given for the swooning are that the *Imam* was a mean man and fainted when he saw the vast quantity of oil used; or that he fainted because the richness overpowered him.

6 *long aubergines*
3 *chopped onions*
3 *large chopped and peeled tomatoes*
2 *sliced tomatoes*
Crushed garlic to taste
1–2 *teaspoons sugar*

Plenty finely chopped parsley
Salt and pepper
½ *pint hot stock or water*
½ *pint olive oil* – (see what I mean?)
Juice 1 lemon

Cut off and discard the green end of the aubergines and make 3 slits in each stretching from end to end. Do not peel them. Sprinkle a little salt inside the slits and leave for 20 minutes. Then gently squeeze each aubergine to rid it of excess water. Heat the oil and fry the aubergines for 5 minutes or until they begin to wilt, turning 2 or 3 times. Take them from the pan and put aside until required. In the same pan fry the onions until they are a golden brown. Also take these from the pan and put into a basin.

Add to the onions the chopped tomatoes, parsley, garlic, salt and pepper. Mix all this well together and stuff the mixture into the slits of the aubergines. Arrange the aubergines in a baking dish and pour over them the olive oil in which you fried the onions. Cover the aubergines with the sliced tomatoes, pour in the stock, the lemon juice, sugar and a little more salt. Cover the pan and bake in a moderate oven until the aubergines are quite soft. Leave to cool before taking them from the pan and then serve quite cold. At least, this is the Balkan way of serving this dish. It is just as good served hot, I think even better.

Sugar is optional, being added merely to reduce the acidity of the tomatoes.

If, like the *Imam*, you find this dish rather rich, do not swoon, but make a few alterations instead. For example, use half the quantity of olive oil and do not pre-fry either the onions or the aubergines. Instead, simply mix the vegetables with some of the oil, using the remainder for cooking.

But, if you do this, although you will have a palatable dish, it will not be a real *Imam Bayildi*.

'LITTLE SHOES'
(Stuffed Aubergines)
PAPOUTSAKIA

6 *aubergines of medium size*	1 *tablespoon finely chopped*
4 *oz butter*	*parsley*
1–2 *finely chopped onions*	*Salt and pepper*
6–8 *oz minced meat (veal,*	1 *pint béchamel sauce*
lamb or beef)	(see page 151)
½ *cup tomato juice*	*Grated Parmesan cheese*

Wash the aubergines and cut them in halves lengthwise. Scoop out the pulp, chop this finely and fry the empty cases in a little butter until they begin to soften. Remove from the pan and arrange in a baking dish.

Add all but one ounce of the remaining butter to the frying pan. Heat this, then add the onions, brown them; add the meat, let this brown, then add the pulp, parsley, salt and pepper, and finally the tomato juice. Cook over a moderate heat until the mixture is fairly dry. Take it from the stove, leave until cool, then add grated cheese to taste. Fill the empty cases with this mixture. Cover each with a layer of *béchamel* sauce and sprinkle with grated cheese. Add about half a cup of boiling water to the pan, and the remaining butter and bake in a moderate oven until the sauce is brown and the aubergines soft – about 30 minutes. Serve hot.

AUBERGINE FRITTERS
MELITZANES TIYANITES

Slice as many aubergines as required, about ¼ of an inch thick. Sprinkle the slices with salt and put between two plates for 2 hours. Wipe free of salt and moisture, lightly coat in flour and fry in deep boiling olive oil until browned on both sides. Serve hot.

I recommend fried aubergine served with beaten yoghourt flavoured with crushed garlic. The aubergine should be very hot and the yoghourt cold – this is not Greek but typically Balkan.

RUNNER BEANS
FASSOLAKIA FRESKA

Trim as many runner beans as required, then break each into 2 or 3 pieces. Fry some onions in a little oil or butter until they begin to change colour. Add about a tablespoonful of tomato *purée*, sufficient boiling water to cover, bring to the boil, add the beans and cook slowly for ¾ of an hour. Season with salt and pepper to taste.

To 2 pounds of beans 1 medium–sized onion would be sufficient. To be served as a main course.

GREEN BEANS WITH TOMATOES
FASSOLAKIA FRESKA ME DOMATES

2 *lb green beans* (*French or string*)	About 1 *cup olive oil*
	Salt and pepper
1 *onion*	*Sugar*
1 *lb tomatoes*	*Chopped parsley*

Peel and chop the tomatoes and the onion. Wash and trim the beans, snap them into halves if they are very long but do not slice them thinly in the usual English manner. Heat the olive oil, lightly fry the onion, add the beans and simmer until they begin to soften. At this point add the tomatoes, salt, pepper and parsley, a little sugar and just enough water to cover. Continue to cook slowly until the beans are tender, about 40 minutes is the Greek timing.

Beans cooked in this way are usually served as a main course but they can be offered as an accompaniment to a meat dish. The amount of oil is probably rather excessive for the British palate but it can be reduced by half or even more. This quantity of beans would be enough for 4 people if served as a main course.

Not all Greek cooks use sugar when cooking tomatoes – its purpose is to reduce the acid content. Many modern Greek housewives are also beginning to disapprove of large quantities of olive oil being used and of pre-frying their vegetables before boiling them.

BRAISED CABBAGE
LAHANA YAHNI

1 *large cabbage*	2 *small, thinly sliced carrots*
2 *medium-sized, finely chopped onions*	*Salt and pepper to taste*
	A few capers
1–2 *chopped stalks celery*	2 *oz olive oil*
2 *chopped tomatoes*	

Discard the outer, coarse leaves and the stalks of the cabbage, cut it into 4 quarters and each quarter again into 2 pieces. Remove any really thick stem. Wash the cabbage thoroughly and drain. Heat the oil and lightly cook the onions, add the celery, tomatoes, carrots, salt and pepper and lastly the cabbage, with just enough water to prevent sticking or burning. Cook for 10 minutes, add the capers and continue to cook until the cabbage is tender.

The olive oil can be omitted if you like: the cabbage is still very good cooked with this mixture of vegetables.

STUFFED CABBAGE LEAVES
(with pork and rice)
LAHANA DOLMATHES ME HIRINO

1 *very large cabbage*	*Salt and pepper*
2 *lb minced pork*	*Spice*
6 *oz rice*	*Egg and lemon sauce*
2 *oz butter or olive oil*	(see page 152)
1 *chopped onion*	

The usual spice in this stuffing is aniseed – but caraway, cinnamon or any other spice may be used provided it matches with pork – and incidentally many Greeks feel that only a pork stuffing marries with cabbage. This is not my opinion. I have made cabbage *dolmathes* many times and found that all varieties of meat or meatless stuffings produce a very palatable dish.

Heat the butter or oil and lightly fry the onions. Add the pork, rice, salt and pepper and the spice. Cook very slowly for about 10 minutes, stirring almost all the while. Take from the heat.

Cook the cabbage in boiling, salted water long enough to soften the leaves, 5 or 10 minutes. Drain and when cool enough to handle separate the leaves. Lay these flat on a table and trim the thick centre vein – this is to make the leaves more pliable. Put on to each leaf about a tablespoonful of the meat mixture (the actual amount depends on the size of the leaf.) Roll each leaf carefully into a package, as described for vine leaf *dolmathes* on page 115. Arrange the *dolmathes* in a large shallow pan in neat rows and close together. If you need to make a second layer put spare cabbage leaves on top of the *dolmathes*, then arrange remaining *dolmathes* on top of the leaves. Add water to cover and cover with a plate to keep the *dolmathes* steady. Put on the lid of the saucepan and cook slowly for at least 1 hour. Remove the *dolmathes* carefully from the pan and serve hot with an egg and lemon sauce which you can prepare while the *dolmathes* are cooking.

Sufficient for between 4 and 6 people – but it is difficult to say exactly since the cabbage leaves vary so much in size, appetites vary even more, and some people like to put more meat in the leaves, others less.

STUFFED CABBAGE LEAVES
DOLMATHES LAHANA

16 *cabbage leaves*
6 *oz rice*
2 *finely chopped onions*
1–2 *crushed cloves garlic*
1 *tablespoon pine-nuts*
1 *tablespoon sultanas or currants*

Pinch ground nutmeg or cinnamon
2–3 *finely chopped tomatoes*
Salt and pepper
3 *tablespoons olive oil*
Tomato and lemon juice (optional)
Flour or cream

The cabbage leaves must be fairly large, whole and fresh, and as it takes only a minute or so to make them pliable it is better to make the stuffing first.

Heat the oil and fry the rice for 2 or 3 minutes, then add the onions, garlic, sultanas (or currants) and pine-nuts. Stir almost all the while and let these ingredients cook slowly until a golden brown, but not too dark. Add the tomatoes, the nutmeg or cinnamon, salt and pepper. Continue simmering for about 5 minutes more. Put aside until required, but keep hot.

Blanch the cabbage leaves in boiling water to make them pliable. Spread the leaves out on a table and trim away the thick centre vein – this makes the leaves easier to roll. Put a small portion of the stuffing on to each leaf, roll it up carefully, tucking in the edges (as described for Vine Leaf *Dolmathes* on page 115). Pack the *dolmathes* close together in a saucepan, cover with salted water or tomato juice, sprinkle with lemon juice and place an upturned plate over them to keep them steady. If the *dolmathes* have plenty of space they will swim around and possibly break. Cover with the saucepan lid and cook very slowly for $\frac{3}{4}$ of an hour. Take the *dolmathes* from the pan when cooked, keep them hot while you thicken the sauce – this can be done with cream or with a flour and water paste. Serve the *dolmathes* and their sauce separately.

CAULIFLOWER COOKED IN TOMATO JUICE
KOUNOUPITHI YAHNI

1 *large or 3 small cauliflowers*	*Handful finely chopped parsley*
2 *large, finely chopped onions*	*Salt and pepper*
1 *tin tomato juice*	2 *oz oil*
1–2 *pounded cloves garlic*	*Flour* (optional)

Thoroughly wash the cauliflower, remove the coarse stalks and
separate the flowerets. Heat the oil and fry the onions and the
garlic until a golden brown, then add the tomato juice, salt,
pepper and parsley and bring this to the boil. Add the cauliflower and cook it until tender. Serve the sauce separately –
this can be thickened with flour.

CELERIAC WITH EGG AND LEMON SAUCE
SELINORRIZES AVGOLEMONO

About 1 *lb celeriac*	*Egg and lemon sauce*
4 *oz butter*	(see page 152)
Salt and pepper	

Wash and peel the celeriac and cut it into cubes. Heat the butter
and brown the pieces, add salt and pepper and enough water
or stock to cover. Cook until tender. Prepare the egg and
lemon sauce, using some of the liquid from the celeriac to thin
it. Take the pan from the fire and pour the sauce into it, mixing
it with the celeriac. Return it to the stove to re-heat but take it
off before the sauce actually boils. Cover and leave to 'settle'
for 2 or 3 minutes, then serve hot.

Celery can be used in precisely the same manner as celeriac
except that it takes half the time to cook.

STEWED MARROW OR SQUASH I
KOLOKITHAKIA YAHNI I

Many years ago, when I was in America for the first time, I
was offered squash – Hubbard squash to be exact. I asked the
waitress, 'What is squash?' and she replied (rather tersely, I
thought), 'Squash is squash'. She was more or less right, squash

is squash. Eleanor Sinclair Rohde in her book, *Uncommon Vegetables and Fruits* (Country Life), mentions ten different kinds of squash that can be grown in England. With this particular recipe you can use pumpkin, cucumber, baby marrows, or custard marrows, etc.

1 *lb marrow or squash*	4 *peeled and chopped tomatoes*
¼ *cup olive oil*	½ *cup water*
2 *large chopped onions*	*Salt and pepper*
1 *tablespoon finely chopped parsley*	*Grated cheese*

Cut the marrow into one-inch cubes. If the vegetable is young there is no need to peel it first, scraping is enough, but this is a matter for personal preference. Heat the olive oil, lightly brown the onions, then add the tomatoes, salt, pepper, parsley and water. Cook for 5 minutes, stir until blended, then add the marrow, cover and cook slowly for about 30 minutes.

Serve hot with grated cheese.

When using marrows, ideally they should be small, not more than 5 inches long and nicely plump. At this stage they have a delicate flavour.

STEWED MARROW II
KOLOKITHAKIA YAHNI II

2 *lb marrow (or similar squash)*	*Handful finely chopped parsley*
1 *lb tomatoes*	*Salt and pepper to taste*
½ *lb finely chopped onions*	½ *cup olive oil*

Peel the marrow, scrape out the seeds and cut the flesh into small pieces, roughly the size of an egg. Peel and chop the tomatoes into fairly small pieces.

Heat the oil, lightly brown the onions, add the tomatoes and when these are soft add the marrow, salt, pepper, parsley and a very little water, only enough to prevent the vegetables from burning. Bring to the boil, then cook more slowly until the marrow is tender but not a squashed mass.

Serve with a garlic sauce (see page 152).

Enough for 6 people and meant to be served as a main course.

MARROW PIE (Greek-American)
KOLOKITHOPITA

2 *lb marrow*   1 *lb sliced tomatoes*
3 *thinly sliced onions*   ½ *cup soft breadcrumbs*
½ *cup finely chopped parsley*   ½ *cup olive oil*
  and dill (mixed)   *Salt and pepper*

Scrape or peel the marrow and thickly slice it. Rub a baking tin with oil, cover the bottom with a layer of marrow, and spread with onion, tomato, breadcrumbs, salt, pepper, parsley and dill. Repeat this until all the ingredients are used up, with tomatoes as the top layer. Pour olive oil over the top, distributing it evenly. Bake in a moderate oven for about 1 hour – longer if necessary, until all the vegetables are soft.

This quantity is sufficient for 6 people. I usually add also either some tomato juice or a little stock to the pie, as it can sometimes be a little dry.

MARROW FRITTERS
KOLOKITHOKEFTETHES

1½ *lb marrow*   2 *tablespoons melted butter*
1 *large, finely chopped onion*   1 *lb soft breadcrumbs*
3 *tablespoons finely chopped*   2 *eggs*
  parsley   *Salt and pepper*
3 *tablespoons grated cheese*   *Olive oil and butter for frying*

Peel the marrow, scrape out the seeds, cut into halves and cook in boiling, salted water with the onion until soft. Drain absolutely free from water then mash until smooth. Put the mashed marrow into a mixing bowl, add salt and pepper, cheese, breadcrumbs, the melted butter, then add the eggs without beating them first. Mix all this together and leave for 1 hour. Shape into rissoles – any size you like – and fry in a mixture of equal parts olive oil and butter until brown.

Enough for 4 to 6 people.

LADIES' FINGERS WITH TOMATOES
BAMIES ME DOMATES

1 *lb ladies' fingers*
6 *peeled and chopped tomatoes*
½ *cup olive oil*
½ *cup vinegar*

2 *large chopped onions*
Handful finely chopped parsley
Salt and pepper

Wash the ladies' fingers, carefully trim off the stems, taking care not to cut into the flesh. Put them into a bowl, pour the vinegar over them and leave for 30 minutes. Rinse thoroughly.

Heat the olive oil and brown the onions, add the tomatoes and cook slowly for 5 minutes. Add the ladies' fingers, parsley, salt, pepper and enough hot water to cover. Cook slowly for ¾ of an hour.

Failing fresh ladies' fingers, the tinned variety can be used, but cooking time will be less, although with such dishes it does not really matter how long they are cooked as long as the vegetables are tender. The amount of oil can easily be reduced to half, which is better for the average non-Mediterranean palate. The reason for soaking the ladies' fingers in vinegar is to take away some of their stickiness. This is meant to be a main dish and not an accompanying vegetable to meat.

STUFFED PEPPERS
PIPERIES YEMISTES

To stuff peppers, you can use any of the stuffings prepared for *dolmathes* or tomatoes. Cut around the stalks very carefully and remove them but put on one side, to be returned later as little lids. Carefully take out the cores and seeds and continue as for stuffed tomatoes, (see page 139). Some cooks prefer to soften the peppers in boiling water before stuffing but usually the peppers become soft enough during cooking. Whether the peppers (*capsicum*) are green, red or yellow does not matter, the flavour is the same. However, variety in colour does add to the appearance of a dish of stuffed peppers. When serving stuffed vegetables I like to mix them in any case: tomatoes, aubergines, *courgettes* and peppers all appear at the same meal.

POTATO PIE
(Greek Shepherd's Pie)
PATATES PURÉE ME KREAS

3–4 *floury potatoes*   2 *crushed cloves garlic*
1 *lb minced lamb or beef*   *Butter*
2 *minced onions*   *Salt and pepper*

Cook the potatoes in their skins until very soft. As soon as they
are cool enough to handle, peel and mash them until quite
smooth. Add salt and pepper and enough butter to make the
potatoes creamy. It is worthwhile taking the trouble to whip
the potatoes with a wire whisk.

Heat a little butter in a pan, add the meat, stir it well, and as
it begins to change colour add the garlic and the onions. Cook
gently for about 10 or 15 minutes, add salt and pepper. The
onions should become soft but not brown.

Rub a casserole lightly with butter, then spread it with half
of the mashed potatoes. Cover with the meat mixture, then
with the remainder of the potatoes. Dot the top with butter
and bake in a moderate oven until the potato has browned.

This is sufficient for between 5 and 6 people. Some Greeks
add chopped tomatoes as well, cooking these with the meat
and onions until soft.

POTATOES COOKED WITH TOMATOES
PATATES YAHNI

There are many Greek vegetable dishes cooked in this manner,
usually with olive oil, but butter or other cooking fat may be substituted.

2–3 *lb potatoes*   ½ *cup olive oil*
1 *lb chopped onions*   *Salt and pepper*
1 *lb peeled and chopped tomatoes*

Wash and peel the potatoes and cut into uniform sizes. Heat
the oil and fry the onions until they are a golden brown. Add
the tomatoes, simmer until soft, then add the potatoes, salt
and pepper and enough hot water to cover. Cook until the
potatoes are soft and the sauce is thick.

Usually served as a main dish.

POTATO CROQUETTES
PATATES KROKETES

1 lb potatoes
1 oz butter
1 small, finely chopped onion
½ tablespoon finely chopped
  parsley

Salt and pepper
2 oz grated cheese
2 well beaten eggs
Olive oil for frying
Flour

Wash and cook the potatoes in their skins until very soft, peel
as soon as possible and then mash them until smooth. Add the
butter, onion, salt, pepper, parsley and 1 egg. With floured
hands form this mixture into rounds, quite small; roll them in
the remaining egg, coat with cheese, then fry in deep, boiling
oil until a golden brown. Serve very hot.

Potato croquettes are often served as appetizers with drinks.

POTATO OMELETTE
OMELETTA ME PATATES

3 medium potatoes
4 eggs
Little grated cheese

3 tablespoons grated onion
Butter or cooking fat
Salt and pepper

Wash and peel the potatoes and cut into very thin strips. Put
enough butter into a frying pan and fry first the onion till a
light brown, and then the potatoes. Beat the eggs, add the
grated cheese, salt and pepper and pour this mixture into the
pan over the potatoes and onions. Continue to cook over a
medium heat until the eggs have set.

This type of omelette is not folded but usually slid flat on to
a hot plate for serving. If you possess one of those frying pans
which can also be used at table, all the better.

SPINACH WITH RICE
SPANAKORIZO

2 lb spinach
2 leeks (optional)
2 medium onions

4 oz rice
½ cup olive oil
Salt and pepper

Thoroughly wash the spinach and break it into small pieces.
Clean and chop the remaining vegetables. Heat the olive oil,
add the spinach and chopped vegetables and cook until brown.
Add salt and pepper and continue cooking until the mixture is
soft. Add 1 pint of water, bring this to the boil, then add the
rice and cook until the rice is tender – from 15 to 20 minutes.

If using the leeks, remember to use as much of the green
part as possible.

SPINACH PIE WITH CHEESE I
SPANAKOPITA I

2 lb spinach
1 tablespoon finely chopped dill
2 tablespoons finely chopped parsley
2–3 large, finely chopped onions

½ lb mashed feta cheese
10 sheets of phyllo pastry
(see page 162)
1 cup olive oil
Salt and pepper

Thoroughly wash the spinach, chop it finely, sprinkle it with
salt and pepper and leave it for 1 hour. Squeeze it to remove its
bitter liquid. Heat the olive oil and fry the onions until brown,
add the spinach and cook this until tender, stirring all the time.
With a perforated spoon take it from the pan and put it into a
bowl. Crumble the *feta* cheese into the bowl, add pepper,
parsley and dill. Mix well. Let the olive oil cool.

Brush with oil a 3-inch-deep baking tin – it should be about
12 inches in length and about 8 inches wide – and line it with
1 sheet of pastry. Brush this with oil, add 4 more sheets of pastry
brushing each with oil. Cover the last sheet with the spinach
mixture, add the remaining pastry, each sheet brushed with oil.
Score the top sheet into squares – using a sharp, pointed knife –
sprinkle the top lightly with water, to prevent the pastry from
curling upwards, and bake the pie in a moderate oven until the
top is a golden brown, about 40 minutes. Cool slightly before
cutting into squares and serve either hot or cold.

If *phyllo* pastry is not available use flaky pastry and make a
pie in the usual way.

SPINACH PIE II
SPANAKOPITA II

4 *lb spinach*	*Salt and pepper*
Bunch mixed herbs	*Olive oil for frying*
Anise or aniseed to taste	10 *sheets phyllo pastry*
1–2 *finely chopped onions*	(see page 162)

The bunch of herbs in Greece would include many mountain herbs and certainly some chopped dandelion. Anise or aniseed is a popular Greek flavouring. If you do not care for this flavour, then leave it out. But highly flavoured herbs do improve the flavour of the pie and it will be more interesting if you can get them.

Wash the spinach – you can sprinkle it with pepper and salt and leave for an hour as in previous recipe – and then cook it in a pan without adding any more liquid than that which adheres to its leaves. Add the herbs, finely chopped, salt and pepper and cook the spinach until tender. In the meantime heat some olive oil and fry the onions until soft and beginning to brown. Take the onions from the pan, stir them into the spinach and chop this mixture until everything is blended and smooth. Line a greased pie dish – 3 inches deep by about 10 inches wide and 6 or 8 inches across, with 1 sheet of pastry, add 4 more sheets, brushing each sheet with oil. Spread the top layer with the spinach, add remaining sheets, brushing each with oil, sprinkle the top layer with a little water and bake the pie in a moderate oven until the pastry is a golden brown, about 40 minutes. If the pastry begins to brown too quickly cover it with paper or lower the heat.

STUFFED TOMATOES I
DOMATES YEMISTES I

8 *large, firm tomatoes*	2 *tablespoons finely chopped mint*
1 *teacup rice*	
1 *teacup olive oil*	2 *tablespoons finely chopped parsley*
2 *finely chopped onions*	
1 *oz currants*	*Salt and pepper to taste*
1 *oz pine-nuts*	*Breadcrumbs*

Only because it looks nicer, choose tomatoes of uniform size. Slice off the stem end of each and scoop out the pulp, core and seeds. Chop this finely and sprinkle the inside of the tomatoes with a little salt and pepper.

Heat the oil and fry the onions to a golden brown. Stir in the tomato pulp, the rice, mint, parsley, salt, pepper, currants and pine-nuts. Simmer for 2 minutes, then add ½ a pint of water and cook slowly until the rice begins to soften, about 7 minutes.

Pack this mixture into the empty tomato cases, but do not completely fill them as the rice will swell. Replace the sliced-off tops and arrange the tomatoes in an oiled baking tin. Brush each tomato with oil and sprinkle with breadcrumbs. Bake in a moderate oven for about 45 minutes. Serve hot or cold, although cold is more usual in Greece.

Instead of first frying the stuffing, you can mix the chopped tomato pulp with the remaining ingredients in their raw state. This produces a slightly less rich dish.

STUFFED TOMATOES II
DOMATES YEMISTES II

About 12 *firm tomatoes*
2–3 *large chopped onions*
10 *oz rice*
4–5 *crushed cloves garlic*
1 *large cored and finely chopped*
  pepper
Handful chopped parsley

1 *tablespoon chopped mint*
1 *tablespoon chopped currants*
1 *tablespoon pine-nuts*
1 *cup olive oil*
Salt and pepper
1 *oz tomato purée*

Carefully cut round the upper part of the tomatoes at the stalk end. Remove the tops but keep these to use later as a lid. Scoop out the core and the pulp. Put the hollowed-out tomatoes in a shallow baking dish, sprinkle with salt and leave until the filling is ready.

Chop the core into minute pieces and mix with the pulp. Put the chopped onions into a pan, add water to cover, bring to the boil and cook for 3 minutes. Drain off the water, add half the olive oil and simmer the onions. Add the tomato pulp and just cover with hot water. Bring to the boil, add the garlic,

parsley, pepper, mint, seasoning, currants, pine-nuts and finally
the rice. Blend well and remove from the heat – the rice has not
even begun to cook at this stage and the mixture should be
comparatively loose. Fill some of this into each of the hollowed-
out tomatoes and put back the 'lids'. Put the remaining olive
oil into the pan, add the tomato *purée*, diluted with enough
water to make a thin gravy, and pour this over the tomatoes.
Bake in a moderate oven until the tomatoes are tender and the
rice has cooked, roughly about 40 minutes. Where there is no
oven available the tomatoes can be cooked, covered, on the
top of the stove.

TOMATOES STUFFED WITH MINCED MEAT
DOMATES YEMISES ME KIMA

Slice off the stalk end and scoop out the pulp from as many
large and firm tomatoes as you require – they should, if possible,
be of uniform size. Chop the pulp and core. Heat some olive oil
and lightly fry some minced onion until brown, add a good
quantity of raw minced meat, brown this, then add the tomato
pulp, salt, pepper and chopped parsley. Stir this mixture together,
fry it for a few minutes and almost fill the empty tomato cases.
Sprinkle the open tops with breadcrumbs. Put into a shallow
baking tin, add enough hot water to prevent burning and bake
in a moderate oven until the tomatoes are soft.

Aubergines, peppers, onions and *courgettes* can all be stuffed
and baked in the same manner.

For such recipes it is not too easy to give fixed quantities,
since it depends so much on the size of the vegetables to be
stuffed and individual taste. I think the experienced cook can
easily decide how much stuffing goes into a tomato – and
there are other recipes in this section which can act as a guide.
Cooked minced meat can be used instead of raw.

TOMATOES STUFFED WITH AUBERGINE
DOMATES YEMISTES ME MELITZANES

8–10 *large, firm tomatoes*   *Salt and pepper*
2 *medium-sized aubergines*   3 *oz grated cheese*
2 *medium-sized minced onions*   2 *beaten eggs*
3 *oz olive oil (or butter)*   *Sugar*
½ *cup fine breadcrumbs*
3 *tablespoons finely chopped parsley*

Cut off the tops of the tomatoes and scoop out the pulp. Sprinkle
the insides with salt and a little sugar and arrange them in a
baking dish.

Without peeling, cut the aubergines into very small pieces.
Heat 2 ounces of oil, add the onions and simmer until they have
become a light brown. Add the tomato pulp with the core
(chopped into small pieces) and simmer for 5 minutes, then add
the chopped aubergine and cook this until it is soft. Add half
of the breadcrumbs, parsley, salt and pepper, cook and stir
for 2 or 3 minutes. Remove from the fire and cool a little. Add
the cheese and when this is completely blended into the mixture
stir in the 2 eggs. Do this briskly otherwise you might find yourself
with a curdled omelette. Beat the mixture before putting it into
the tomatoes. Sprinkle the open top with the remaining breadcrumbs and oil. Put into a baking pan with hot water and bake
in a medium oven until the tomatoes are tender.

The tomatoes should be really large and, if possible, all of
uniform size.

SHRIMP STUFFED TOMATOES
DOMATES YEMISTES ME YARITHES

Drop as many tomatoes as required into boiling water and
leave for a minute or so, then peel. Leave until cold, before
cutting off the tops and carefully removing the pulp. Fill the
empty cases with cooked shrimps which have been mixed with
salad cream or mayonnaise. Chill before serving.

The pulp should be saved and used either in a soup or sauce.

BUTTER BEANS COOKED WITH TOMATOES AND ONIONS
FASSOLIA YIYANDES PLAKI

1½ lb dried white beans	1 cup olive oil
1½ lb chopped onions	1 teaspoon sugar
2 chopped cloves garlic	Salt and pepper
1½ lb peeled and chopped tomatoes	2 tablespoons finely chopped mint

Soak the beans overnight and next morning cook them rapidly in water for 5 minutes. Drain, return them to the stove with fresh salted water and leave to cook until they are tender. Thoroughly drain them, keep the water, and in this cook the chopped onions for 5 minutes. Now drain off the water from the onions and add a quarter of the olive oil and cook the onions in this until they begin to brown. Add the beans, the tomatoes, garlic, remaining oil, salt, pepper, sugar and mint and continue cooking very slowly for another 30 minutes.

Both the onions and the tomatoes should be very finely chopped. Instead of fresh tomatoes you can use tinned (but first rub them through a sieve), or thick tomato juice. The quantity of mint can be reduced to taste, or, if preferred, use parsley.

DRIED BEANS BOILED WITH VEGETABLES
FASSOLIA YAHNI

This recipe can be used with all types of dried beans.

1½ lb white dried beans	4 medium-sized, coarsely chopped carrots
1 cup olive oil	
1 heaped tablespoon tomato purée	1 bunch chopped celery
	Salt and pepper
1–2 chopped onions	Bicarbonate of soda

Soak the beans overnight. Next morning put them into a large saucepan with plenty of water. Cover and bring them to the boil. Cook quickly for 20 minutes. Then add a pinch of bicarbonate of soda and continue to cook rapidly for another 15 minutes. Drain them well, add the olive oil, tomato purée (diluted

with a little water), the onions, carrots, celery, salt and pepper.
Add hot water to cover and bring this once to the boil, reduce
the heat and continue cooking until the beans are quite tender.

MIXED LENTILS AND NOODLES
(Rhodes)
ALVEROF (FAKI ME PASTA)

1 *lb lentils*   2 *quarts cold water*
12 *oz noodles*   *Salt and pepper to taste*
1–2 *large, finely chopped onions*   ½ *pint boiling water*
Olive oil or butter for frying

Put the lentils into a pan with the water, cover and bring to the
boil over a quick heat. Reduce the heat to moderate and continue cooking until the lentils are just soft. Add the noodles,
broken into squares, salt and pepper, then the boiling water.
Continue cooking over a good heat until the noodles are tender,
about 20 minutes.

While this is cooking, fry the onions in oil or butter until
brown. Strain the lentils and noodles, turn out on to a large,
heated platter and garnish with the fried onions.

This is sufficient for 6 to 8 people and should be served very
hot.

DRIED WHITE BEANS WITH PORK
FASSOLIA ME HIRINO

Soak 1 pound of beans overnight and next morning cook them
rapidly in water for 5 minutes. Drain, return them to the stove
with fresh, salted water and leave to cook until they are tender.
Drain. (The water can always be used as a basis for a soup.)

Fry in a little butter or oil 1 pound of pork cut into cubes or
slices, add 1 large, minced onion, tomato juice to cover, salt
and pepper and cook until the meat is tender, adding from time
to time a very little hot water. When the meat is tender, add the
drained beans, blend well, continue to cook for another 10
minutes, then serve hot.

CHICK-PEAS
REVITHIA YAHNI

Soak 2 pounds of chick-peas overnight, or better still for 24 hours. Drain and put them into a towel and then rub back and forth until the skins of the chick-peas are rubbed off. Put the peas into a pan with plenty of water and cook for 4 hours. When they are soft, flavour with crushed garlic, quite a lot of chopped onion, tomatoes, mint or parsley, salt and pepper. Cook gently for another 20 minutes – the heat should be low but the chick-peas must be boiling all the while. The best way to cook chick-peas is to have them on the side of a large coal- or coke-burning stove.

This would be considered rather in the nature of a Lenten dish, or a dish for a canteen or families with hearty appetites. Sometimes pieces of pork are added or garlic sausage – although this latter is more of a Spanish custom than Greek. Two pounds of chick-peas makes a solid meal for 6 to 8 people.

Rice and Pasta

PILAFIA KE PASTA

PILAU
PILAFI

A basic recipe which can be adjusted to suit individual tastes.
If you do not care for the flavour of tomato, omit the tomato
paste.

1 *lb long grain rice*	1 *tablespoon tomato paste*
2 *pints boiling meat stock*	*Salt and pepper to taste*
4 *oz olive oil*	

Dilute the tomato paste with some of the stock. Heat the oil
and add the rice. Stir and cook over a medium heat for 5 minutes
– the rice becomes almost transparent. Add the stock to the pan
but do it fairly slowly for when the stock touches the pan it
causes an alarming, sizzling noise. Add salt and pepper, cover and
cook over a slow heat for about 20 minutes. By this time all the
liquid will have been absorbed and the rice will be tender but dry.

To help the drying process most Greek and Balkan cooks
wrap the saucepan lid in flannel or a napkin and then clamp
the lid on tightly. The cloth absorbs the steam rapidly, prevents
further swelling of the rice and you can keep it in the pan longer.

TOMATO PILAU
PILAFI ME DOMATES

1 *lb long grain rice*	2 *tablespoons tomato paste*
2 *pints light meat stock*	4 *oz olive oil*
4 *large, peeled and chopped tomatoes*	*Salt and pepper*
	1 *teaspoon sugar* (optional)

Heat the oil in a saucepan and fry the rice for 5 minutes. Add
the tomatoes and simmer for 10 minutes. Dilute the tomato

paste with the stock, add salt, pepper and sugar and pour this into the pan; bring to the boil, lower the heat and cover tightly. Cook for 10 minutes. Lower the heat to almost nothing and continue for another 30 minutes, preferably with the lid wrapped in a napkin.

BAKED RICE PILAU
(Greek-American)
PILAFI TOU FOURNOU

1 *lb long grain rice*   *Salt to taste*
2 *pints boiling stock*

Thoroughly wash the rice and soak it in boiling water for 30 minutes. Drain and shake it dry. In the meantime bring the stock to boiling point in a casserole. Heat the oven to its highest temperature, stir the rice into the stock, add salt, cover and put the casserole into the oven. Lower the heat and bake the rice for 15 minutes.

Remove the cover, wrap it in a cloth and replace it, then turn off the heat and leave the casserole in the oven for 30 minutes. Serve the pilau either in the casserole or turn it out on to a hot platter. If all the liquid has been absorbed, as it should be, it will turn out in the shape of the casserole. Garnish it with anything you like, fish if you have used a fish stock, meat or chicken or baked tomatoes. Or you can mix all kinds of things such as chicken livers, strips of meat or chicken, parsley or other herbs with the rice while it is cooking.

TWO-TO-ONE PILAU
DYO-M' ENA PILAFI

1 *cup rice*   *Butter*
2 *cups water*

Bring the water to the boil, add the rice and cook until tender, about 15 minutes. Cover the pan with a napkin to absorb any remaining water and also to prevent any futher swelling of the rice. Heat the butter until it bubbles, then pour this into the rice. Run a fork lightly through the grains to let the butter penetrate. Serve at once.

Tomatoes or tomato juice can be added but the quantity of liquid must always be just 2 cups.

Enough for 2 people if a half-pint measuring cup is used. Instead of water a light stock may be used which, of course, improves the flavour of the pilau.

PILAU WITH MUSSELS
MYTHIA PILAFI

1 *quart fresh mussels*   *¼ cup olive oil*
2 *cups rice*   1 *glass white wine*
4½ *cups water*   *Salt and pepper*
1 *finely chopped onion*

Wash the mussels thoroughly in several waters, scrubbing or scraping their shells. Heat the oil, add the onion and fry it until it begins to brown. Add the mussels, stir once or twice and leave until the mussels begin to open, then add the wine, water, salt and pepper. Bring the liquid to the boil, lower the heat, then cook the mussels gently for 10 minutes. By this time the mussels should be quite open – if they are not, then they are not fresh. With a perforated spoon take the mussels from the pan, put aside, and throw the rice into the mussel stock. Let this boil for 15 minutes while you deal with the mussels. Open the shells, discard these, and remove the edible flesh, discarding the dark part. Return the mussels to the pan just 5 minutes before the rice is ready. As soon as the rice is tender, take the pan from the fire, cover it with a napkin, clamp on the lid, and put the saucepan on the side of the stove. Leave for 20 minutes, by which time all the moisture in the rice will have been absorbed.

SHRIMP PILAU
GARITHES PILAFI

2 *pints fresh shrimps or small*   1½ *cups rice*
  prawns   *Salt and pepper*
½ *cup olive oil*   *Pinch marjoram*
2 *finely chopped onions*

I have given the quantity of rice in cups to make sure that your measurements will be accurate, as this is the basic Greek pilau rule, 2 liquid to 1 rice. Use half-pint measuring cups.

If you buy uncooked shrimps or prawns they must be cooked until they are pink – so put them into boiling, salted water and cook them until they turn a bright pink. Drain (keep the liquid), rinse in cold water, peel them and remove the black strip. (If you use tinned prawns or shrimps, drain from the liquid in which they are tinned and soak them in cold water with a piece of potato to remove excessive salt before using.)

Heat the olive oil in a heavy saucepan and lightly fry the onions, until soft but not brown. Add the rice and cook for 5 minutes or until the rice becomes almost transparent. Add the shrimp water, which must be boiling, plus enough water to make 3 cups. Bring the rice and the water to the boil, add salt, pepper and marjoram to taste, lower the heat, add the shrimps, cover tightly (wrap the lid in a cloth for better steam absorption) and cook until the rice is tender. Leave for 20 minutes, still covered, on the side of the stove.

SPAGHETTI WITH A MEAT SAUCE
SPAGHETO ME KIMA SALTSA

1 *lb spaghetti*	4–6 *peeled and chopped*
1 *lb minced beef*	*tomatoes*
2 *finely chopped onions*	½ *teaspoon ground cinnamon*
2–3 *crushed cloves garlic*	3 *tablespoons olive oil*
1–2 *bayleaves*	*Salt and pepper*
2 *tablespoons tomato paste*	*Water*

A recipe from Rhodes but popular throughout Greece.

Heat the pan and *sauté* the meat for 5 minutes, frequently shaking the pan. Add the oil, when this is hot add the onions, garlic and tomatoes. Simmer for about 10 minutes. Add the tomato paste diluted with 1 cup of water, salt, pepper, cinnamon and bayleaves, stir well and bring to the boil. Reduce the heat to very low and continue to cook gently for 30 minutes or until the meat is quite tender and the onions and tomatoes reduced to a thick sauce.

While this is cooking, bring a saucepan of salted water to

the boil, gradually add the spaghetti, letting the water cook
rapidly all the while. Cook the spaghetti quickly for 15 minutes.
Drain and shake dry – you can pour a little olive oil over it if
you like – arrange on a very hot platter, slightly indent the
middle, then pour the meat and tomato sauce into the hollow.
Serve at once.

NOODLES WITH LENTILS
(Rhodes)
PASTA KE FAKI

Another recipe with a strong Italian influence.

Noodles
Flour, about 12 oz   Pinch salt
Water

Mix the flour, salt and water to a dough and knead until pliable.
Roll out very thinly – it is better to use a very thin roller and let
the pastry wind itself around this as you roll. If you have only
the usual rolling-pin, then continue rolling until the dough is
thin. Cut it into noodle shapes, they should be roughly ½ an
inch wide by 2 inches long.

1 lb lentils   Salt and pepper
1 finely chopped onion   Butter

Cook the lentils until soft in plenty of water. Add the noodles,
salt and pepper and continue to cook until these are tender,
about 10 minutes should be long enough. Chop and brown the
onion in butter. Drain the lentils and noodles, turn on to a
dish and garnish with the fried onion.

Commercially made noodles may also be used.

Sauces
SALTSES

Greek sauces are quite individual and there are not many of them. But it was the Greeks who invented sauces. Orion, who is one of the seven sages of the culinary arts, invented the white sauce, while Lampriades, another culinary sage, introduced the brown sauce. There was yet another sauce of great antiquity and fame, a fish sauce invented by the poet Menander, but, although its fame has come down through some twenty centuries of cooking, the recipe has been lost.

But Greeks still feel strongly on the question of sauces. Xenophon, the cook of a Greek friend of mine, was in search of a job because his master had left Athens. He was offered one in a good, even exclusive, restaurant, but he refused. Asked the reason for his refusal he replied, 'Working in a restaurant would ruin my sauces – they even put flour in a mayonnaise.' Now he is happy working for some French archaeologists who simply adore his sauces.

BÉCHAMEL SAUCE
SALTSA BÉCHAMEL

Used in a great number of Greek recipes, it is simply white sauce with a slight difference.

2 oz butter	Salt and pepper to taste
2–3 oz flour	Good pinch nutmeg
1½ pints milk	

Scald the milk. Heat the butter in a saucepan and gradually work in the flour until smooth. Slowly add the milk, stirring it all the while, add nutmeg, salt and pepper and cook very slowly until the sauce is thick and there is no odour of flour. It is better to cook for 15 or 20 minutes, stirring all the while.

EGG AND LEMON SAUCE
SALTSA AVGOLEMONO

This extremely good sauce is the national sauce of Greece. It
is simply egg and lemon beaten together and stirred into whatever dish requires it. It is frequently used for flavouring soups,
and just as often with meat, fish, vegetable and poultry dishes.
All that is essential is that the dish which is to be flavoured with
this sauce has some liquid, from which to take 2 or 3 tablespoonfuls. This is stirred into the egg and lemon and then
the sauce goes into the pan.

4 egg yolks   2–3 tablespoons hot broth
4 tablespoons lemon juice

Beat the egg yolks until fluffy and light, then slowly add the
lemon juice, beating all the while. Gradually add 2 or 3 tablespoons
of the liquid from the dish you have prepared. Then the sauce
is stirred into the dish you are making. Leave for 5 minutes
on the side of the stove – above all do not let the sauce boil,
and keep the pan covered.
    Instead of 4 egg yolks you can use 2 or 3 whole eggs.

GARLIC SAUCE WITH POTATOES
SKORTHALIA ME PATATES

Skorthalia or garlic sauce is a favourite of the Greeks and is
eaten with many types of meat, fish and vegetable dishes although
the most important marriage is skorthalia with salt fish. There
are several ways of making it, with potatoes, with nuts, with
breadcrumbs or with flour.

6 medium-sized potatoes   ¾ cup olive oil
4–6 cloves garlic   Strained juice 2 lemons
1 teaspoon salt

Wash the potatoes and boil them in their skins until soft. Peel
them as soon as they are cool enough to handle and pound in a
mortar. Crush the garlic with the salt (do this while the potatoes are cooking), mix with the mashed potatoes and continue
to pound until these ingredients are blended and the mixture is

smooth. Gradually add the olive oil drop by drop, alternating with the lemon juice, stirring all the while until you have a thick cream. When you are ready to serve the sauce you can, if you like, dilute it just a little either with fish or meat stock.

GARLIC SAUCE WITH BREADCRUMBS
SKORTHALIA ME YALETTA

2 *cups soft breadcrumbs*	*Juice* 1 *lemon*
¾ *cup olive oil*	*Salt to taste*
6–8 *cloves garlic*	

Pound the garlic to a paste with about 1 teaspoonful of salt. Add the breadcrumbs and beat or pound until the breadcrumbs and garlic are mixed like a paste. Gradually add the olive oil and lemon juice, alternately until you have a sauce of the same consistency as mayonnaise.

A similar sauce can be made with a flour and water paste, using the same quantity of flour, and some Greeks consider this to be much lighter.

GARLIC SAUCE WITH ALMONDS
SKORTHALIA ME AMYGTHALA

1 *medium-sized potato*	*Juice* 1 *lemon*
6 *oz blanched and ground almonds*	1 *teaspoon salt*
	¾ *cup olive oil*
6–8 *cloves garlic*	

Cook the potato until soft (preferably in its skin) and, while it is cooking, crush the garlic and salt in a mortar and pound until smooth. Add the almonds and pound until a smooth paste is formed. By this time the potato will be cooked. Peel this and mash it until smooth, then add it to the almond-garlic paste. When well blended, add the olive oil and lemon juice, drop by drop until you have a thick sauce, stiff enough to hold its shape.

GARLIC AND EGG SAUCE
(Instanbul-Greek)
SKORTHALIA ME AVGO

4 *cloves garlic*   *Olive oil*
1 *teaspoon salt*   *Lemon juice or wine vinegar*
2 *egg yolks*

Pound the garlic with the salt to a pulp, beat in the 2 egg yolks
and then gradually add, drop by drop, enough olive oil to
make a sauce of mayonnaise consistency. Loosen with either
lemon juice or wine vinegar.

PISTACHIO SAUCE
SKORTHALIA ME FYSTIKIA

4 *oz pistachio nuts*   *Olive oil*
2 *oz soft white bread*   *Lemon juice or wine vinegar*
4 *cloves garlic*

Pound the nuts (peeled, of course) in a mortar with the garlic
until the mixture is smooth. Soak the bread in water and squeeze
it dry. Mix with the nuts and work the mixture till smooth.
Gradually add enough olive oil to make a thick sauce, then loosen
it with either lemon juice or wine vinegar.

LEMON AND MUSTARD SAUCE
SALTSA MOUSTARTHA

Juice 2 lemons   1 *teaspoon dried mustard*
Double this quantity olive oil   2 *cloves crushed garlic*
Salt and pepper to taste   *Chopped parsley*

Put the lemon juice – well strained – into a bowl and gradually
add the olive oil, salt, pepper, mustard and garlic. Stir together
until blended, then strain. Serve in a sauce-boat sprinkled lightly
with finely chopped parsley.

MAYONNAISE SAUCE
SALTSA MAYIONEZA

There are several ways of making mayonnaise sauce. This is a
typical Greek method of which Zenophon would not approve.

1 *cup pure olive oil*	2 *tablespoons lemon juice*
1 *cup good quality vinegar*	1 *egg yolk*
1 *tablespoon dry mustard*	1 *oz flour*
½ *teaspoon salt*	

Stir the flour in a bowl and mix with a little water to a paste.
Add mustard, salt and egg yolk. When blended, add a few
drops of vinegar and a few drops more of water. Add the oil,
a little at a time, stirring briskly all the while. When the mixture
is quite thick, add the lemon juice and the remaining ingredients
and stir until smooth. If it is a little too stiff, cautiously add a little
more lemon juice.

TOMATO SAUCE I
SALTSA DOMATES I

1½ *lb tomatoes*	1 *teaspoon cornflour*
½ *pint water*	1 *oz butter*
1 *teaspoon sugar*	*Salt and pepper*

Peel the tomatoes (dip them into boiling water first to make
this operation easier). Slice them thickly and put into a pan,
without adding any liquid, and simmer gently until they begin
to soften. Add remaining ingredients and continue cooking
until the tomatoes are soft. Rub through a strainer and use as
required.

Sometimes chopped onion is added. It is first lightly fried
in butter until soft and put in the pan at the same time as the
cornflour, etc.

This is a sauce for immediate use. It is easier to mix the cornflour with water to a paste before using it.

TOMATO SAUCE II
SALTSA DOMATES II

3 *lb tomatoes*	*Salt and pepper*
1 *small, chopped onion*	1 *teaspoon sugar*
1 *finely chopped carrot*	1 *oz flour*
1 *finely chopped stick celery*	1 *oz butter*
Garlic to taste	

Wash the tomatoes and cook them with the vegetables, garlic
and seasoning until very soft. Rub through a sieve. Heat the
butter, stir in the flour and cook for a minute or so. Add the
strained tomato sauce and the sugar, stirring all the while, and
cook slowly until the sauce is thick.

For immediate use but will keep for a while, especially if
stored in a refrigerator. The above quantity will make about
2 pints of sauce – much depends on the juiciness of the tomatoes.

TOMATO SAUCE III
SALTSA DOMATES III

12 *lb tomatoes*	6 *tablespoons salt*
2 *lb onions*	1 *teaspoon pepper*
1–2 *cloves garlic*	½ *pint vinegar*
1 *grated nutmeg*	4 *oz sugar*
1 *tablespoon ground ginger*	

Chop the tomatoes and onions coarsely and put into a large
saucepan with the garlic, nutmeg, ginger, salt and pepper, and
cook very slowly until the tomatoes are soft – cook for at least
2 hours. Rub this through a sieve and leave until cool. Add the
vinegar and sugar, return the sauce to the pan, and continue to
cook until the sauce is thick. Cool and pour into bottles.

SALAD DRESSING OR SAUCE
LADOXITHO

¾ *cup olive oil*	¼ *teaspoon dry mustard*
¼ *cup vinegar*	*Pinch salt and pepper*

Put these ingredients into a jar, seal and shake until blended.
Chill before serving.

Salads
SALATES

When the Greeks talk of salads they do not mean a mixture of
lettuce, cucumber, beetroot and spring onions, garnished with
a mayonnaise sauce. Generally vegetables used for salads are
simply dressed with olive oil – not always by any means to
the foreigners' taste. Greek salads are made from a large choice
of vegetables, including many wild varieties, or herbs from the
mountains. These are all prepared in the manner of spinach
salad (see page 160). Especially popular are dandelion leaves,
a salad so nicely rendered in Zonar's menu as 'tandel lion'.
Dandelion is credited with the curing of many ills, particularly
those of the stomach. Also a salad can be what we would call a
purée, such as aubergine or *taramo* salad; or dried beans cooked
and served in a dressing; or beetroot, cooked and sliced, served
with any of the *skorthalia* or garlic sauces.

FISH ROE SALAD (BOTARGO)
AVGOTARAHO: TARAMOSALATA

According to the *Oxford Dictionary* botargo is a relish of mullet
or tunny fish roe. The Greek word comes from *tarihkion*,
which means pickled or pickle. Sometimes *avgotaraho* goes
under the name of 'red caviare'. It has a unique flavour, is as
thick as caramel, extremely rich, and adheres somewhat to the
teeth and the roof of the mouth. It is not known much in Britain,
although Samuel Pepys records on June 6th, 1661, 'We stayed
talking and singing and drinking great draughts of claret, and
eating botargo and bread-and-butter till twelve at night.' As he
does not mention it with any kind of explanation it must have
been well known, like so many other items of diet which are
now considered exotic. Botargo in those days was called, 'a
sausage made from the eggs and the blood of the mullet'.

The method of collecting the eggs from the grey mullet is interesting. The collecting grounds in Greece (there are others in Turkey and in some Arab countries as well) are called *tzenios* and the area around is cleared of all seaweed, which is replaced by an ingenious system of 'cane weirs'. In August, when the female grey mullet is ready to spawn and is looking for a quiet spawning ground, she is tricked into the false weirs and at once speared with amazing dexterity by fishermen lying in wait for her in flat-bottomed boats. The roe, which is in two sections, is immediately removed from the belly, cleaned of all its membranes, soaked in brine for several hours, and then put into the sun to dry. The dried roe can be eaten at once, but it is generally covered with a thick coating of beeswax in order to preserve it. This is, of course, removed for eating. In this stage the roe is called 'red caviare' and is sliced and eaten as an appetizer. I find it irresistible and can eat far too much of it.

To make *taramosalata* you put into a mixing bowl as much roe as will be required – say about 4 ounces – and mix it with and equal quantity of bread, which has been soaked in water, squeezed dry and then pounded until smooth. When the roe an the bread are really well blended, gradually add olive oil until the mixture has the consistency of a soft, but not too soft, *purée*. Then add just enough lemon juice to loosen it slightly. Some people add a minute quantity of water to make the *purée* even lighter and creamier, others an egg yolk, previously well beaten. Then again the quantity of bread can be reduced. It should be served as an appetizer. In Britain it can be served as and unusual but delicious prelude to a small dinner – or a large one for that matter. Failing grey mullet roe quite a good salad can be made with cod's roe but this will not, of course, have the same flavour.

Incidentally, when I talk of red caviare I do not mean the loose variety. Botargo is definitely dried and firmly pressed.

AUBERGINE SALAD (or *PURÉE*)
MELITZANOSALATA

2 *aubergines – fairly large*   *Salt and pepper to taste*
1 *medium-sized grated onion*   *3 oz olive oil*
1 *tablespoon chopped parsley*   *Juice half a lemon or vinegar*
1 *crushed clove garlic*

Remove the green ends and grill the aubergines until the skins
turn brown and begin to break. (This is best done over a charcoal fire.) As soon as you can handle the aubergines rip off all
the skin and pound the flesh in a bowl. Add the onion and garlic
and continue to pound until the mixture is smooth, adding
salt and pepper as you work – Greeks add rather more salt
than we are apt to. When the mixture is reasonably smooth,
add the olive oil gradually until it is like a stiff mayonnaise.
Beat in the parsley and the lemon juice. Serve cold.

The nicest way to eat this and other similar *purées* is to scoop
it up with chunks of soft, brown bread.

WHITE BEANS IN OIL
FASSOLIA SALATA

By this I mean the large, dried beans called butter beans in
Britain or giant beans by the Greeks.

Cook the beans in the usual manner and when they are drained
but still warm coat them with olive oil, sprinkle lightly with
grated onion and a little chopped parsley. Serve cold.

BRAIN SALAD
MIALA SALATA

Soak as many brains as required in cold water for at least one
hour – this is to whiten them. Put them into a pan with fresh
water, salt, pepper, a little parsley, some lemon juice, a dash of
chopped onion and bring to the boil. Simmer gently for another 20 minutes, or until the brains are tender. Drain and
cool; then remove skin and membrane and drop the brains into
cold water. Leave for 30 minutes.

Cut the brains into pieces – size is a matter for individual taste – pat dry and serve with an olive oil and lemon dressing, sprinkled lightly with finely chopped parsley.

CUCUMBER AND YOGHOURT SALAD
TZATZIKI

1 *pint or lb yoghourt*   1 *tablespoon olive oil*
1 *clove garlic*   1 *tablespoon vinegar*
1 *small grated cucumber*   *Salt*

Beat the yoghourt, add the remaining ingredients and then chill. In Macedonian Greece *tzatziki* is served as a soup.

GREEN BEAN SALAD
SALATA FASSOLAKIA

You should use either very young runner beans for this salad or French beans, small enough to leave whole, with only the ends trimmed. With beans which are long but tender, break them into halves. Cook them in just enough boiling water to cover with a little bicarbonate of soda added, and salt and pepper. When they are tender, pour away any remaining water and replace it with enough olive oil to coat each bean. Leave until cool, then add about 2 tablespoonfuls of lemon juice, and some crushed or finely chopped garlic. Stir with a wooden spoon and serve when really very cold.

Very good also with a garlic sauce.

SPINACH SALAD
SPANAKI SALATA

Wash as much spinach as required, removing all coarse leaves and thick stalks. Cook it in a saucepan without adding water for 15 minutes. Drain it thoroughly and arrange in a salad bowl. Add an olive oil and lemon dressing, salt and pepper, stir it round and round until all the spinach is well covered with the dressing, and serve either hot or cold – the latter is preferable.

Pastries, Cakes, and Sweet Dishes

YLYKA

Many Greek pastries and sweet dishes are of ancient origin
and they are quite different from those we are used to eating
in Britain, or for that matter, in France. Generally speaking,
Greeks do not finish a meal with a sweet dish: when they eat
sweets it is for a special occasion, such as a wedding, or a name-
giving ceremony and, of course, on the many days of festival.

So in this way Greeks do eat large quantities of sweet dishes
in some form or other. And I think it is fair to say that never
have I seen quite so many sweets or pastry shops as in Athens
– except perhaps in Istanbul. Shop after shop is filled with
honey-flavoured sweet pastries, with row after row of cakes
and pastries wrapped in gold, silver or scarlet paper, looking
very luscious and tempting.

I remember one day I was taken by a Greek friend to Lutosi,
which is near Corinth, simply to eat pastries. There were all
varieties of *baklava* and *kataifi* – one variety I remember was
called *Laïs*, after a well-known courtesan of that name whose
love was so sweet. There was *melogarida*, which is honey and
walnuts pressed together to such a sticky, hard mass that it
becomes almost like a wafer biscuit – and is excellent. I ate
karithopita, or Athenian walnut cake, and chocolate cake,
marzipan and fruit cake – never have I eaten so many cakes in
one session. And then my charming hosts went to the great
glass counters and, in consultation with one of the girl assistants,
picked me out a variety of their choicest silver- and gold-wrapped
pastries. Fortunately the wrapped pastries were made to last –
I was not expected to have another pastry-eating session that day.

Almost all Greek pastries seem to be soaked in honey – and
seem at first glance to be difficult to prepare. If you are able to
buy Greek *phyllo* pastry, nothing could be easier than making
a *baklava* pastry and for a change it is really to be recommended.
Oddly enough, sweet though this pastry is, I do suggest you try

it with Devonshire cream. This is not Greek taste, but in Istanbul we used to eat all these honey-soaked pastries with a portion of *kaimak* – which is a thick cream so firm that it can be cut into slices.

The *halvah* recipe I have given is not the same *halvah* that we buy in Soho – or when travelling in the Middle East. Almost all sweet dishes made with semolina and nuts become *halvah* – right through to India. The *halvah* of the shops is a sticky, almost crisp-textured sweet, heavily flavoured with sesame, available only in winter since it melts easily. It is absolutely delicious – but like so many good things, figure shattering.

Turkish delight or *loukoum*, although available in Greek shops, is really Turkish – the secret of its preparation still being in the hands of one Istanbul family. Other firms make it – but it is not quite the same. Cypriot Greeks also prepare *loukoum*.

I have not mentioned ice-cream in this section, which may seem to some students of Greece rather odd, as Athens is famous for its ice-creams. Most of the Greek ice-cream gets its richness from the ewes' milk with which it is made and even if I gave recipes the flavour would not be quite the same. But ice-cream has always seemed to me to be better throughout the Balkans than the ice-cream we serve in Britain – probably because in our sad summers we do not have the violent urge to cool ourselves with ice-cream. In the Balkans and Greece one does.

GREEK PASTRY I
PHYLLO

Phyllo is a plain, paper-thin pastry used in most Greek pastries and pies, whether savoury or sweet, and requires an expert to make it properly. It is bought by the pound in Greece (and in the Balkan countries as well as in the Middle East) in shops which sell only *phyllo* and *kadaifi* pastry.

The dough for making *phyllo* is simple enough – flour and water mixed to a stiff paste. From this pieces are broken and rolled into balls roughly the size of a tennis ball. At this stage an expert must take over. First he tosses a ball of dough back and forth between his large, capable hands, then up and down and along his brawny arms, until it becomes like a thin circle of parchment paper. Then it is twirled round and round in the air until it becomes even larger and thinner – a fascinating operation to watch, as good as any juggler's act. After this the round of pastry is thrown with unerring aim on to a specially constructed round metal disc, about the size of a small table in diameter, and stretched and stretched and stretched until the almost agonized watcher feels it must break, that this stretching cannot go on any longer – but it does. Finally, when everyone is satisfied that the pastry has reached the limit of its endurance, it is cut into sizes suitable for making the pies and pastries to which the people of Greece are accustomed. In Britain *phyllo* can be bought in those shops which specialize in Continental items of food or usually wherever there is a large community of Greeks and Cypriots.

Home-made *phyllo* cannot compete with the professional variety, but even so a passable imitation is possible. You need to mix as much plain flour, baking-powder and water as required to a stiff dough. The quantity of baking-powder to flour is 2 teaspoonfuls to every 2 pounds of flour. Knead it as much as you are able and set it aside for 2 hours. Then, like the professionals, break off pieces of about tennis ball size and roll these out until the pastry is very thin. It can be done; I have done it myself and made a passable imitation of Greek pies. I use a thin rolling pin and when the pastry is really thin I roll it round the pin and roll it back and forth until the pastry becomes – well, not quite paper thin, but very thin.

When using home-made *phyllo* use less than half the quantity of pastry called for in the recipe.

GREEK PASTRY II
KATAIFI

This, like *phyllo*, is made by professional pastry makers. The dough, however, is much thinner and squeezed through a tin with a perforated bottom straight on to the metal disc which, however, is hot. The pastry is not cooked on the disc but merely set into long thin strands which look very like strands of spaghetti. It is sold in the same kind of shops which sell *phyllo*.

ALMOND STUFFED ROLLS
FLOYERES

6 *sheets phyllo pastry*   1 *beaten egg*
4 *oz almonds or walnuts*   *Fresh butter – slightly melted*
2 *oz sugar*

Syrup
½ *lb sugar*   1 *teaspoon lemon juice*
1 *pint water*   1 *small piece cinnamon*

Six sheets *of phyllo* pastry will make 24 rolls.

Blanch the nuts and either grind or crush them. Mix with
the egg and sugar. This makes the filling.

Cut each sheet of *phyllo* into 4 strips and brush each strip
with butter. Put a heaped teaspoonful of the filling on to one
end of each strip of *phyllo* and roll up each in the manner of a
swiss roll. Arrange these on a buttered baking dish and bake
in a moderate oven until a golden brown, about 25 minutes.

Put the syrup ingredients into a shallow pan and bring to the
boil, then simmer until the syrup is of a medium thickness. As
soon as the turnovers are ready, take them from the oven and
put 2 or 3 into a perforated spoon and dip them into the still
simmering syrup. Do this once or twice then put the rolls on
to a large platter. When all the rolls have been dipped in the
syrup leave them until cold. *Floyeres* will keep for several days
– at least they will in theory, but in practice they usually disappear rapidly, for in Greece they are very popular.

PASTRY FILLED WITH WALNUTS AND STEEPED IN SYRUP
BAKLAVA

A sweet, nut-filled pastry which the traveller begins to discover
as soon as he arrives in the Balkans. Whether it was invented
by the Greeks or the Turks (or the Russians) is always a matter
of argument between Hellenophiles and Turcophiles.

1¼ *lb phyllo pastry (about 25 to*   1 *lb unsalted butter – melted*
30 sheets)   1 *tablespoon ground cinnamon*
¾ *lb blanched and chopped walnuts*   *(or to taste)*

Syrup

½ pint honey	1½ pints warm water
8 oz sugar	1 teaspoon lemon juice

For *phyllo* pastry see page 162.

Mix the walnuts with the cinnamon. Butter a flat baking tin to match the size of your sheets of pastry, usually around 16 by 12 inches, and line it with 1 sheet of pastry. Brush this lightly with melted butter. Add another sheet, butter this and sprinkle lightly with the cinnamoned walnuts. Add 2 more pastry sheets brushed only with butter, then another with butter and walnuts, and repeat this operation until you have about 8 or 10 pastry sheets left. By this time all the walnuts should be finished. Add the last sheets brushed with butter. Dip a sharp knife into boiling water and score through the first 4 sheets making squares of a serving size. Sprinkle the top sheet of pastry with water (this is to prevent it from curling upwards). Put the *baklava* in a moderate oven and bake for about 1½ hours. Let it cool before adding the syrup.

While the *baklava* is baking make the syrup. Boil all the syrup ingredients together until the mixture is syrupy but not too thick. While it is still boiling pour it slowly over the cooled *baklava*. Cool again before serving, by which time most of the syrup should be absorbed.

There are some cooks who add a piece of cinnamon to the syrup, others who sprinkle each sheet of pastry with sugar, but this makes the baklava even sweeter than it is already.

Instead of squares the top sheets of pastry can be scored into diamond, oval or oblong shapes.

SWEET PASTRY ROLLS
KATAIFI

Professionally made *kataifi* rolls look rather like stuffed Shredded Wheat – but here the resemblance ends. Non-professional cooks make their *kataifi* in the manner described overleaf – the flavour is the same, they do not look quite so elegant.

Filling
¾ lb blanched and chopped walnuts   4 oz sugar
6 oz melted butter   ½ teaspoon cinnamon

Syrup
1 lb sugar   Lemon or orange rind
1½ pints water   1 teaspoon lemon juice

There are two ways of preparing *kataifi*. Correctly and more
professionally you spread out enough of the *kataifi* pastry in
your left hand to cover it, sprinkle it with filling and then gently
close the 2 ends, pressing them artfully together. Less professional but more simple is to lay half the *kataifi* pastry in the
bottom of a shallow baking tin, spread this with walnuts, sugar
and cinnamon, add half the butter and then cover with the
remaining *kataifi*. Pour the remaining butter over the top layer
of *kataifi* and bake in a very moderate oven for about 1½ hours.
Boil the syrup ingredients together until you have a medium-
thick syrup and pour this over the *kataifi* while it is still hot.
Cover with a napkin so that the steam will be absorbed and the
surface becomes soft. Cool and cut into squares or diamonds
to serve.

Actually making *kataifi* is not difficult but for some mysterious
reason, just as one's cherished pastry recipes sometimes fail,
so do the *kataifi* rolls. Even cooks who normally can make
perfect *kataifi* sometimes find they are too hard and cannot be
broken, or sometimes the syrup goes wrong and they become
too soggy. But when they are good, they are very very good.

VANILLA CREAM PIE
GALATOBOUREKO

20 *sheets phyllo pastry*   6 oz melted butter

Filling
4 pints milk
1 lb sugar   6 oz semolina
6 eggs   A few strips lemon peel
                                        Vanilla flavouring to taste

Syrup

1 *lb sugar*	1 *teaspoon lemon juice*
2 *pints water*	*A little lemon peel*

Heat the milk to scalding point and take from the heat. Beat the eggs with the sugar until thick and creamy, add vanilla flavouring and lemon peel, stir well, then gradually add the semolina, beating all the time. Slowly add the scalded milk and then put the mixture back into the saucepan. Cook over a low heat until the mixture thickens, stirring all the time. Take the pan from the heat and continue stirring or beating until the mixture is quite cool.

Butter a baking tin somewhat smaller than your sheets of pastry and line it with 1 sheet of pastry; the edge of the pastry should come up above the top of the tin. Add the semolina-cream and turn back the edges of the pastry over the cream to keep this from oozing out. Cover with remaining sheets of pastry, each spread with melted butter. With a sharp knife trace or score the first 4 sheets of pastry into serving sections, either in squares or diamonds, sprinkle the top layer with water and bake in a moderate oven for about 1½ hours.

Boil the syrup ingredients to a medium-thick syrup and pour this over the pie when you take it from the oven – it is better to do this gradually. Cool before serving.

Greeks prefer to use vanilla crystals for flavouring rather than essence. I prefer to use vanilla bean but it is a matter of personal preference.

Enough for about 12 people.

Failing *phyllo* pastry the filling is excellent when used in the same way as in a custard-cream pie.

GREEK SHORTBREAD
KOURABIETHES

Kourabiethes, traditionally, are made both for the New Year celebrations and for Christmas. It is claimed that their history can be traced back to the days of St. John Chrysostom who is said to have mentioned *kourabiethes* during one of his sermons. Each shortbread or *kourabiethes* should be stuck with one clove to represent the Three Wise Men who brought spices to the Christ Child.

Kourabiethes, like Christmas puddings or mince pies, must be made with loving care and housewives like to specialize in them. One Greek friend of mine refuses to eat them anywhere but in her mother's home. She says the quality of flavour depends absolutely on the creaming of the butter and this should be done with the hand and fingers for at least 30 minutes. She remembers her mother sitting happily in their large kitchen, her hands deep in creamy butter, beating and beating, and, she adds, her mother's *kourabiethes* were the best in the whole of Greece. This is her mother's recipe, but how much you beat will depend on time, modern conditions and patience. I think a modern rotary mixer can bring the butter to the creaminess desired, although my friend thinks not.

2 *lb flour – approximately*	1 *teaspoon vanilla essence*
1 *lb unsalted butter*	2 *egg yolks*
6 *oz sugar*	*Rosewater*
1 *teaspoon baking-powder*	*Icing sugar*
1 *tablespoon ouzo* (see page 213)	*Cloves*

Sift the flour with the baking-powder twice or thrice. Cream the butter with the sugar and then add the *ouzo* and the vanilla, the egg yolks and gradually enough flour to make a soft but firm dough. If there is not enough liquid, add either some more *ouzo* or another egg yolk – if you have made the dough too loose, then add more flour. Break off small pieces, pat these into biscuit shapes and place on a floured baking sheet. Insert a clove into each shortbread and bake in a very moderate oven for about 20 minutes, until they are cooked through but not browned. Take from the oven and while still hot sprinkle with icing sugar and then rosewater. Do this once more, then cool. *Kourabiethes* will stay fresh for 2 or 3 weeks.

SHORTBREAD WITH ALMONDS
KOURABIETHES ME AMYGTHALO

Prepare as in the preceding recipe but add 2 ounces of blanched and chopped almonds and 2 or 3 toasted and chopped almonds.

ALMOND PEARS
AMYGTHALOTA

1 *lb blanched almonds*	*Orange flower water*
8 *oz castor sugar*	*Icing sugar*
3 *egg whites*	*Butter*
3 *oz soft breadcrumbs*	*Cloves*
Vanilla essence to taste	

Mix the almonds with 1 ounce of sugar and grind them until very fine. Add remaining sugar, vanilla essence, egg whites and the breadcrumbs. Knead this mixture to a dough, then break off small pieces. Shape these into 'pears' and at the end of each insert 1 clove to represent the stalk. Arrange on a buttered baking sheet and bake for 15 minutes in a moderate oven. When the almond pears are cool, dip them quickly into orange flower water and then lightly coat with icing sugar.

You can, of course, use commercially ground almonds.

The cooks of the island of Hydra, just off the mainland, are known for their particular version of almond pears and they are worth asking for – the Amygthalota, I mean, not the cooks.

ATHENIAN WALNUT CAKE
KARITHOPITA ATHINAIKI

1½ *lb flour*	8 *eggs*
1½ *lb shelled walnuts*	2 *teaspoons cinnamon*
10 *oz sugar*	2 *teaspoons baking-powder*
4 *oz butter*	

Syrup

12 *oz sugar*	1–2 *wine glasses brandy*
1 *pint water*	(optional)

Coarsely grind the walnuts and put aside 2 tablespoonfuls. Separate the egg yolks from the whites and beat the latter until stiff. Beat the butter and sugar together until creamy, add the egg yolks one by one, beating all the while. Add half the beaten egg white and the cinnamon. Still beating, gradually add the flour, baking-powder and the walnuts. When all this is blended, fold in the remaining egg white. Turn the mixture into a buttered cake tin, preferably oblong and in size about 12 by 9 by 2 inches. Sprinkle with the remaining walnuts and bake in a moderate oven for about 30 or 40 minutes.

While the cake is baking make a syrup by boiling the sugar and water together until the sugar is dissolved and the mixture thickens. At this point add the brandy. When the cake is baked take it from the oven and pour the hot syrup over it.

Serve cold. *Karithopita* will keep for 2 or 3 days.

YOGHOURT CAKE
YAOURTOPITA

1½ lb flour
½ pint yoghourt
2 teaspoons baking-powder
Good pinch salt
8 oz butter

6 oz castor sugar
5 egg yolks
5 egg whites, stiffly beaten
Icing sugar

Cream the butter and sugar until light and fluffy, add the egg yolks one by one, beating vigorously after each addition, then, when this mixture is well blended, add the yoghourt, beating all the while. Sift the flour, baking-powder and salt into the creamed mixture and beat again until the flour is thoroughly blended into it. Fold the egg whites into the cake batter and pour it into a buttered cake tin and bake in a moderate oven for about 1 hour. Take from the oven and cool on a cake-rack (out of the tin). When cool, dust generously with icing sugar.

This is an extremely moist but light cake. Some people like to add grated lemon rind to the ingredients or just a whiff, as it were, of vanilla essence.

BAKED SEMOLINA CAKE
HALVAS TOUFOURNOU

1 lb coarse semolina
9 oz butter
2 oz sugar
8 teaspoons baking-powder
8–10 oz coarsely chopped almonds

1 small glass brandy
1 tablespoon ground cinnamon
4 egg yolks
4 stiffly beaten egg whites

Syrup
1 *lb sugar*   1 *teaspoon lemon juice*
1½ *pints water*   1 *small glass brandy* (optional)
1 *small piece cinnamon*

Beat the butter and sugar together until very creamy. Add the
egg yolks, one by one, beating well after each addition. Add
the semolina and, while still beating, the baking-powder, cinnamon, brandy and nuts. Finally fold in the egg whites. Pour
this mixture into a buttered cake tin and bake in a medium
oven for 10 minutes, lower the heat and bake until the cake is
cooked through, about another 40 minutes. Test with a knife,
which should come out clean if the semolina is cooked.

While the cake is baking, make the syrup. Put the sugar,
water, cinnamon and lemon juice into a pan, bring to the boil,
then cook slowly until the mixture thickens. Remove the cinnamon and stir in the brandy. Pour the syrup (it must be hot) over
the cake as soon as you take it from the oven.

For some unknown reason most Greeks call this cake *Halvas
Tis Rinas*. Rina is the name of a woman. As one Greek friend
of mine explained to me, 'When we talk of *Halvas Tis Rinas*
we always know that it is *halvas* which has been baked in a hot
oven – although exactly why I do not know.' The quantity of
cinnamon can be reduced to taste.

EASTER HALVA CAKE
HALVAS

2 *cups coarse semolina*   4 *oz chopped blanched*
6 *oz butter*   *almonds*
6 *oz sugar*   4 *eggs*
                                                    1 *teaspoon ground cinnamon*

Syrup
1 *lb sugar*   1 *teaspoon lemon juice*
2 *pints water*   1 *inch piece cinnamon*

Cream the butter, add the sugar, continue creaming, then add
the eggs one by one and beat until the mixture is very creamy
indeed. Add the semolina, still beating, and lastly the nuts and
the cinnamon.

Half fill a 9-inch diameter, 3-inch deep baking tin or cake tin (grease the tin first with a little butter) and bake the *halva* in a moderate oven for about 40 minutes. Boil the syrup ingredients together to a thick syrup and, as soon as you take the *halva* out of the oven, pour the syrup over it. (Of course, remove the piece of cinnamon.) Cool and cut into squares to serve.

A slightly less elaborate version of the previous recipe.

NEW YEAR'S CAKE
VASILOPITA

Vasilopita or New Year's cake is served at the stroke of midnight on New Year's Eve – a date which is one of the most important in the Greek calendar. Celebrating begins fairly early in the evening and relatives and close friends gather together for a party in the largest house in the family circle.

Guests arrive at all times in the evening and are greeted sometimes with spoon sweets (see page 189) and liqueurs or with Turkish coffee and, of course, *kourabiethes* (see page 167) and other Greek delicacies. Groups of boys go from house to house singing the songs of St. Basil, the patron saint of the Greek New Year, and come into the house to wish the family good fortune and happiness in the coming year. In return they are offered drinks and *kourabiethes* and usually some hard cash as well.

Good fortune is important and on New Year's Eve the Greeks like to try and discover what their luck is going to be in the coming year. This they try to assess at the gambling table – either at baccara or the roulette wheel. In every house dining tables are stretched to their fullest and overnight Greece becomes one vast Monte Carlo and each house a miniature casino.

Just before midnight all gambling ceases – temporarily – and the table is cleared for the dramatic appearance of the enormous *Vasilopita*, with its lucky coin, another foreteller of luck or otherwise. The arrival of the *Vasilopita* is a moment cherished by all Greeks and even the youngest are allowed to stay up – if they can keep their baby eyes open.

By this time it is midnight, bells clang and shots are fired outside. Everyone begins excitedly to kiss and hug their nearest and dearest and cry happily, '*Hronia polla*', which roughly means, 'many happy new years'. All lights are switched on and the host stands ready to cut the cake. He flourishes his knife, then makes the sign of the cross over the cake before he begins to cut the first slice, which is offered either to Panayia (the Holy Mother) or to St. Basil. This piece is put aside, then he cuts large slices for the family in order of age, next for the relatives and friends and finally for the servants. What is left over is given the next day to the poor. The traditional *Vasilopita* must be very large. The piece cut for the Holy Mother or St. Basil is left on the table and it is expected that during the night it will be collected in person.

The cake distributed, the next moment of excitement is the finding of the coin. The fortunate finder is greeted with cheers, for this is a sure sign that he or she will be lucky in the coming year. If the coin is found in the piece left for the Holy Mother or St. Basil, this means luck for everyone assembled. If it is in the cake left over for the poor, then to the poor it must go. But until the coin is found there are some tense moments.

After the cake is cut champagne is served and the table cleared once more for gambling – this time in dead earnest – which is continued until the early hours of the morning, often until dawn, which, on New Year's Day, is greeted with a twenty-one-gun salute from Mount Lycabettus. There is, however, still one more chance of good luck – if a handsome blond man should make the first footing across the threshold, then all's right with the world.

NEW YEAR'S CAKE (WITH YEAST)
VASILOPITA I

3 *lb flour*	1 *pint warm milk*
2 *oz yeast*	½ *teaspoon salt*
3 *oz sugar*	½ *teaspoon sesame*
6 *eggs*	1 *teaspoon cinnamon*
4 *oz melted butter*	

Crumble the yeast into a mixing bowl, add half the milk, the salt, and enough flour to make a batter, about 4 or 5 table-spoonfuls should be sufficient. Cover with a napkin and leave for about 1 hour in a warm place to rise.

Put the remaining flour in another large mixing bowl, make
a well in the centre, stir in the yeast batter, add the butter, 5
eggs (one at a time), sesame, and lastly the remaining milk.
Mix this thoroughly. Knead for at least 10 minutes. The dough
must be stiff; if it is not, add more flour; if too stiff, add more
milk. Cover the dough again and leave to rise, this time for 3
hours. Put on to a floured board and knead as you would for
making a loaf of bread. Tear off a handful and shape the remainder into a cake – before rising this should be 1½ inches
thick. Put this into a greased baking tin but leave space for
further rising. Take most of the torn-off piece of dough and
form it into a long sausage shape with your hands and arrange
in a circle on top of the cake. Inside this circle 'write' the number
of the coming year with the remaining dough. Cover the dough
again with a napkin and let it rise another inch. Push a silver or
golden coin into the cake, beat the remaining egg with a little
warm water and sugar and brush this over the top before putting
it into the oven. Bake in a moderate oven until brown.

Sometimes chopped almonds are sprinkled over the top of
the *Vasilopita* before baking.

This is a typical *Vasilopita* but each family has its own variations of this basic recipe.

NEW YEAR'S CAKE (WITHOUT YEAST)
VASILOPITA II

3 lb flour   4 oz melted butter
6 eggs   3 teaspoons baking-powder
8 oz sugar   Juice and grated rind 1 orange
1 sherry glass brandy   Icing sugar

Separate the egg yolks from the whites. Mix the brandy with
the orange juice and rind. Whisk the egg whites until stiff. Beat
the egg yolks with the sugar until creamy, add the butter and
continue beating for another 5 minutes. Add the brandy and
orange then gradually half the flour and half the egg whites.
Continue beating until the mixture is thoroughly blended.
Add the remainder of the flour and remaining egg whites. Put
the mixture into a greased baking tin and bake in a moderate
oven for about 1½ hours. Sprinkle with icing sugar and serve cold.

This type of *Vasilopita* is more cake-like than the preceding recipe, which resembles a rich coffee-bread.

SWEET BREAD
KOULOURIA

There are several kinds of *koulouria*. Most popular are the small sesame rings and rolls which the delivery boy brings to the house, yelling as he arrives '*freska koulouria*', and with him comes a sweet smell of warm bread and sesame seeds. Or you can buy a *koulouria* at any street corner and munch it on the way to the office or take it with you into the nearest coffee shop and dunk it into your bowl of French coffee. And then there are the sweet *koulouria* – as this recipe – which is more like Danish coffee-bread and also extremely good.

1½ *lb flour*	*Milk or water for mixing*
1 *teaspoon baking-powder*	*Vanilla flavouring to taste*
4–6 *oz sugar*	1 *egg white*
5 *oz butter*	*Pinch salt*
2 *eggs*	

Lightly beat the egg white with a little sugar. This is to be used for glazing the *koulouria*. Cream the butter with the remaining sugar until the mixture is very creamy, almost fluffy. Sift the flour with the baking-powder and salt into a mixing bowl, add the creamed butter and mix well, preferably with your hands. If the dough is too stiff, add a little milk or water. If too loose, add a little more flour. Break off pieces of the mixture and shape into rolls, buns, or bracelet-size rings. Brush with the egg and sugar glaze and arrange the *koulouria* on a lightly greased baking sheet. Bake in a moderate oven for about 15 or 20 minutes, or until the *koulouria* are a golden brown.

There are variations on this theme. For example Cinnamon Rolls are made by using cinnamon instead of vanilla, or you can use sesame, mastic (see page 205) orange or lemon rind, even chocolate or wine must.

GREEK EASTER BREAD
LAMBROPSOMO

2 lb flour
2 oz yeast
¼ pint warm milk
1 pint lukewarm water
Finely chopped rind 1 orange
Pinch salt

Sesame seeds (see page 205)
5 dyed red eggs (see page 204)
1 egg yolk
1 tablespoon cold water
Olive oil

Dissolve the yeast in the milk, leave for 10 minutes. Gradually add 4 ounces of flour, cover with a napkin and leave in a warm place to rise overnight.

Next day sift the remaining flour into a large bowl and make a well in the centre. Add salt and half the warm water and gradually work the yeast batter into the centre of the well, adding as you do so the remaining warm water. When all the flour is mixed into the batter, knead the dough for at least 10 minutes. Add the orange peel and if the dough seems to be too loose add a little more flour. Brush a board with olive oil and sprinkle it generously with sesame seeds. Take enough of the dough from the basin and shape into a long loaf, then roll it over and over in the sesame seeds. Pat the loaf until it is about 2 inches high. Take the remaining dough and divide it into 2 pieces rolling them with the hands into long sausage-shape rolls about twice the length of the loaf. Roll one length of dough in the sesame seeds and when well covered place it along one side of the loaf, pressing it down slightly as you work and bring it along one end. Do the same with the other piece but place this on the other side of the loaf. Make 5 depressions in the loaf, one in the centre, the others at the four points of the compass. Into these depressions put the red eggs. Leave covered with a napkin for 3 hours. Beat the egg yolk with the cold water and lightly brush the top of the loaf, bake in a hot oven – not too hot – for about 45 minutes or until the bread is a golden brown.

There are variations on this theme. The same recipe is used for *Christopsomo*, or Christmas bread, which is decorated with a cross instead of the scarlet eggs and garnished with chopped nuts. The red eggs, according to the Greek Orthodox Church, represent the blood of Christ.

PLAITED BREAD
TSOUREKIA

Plaited bread takes the place of the British Hot Cross Bun during the Easter celebrations and is eaten at breakfast on Easter Day.

4 lb flour
6 oz melted butter
4 oz sugar
5 beaten eggs

½ pint warm milk
Grated rind 1 orange or 1 lemon
2 oz yeast
1 teaspoon salt

Dissolve the yeast with 4 ounces of flour and the scalded milk and mix to a smooth batter. Cover with a napkin and set aside in a warm place to rise for about 4 hours.

Sift the remaining flour into a mixing bowl, add the salt, sugar, orange or lemon rind, and make a well in the centre. Into this pour the yeast batter, the butter, and 4 eggs (one at a time) working the flour into the centre as you add these ingredients. Work to a fairly stiff dough, sprinkle lightly with flour, then cover with a napkin and leave to rise until it doubles its bulk. Turn on to a lightly floured board and knead, then divide the dough into 3 portions. Roll (with the hands) into long ropes, the ends of which should be thinner than the middle. Plait the 3 pieces and turn the ends under, pressing them down. Arrange on a greased baking sheet and leave to rise once more, about 2 hours. Beat the remaining egg and mix it with 1 teaspoonful each of sugar and cold water. Brush this mixture over the top of the bread and bake in a fairly hot oven for about 20 minutes.

The dough can be made into several plaited buns – or rolled round and round, like a Chelsea bun turned on its side. Mothers of small children often shape the dough into dolls or animals, with a red egg as a face. And quite often coarse sugar is sprinkled over the top and even blanched almonds.

HONEY PIE
MELOPITA

Pastry
12 oz flour
5 oz butter

Pinch salt
1½ teaspoons baking-powder

Filling

1½ lb unsalted, fresh myzithra (cottage) cheese	8 oz honey
	5 eggs
6 oz sugar	2 teaspoons cinnamon

First make the pastry. Sift the flour, baking-powder and salt together, then rub in the butter. Add enough water to make a stiff dough. Roll out and line a pie or flan tin, about 10 inches across and 3 inches deep.

In a mixing bowl beat the cheese, sugar and half the cinnamon. Add the honey and when this is thoroughly blended, add the eggs, one by one, beating well after each addition. Rub the mixture through a sieve and pour it into the pie or flan shell. Bake in a slow oven for 45 minutes, then increase the heat and bake for a further 15 minutes. When it is ready insert a knife into the filling – if it comes out clean the pie is ready. Turn off the heat, open the oven door and cool the pie in the oven. Remove and sprinkle with remaining cinnamon. Serve cold.

This is a very good pie and the filling should be thick to get the full flavour.

A recipe not very far removed from those of ancient Greece.

HONEY PUFFS (WITH YOGHOURT)
LOUKOUMATHES I

The best honey in Greece, according to the Athenians, comes from Hymettos, Athens' nearest mountain, where the bees swarm the mountain slopes sucking the perfumed sweetness from the thyme. However, people living in the region of Delphi also claim that theirs is the best honey, produced on the mountain slopes where the gods used to play. British housewives will, of course, use their own favourite brand of honey.

The puffs which are served with a honey sauce should, according to tradition, 'be as light as thistle-down' and are at their best eaten on a cold winter's night in front of the fire. In Greece, should you have an urge to eat honey puffs but no desire to make them yourself, you go to a *kafenion* or coffee shop where you can order a portion, 6 puffs, with some coffee or perhaps a bottle of Negrita, a mineral water of the Vichy type, which helps to wash down the sweet pastries and puffs so popular throughout the country.

1 *pint yoghourt*
8 *oz flour (approximately)*
1 *small glass brandy*

Pinch salt
Grated rind 1 orange or lemon
Olive oil for deep frying

Sauce
1 *cup honey*
Warm water

1 *teaspoon lemon juice*
1 *small piece cinnamon*

Beat the yoghourt and the rind together, add the salt and brandy and beat until the mixture is smooth, then gradually add enough flour to make a mixture of dropping consistency. To check whether the mixture is sufficiently pliable, pull some of it from the bowl and if it breaks it is too dry. As it stretches it should have an elastic quality. Leave for 2 hours.

Heat some olive oil in a deep frying pan until it begins to smoke. Drop small spoonfuls of the batter into this, 2 or 3 at a time. The puffs will swell and should be left until they are a golden brown. Take them from the pan and drain on absorbent paper. Cook the syrup ingredients until you have a medium-thick syrup, remove the cinnamon and pour the liquid over the puffs immediately. Serve at once.

Failing yoghourt, sour milk beaten until smooth is excellent as a substitute. The above quantity will make 3 dozen small puffs. Estimate 6 or 8 per person.

HONEY PUFFS (WITH YEAST)
LOUKOUMATHES II

1 *lb flour*
2 *oz yeast*
½ *teaspoon salt*

Lukewarm water or milk
Olive oil

Syrup
1 *cup honey*
Hot water

1 *teaspoon lemon juice*
Small piece cinnamon

Dissolve the yeast in a little warm water and mix with 4 ounces of the flour. Leave to rise until the batter doubles its size. Add the remaining flour and enough warm water or milk to make a

very soft dough. Cover again and let it stand until the dough
begins to bubble. This will take 4 or 5 hours.

Heat in a deep frying pan plenty of boiling oil until it begins
to smoke. Drop the dough in small spoonfuls into the hot oil
2 or 3 at a time. The puffs will swell and when they are golden
brown take them out with a perforated spoon, drain on absorbent
paper and serve hot with the honey syrup poured over them.

Syrup. Cook the honey with enough water, cinnamon and
lemon juice to make a thickish syrup. Remove the cinnamon
before using.

Greek and Balkan experts usually take a handful of the dough
and squeeze it through one hand so that a bubble forms on top
of the thumb and first finger. Deftly the bubble is knocked off
and dropped straight into the pan. For the amateur, and that
includes myself, spoons are easier.

FRITTERS I
TIYANITES

This is really yet another variety of the honey puffs.

1 *lb flour*	$\frac{1}{4}$ *teaspoon salt*
2 *teaspoons baking-powder*	*Juice* 1 *lemon*
1 *small glass brandy*	*Olive oil for deep frying*

Syrup	Garnish
1 *cup honey*	1 *cup ground walnuts*
1 *small piece ground cinnamon*	
1 *teaspoon lemon juice*	

Sift the flour, baking-powder and salt into a large bowl. Add
enough cold water to make a smooth dough or batter, then add
the lemon juice and the brandy.

Heat the oil until boiling, then drop spoonfuls of the batter
into it, 2 or 3 at a time. When the fritters are swollen and a
golden brown take them from the pan, drain on absorbent paper,
and arrange on a platter. Cook the honey with enough warm
water, cinnamon and lemon juice to make a syrup and pour this
over the fritters. Sprinkle with ground walnuts and serve at once.

Quite often *tiyanites* are served with icing sugar, cinnamon
or ground nuts and no sauce.

NUT TURNOVERS
SCALTSOUNIA

Filling

8 oz walnuts	1 teaspoon mastic (see page
8 oz almonds	205)
1 teaspoon ground cloves	1 teaspoon ground cinnamon
	Honey

Blanch and coarsely grind or crush the walnuts and almonds.
Mix with the cinnamon, cloves, mastic, and enough honey to
blend the mixture without making it too stiff. Leave aside while
you make the pastry.

Pastry

1 cup olive oil	Flour – about 1 lb
1 cup water	Rose or orange flower water
1 teaspoon baking-powder	(see page 206)
Juice 1 lemon	Icing sugar

Mix the first 4 ingredients together, then add enough flour to
make a stiff dough. Roll this out to one-third of an inch thickness on a floured board. Cut the dough into circles and on each
one place a teaspoonful of the nut filling (just how much depends
on how large you make the circles). Fold the pastry over the
filling in the ordinary manner of making turnovers and press
the edges of the dough together. Arrange on a greased baking
pan and bake for about 15 minutes in a moderate oven until the
pastry is a golden brown. Take the turnovers from the oven,
leave until cool enough to handle, then dip them into either
orange-flower water or rose water and sprinkle with icing sugar.

Enough for about 25–30 small turnovers. I have kept the
liquid measurements in cups as it is simpler. Use a teacup of
everyday size.

SWEET FRIED BOWKNOTS
THIPLES

A favourite Greek tea-time sweet, especially with children.

2 lb flour	Ouzo or orange juice
1 teaspoon baking-powder	Water
4 eggs	Olive oil for deep frying
Pinch salt	

Syrup

1½ cups honey	A little lemon juice
1½ cups warm water	Small piece cinnamon

Garnish

Cinnamon	Chopped nuts – preferably
Coarse sugar	walnuts

Sift the flour and the baking-powder, add salt, then the eggs,
one at a time, and enough water, flavoured with *ouzo* or orange
juice, to make a stiff dough. If the dough is too loose, add more
flour; if too stiff, more liquid. Break off small pieces and roll
these out on a floured board until very thin. Cut into strips and
tie into bowknots (or any shapes you fancy). Fry in deep, boiling oil until a golden colour. Do not put too many in the pan
at the same time. Take the bowknots from the pan with a perforated spoon and place them on absorbent paper until all the
thiples are finished.

Make a syrup from the honey, warm water and lemon juice.
Arrange a layer of the *thiples* on a plate, sprinkle lightly with
syrup, cinnamon, sugar and chopped nuts. Arrange another
layer and repeat the sprinkling of syrup, cinnamon and nuts.
Repeat until all the *thiples* are used up. Most of the syrup pours
down into the plate but this can be spooned up and poured
over the *thiples* when serving them.

Two other names for *thiples* are *Avgokalamara* and *Xerotiyana*.
Not all Greeks take afternoon tea. It is an adopted custom
and rather like the French five o'clock tea.

VENETIAN CAKES
FINIKIA

Finikia is the popular name of honey-dipped cakes called *Melo-makarona* and supposed to be taken from a recipe dating back to the Venetians, hence the name.

3 *lb flour*	1 *tablespoon honey*
1 *pint olive oil*	1 *tablespoon lemon juice*
1 *sherry glass brandy*	2 *teaspoons baking-powder*
Juice 2 oranges	6 *oz sugar*
Grated rind 1 orange	1 *teaspoon ground cinnamon*

Syrup
1½ *lb honey*	½ *pint water*
1 *teaspoon lemon juice*	

Garnish
Sesame seeds	*Ground cinnamon*

Warm the oil and beat it until it becomes almost white. Add brandy, sugar and orange juice and beat for 10 minutes. Work in the flour and continue to work the mixture for 15 minutes, then knead for another 15. Add the honey, orange rind, baking-powder, cinnamon, and the lemon juice and knead again for 15 minutes. Shape into very small round cakes. With the back of a fork make designs on the top of the cakes. Arrange on greased baking sheets and bake in a fairly hot oven for 20 or 25 minutes. Leave to cool and meanwhile make the syrup.

Cook the honey and lemon juice with the water to a syrup. Dip the cooled cakes into this and then sprinkle with sesame seeds and cinnamon. This quantity makes a large number of cakes but they will keep for several days, the flavour improving.

SEMOLINA SWEET OR HALVA
HALVAS SIMIGTHALENIOS

1 *glass butter*	3 *glasses sugar*
2 *glasses coarse semolina*	4 *glasses water*

Garnish
Peeled and chopped almonds	*Ground cinnamon*

Cook the sugar and water to a syrup. Heat the butter over a
low heat to boiling point, using a heavy saucepan. Stir in the
semolina and, using a wooden spoon, stir and cook very slowly
until the semolina is a light, golden colour. Add the syrup, stir
it to blend, then take the pan from the heat, cover with a napkin, and leave on the side of the stove, or turn the semolina
into a casserole and put into a warm but not hot oven. Leave
for about 15 minutes. By this time the semolina will have absorbed the syrup and be crumbly. Put it into a glass dish, press it
down firmly and then turn out to serve. Garnish with almonds and
sprinkle with cinnamon.

The secret of *halva* is the slow cooking until it is a golden
brown. This recipe is known as the 1–2–3–4 recipe and is considered infallible. Quite often blanched and toasted almonds
are added, either chopped or halved.

SESAME AND HONEY SWEET
PASTELLI

For those who like the flavour of sesame – and I am one – this
is a delicious concoction.

2 *cups sesame seeds*   1¼ *cups honey*

Cook the honey and sesame seeds together in a thick-bottomed
saucepan very slowly for about 10 minutes, stirring from time to
time until the mixture becomes a golden brown. Test it in cold
water – if it forms into a ball, then it is ready. Pour it on to a
board or a marble slab and pat with the back of a wooden
spoon or spatula until it is flat and about ½ an inch think.

To store, wrap individually in waxed paper and keep in an
air-tight box.

This is one of those nice goo-ey toffee-like sweets that children
usually adore.

APPLE COMPOTE
COMPOSTA MILO

This is simply apples peeled and cut into quarters or halves
and put into a saucepan with water, sugar to taste, a small piece

of cinnamon stick or cloves and lemon juice, and cooked fairly slowly for about 30 minutes.

Pears, peaches, quinces and other similar fruits are dealt with in the same manner.

CUSTARD

CREMA PATISSERI

1 *pint milk*   1 *oz flour or cornflour*
2 *oz butter*   *Pinch salt*
2 *well-beaten eggs*

Mix the flour or cornflour to a smooth paste with a quarter of the milk, add the eggs and beat the mixture until it is thoroughly blended. Heat the remaining milk over a low heat, add the flour and egg mixture, stirring all the while to prevent curdling. Continue to cook until the cream thickens and the odour of the raw flour or cornflour has disappeared. Use as a filling for pastries.

Personally I think cornflour is better for this custard than flour. This custard is a good basis for ice-cream but some vanilla flavouring should be added.

CORNFLOUR PUDDING I

CREMA I

2 *oz cornflour*   1½ *pints hot milk*
4 *oz sugar*   *Cinnamon*

Use a double boiler. Mix the cornflour in a basin with some of the milk to a paste. Bring the remaining milk to the boil in the top of a double boiler and pour it on to the cornflour paste. Stir well and return it to the pan. Add the sugar. Stir and cook until the mixture is very thick. Pour into small glass bowls and sprinkle with ground cinnamon, cool and then chill.

This is the basic recipe for a popular Greek dish which is seldom served after a meal but, like *Rizogalo* (see page 186), eaten between meals as a snack. Sometimes the pudding is sprinkled with ground nuts instead of cinnamon and sometimes a more elaborate version is made, like the following recipe.

CORNFLOUR PUDDING II
CREMA II

2 oz cornflour
4 oz sugar
3 egg yolks

Grated rind small orange or
    tangerine
1 teaspoon vanilla essence
1½ pints milk

Mix the sugar and cornflour with the egg yolks to a paste. Beat
until the mixture is smooth. Heat the milk until it is scalding hot,
then stir carefully into it the egg and cornflour mixture. Strain
(this operation is optional, for if the milk has been added carefully, stirring all the while, the mixture should not have either
curdled or become lumpy). Add the orange or tangerine rind and
pour the mixture into the top of a double boiler. Cook slowly,
stirring all the while until it is thick, then add the vanilla. Pour
the *crema* into glass dishes and sprinkle with cinnamon and
coarsely ground nuts. Cool, then chill. It looks and tastes better
if you use coarsely ground almonds and pistachio nuts mixed as a
garnish.

RICE PUDDING
RIZOGALO

2 pints milk
6 oz sugar
6 oz rice

Ground cinnamon to taste
Lemon rind
2 teaspoons cornflour

Cook the rice with the milk and lemon rind, stirring frequently
until the rice is very soft. Add the sugar and the cornflour (mixed
to a paste) and continue to cook until the mixture is creamy. Cool
and pour into glass dishes, sprinkle with cinnamon, and then put
into a refrigerator and leave until ice-cold.

Some Greek cooks like to add 2 well-beaten eggs to the rice.
If this is done, the eggs should be beaten into the milk before it is
put into the saucepan. However, I think the rice is nice enough
without the eggs.

CHESTNUT PURÉE
KASTANA PURÉE

This is prepared in the same manner as the Italian '*Mont Blanc*' and for those visiting Athens who like chestnuts, especially when *puréed* and served with whipped cream, I suggest a visit to the Restaurant Floca where one can sit on the pavement, watch the crowds go by, ruin one's figure and enjoy a dish of chestnut *purée*.

2 *lb chestnuts*	1 *small glass brandy*
1½ *pints milk*	*Salt*
3 *oz sugar*	*Whipped cream*
1 *teaspoon vanilla essence*	

Make a slit in the skin of each chestnut and cook in plenty of salted water until the skins will peel off easily – about 15 or 20 minutes. Drain, peel and put into the top of a double boiler with the milk, sugar, a pinch of salt, and the vanilla. Cook over hot water until the chestnuts are soft and have absorbed all the liquid. Pour the brandy over the chestnuts, simmer until this is absorbed and then rub them through a coarse sieve. Take small portions and make about 4 discs, roughly 2 inches across. Pile the remaining *purée* lightly on the top of these discs – it should be light and fluffy, so too much spooning will make it flat. Top with whipped cream and chill before serving. Grated chocolate can be sprinkled over the top of the cream.

Absolutely delicious.

WHEAT AND MIXED FRUIT
KOLYVA

This is a traditional dish, made and eaten by orthodox families forty days after the death of a member of the family and on the anniversary of a death. It has no particular recipe since it is simply wheat boiled until soft and mixed with fruit and pomegranate seeds – all of which have a symbolic meaning. Wheat means everlasting life; fruit, joy and sweetness, and pomegranate seeds, plenty.

The custom of eating *kolyva* dates back to pagan days and

was recognized or received the blessing of the Church in the
days of Julian the Apostate who, alarmed at the increasing influence of the Christian Church, planned to annihilate the
Greek community of Constantinople through the simple ex-
pedient of poisoning their Lenten food. This plot, however,
was foiled by the timely warning given to them by the Patriarch,
Head of the Greek Orthodox Church, to whom the plot was
revealed in a dream. He warned his people and told them to eat
only wheat during the period of the Lenten fasts. Having been
saved from death, the Greeks then dedicated several Saturdays
during the year as Soul Sabbaths and to the remembrance of the
dead. Then *kolyva* was eaten – it is an improved or revised version of the pagan *pansperima*, a similar dish also eaten in remembrance of the dead.

Preserves

KOMPOSTES KE YLYKA KOUTALIOU

SPOON SWEETS
YLYKA KOUTALIOU

The offering of 'spoon sweets' to guests is a very old and rather delightful custom. Foreigners, when they first meet it, are apt to be a trifle confused. As one Greek told me, when the tray with its small bowl of preserve, glasses of water, spoons, and usually glasses of liqueur arrives the foreigner, if he does not know the custom, looks nonplussed. Sometimes he takes the whole bowl of preserve, tries to get through it, then says sadly and with some embarrassment, 'I simply cannot eat it all.'

When the tray thus laden arrives, the guest is supposed to take a spoon, and then a spoonful of the preserve, and eat it. Then he drinks a glass of water, still holding the spoon, which, when he has finished the water, he puts into the empty glass, and returns this to the tray. By this time he is ready to take the glass of liqueur or small cup of Turkish coffee. When he has done all this he should wish his hostess and family happiness and good fortune. If, however, the guest, being a foreigner, is rather shy about doing this, the best thing he can do is to smile brightly and express his thanks.

This offering of spoon sweets is a symbol of Greek hospitality, and also, so my husband was told when he first met the Greek Patriarch in Istanbul, a silent sign that, since everyone eats from the same bowl, it is not poisoned. But this legend dates back ages – further back, even, than the days when we had our royal tasters to prevent poisoning, a well-known custom in days gone by but rarely, of course, known today.

AUBERGINE PRESERVE
MELITZANAKIA YLIKO

For this recipe you require ripe but small aubergines. Wash as
many as required, score them once with a sharp knife and put
into a pan to boil – using not too much water and taking care
they do not overcook to a mush. Drain and dry in a napkin.
Insert one blanched almond deeply into the aubergines – it must
be deeply inserted otherwise it will come out during cooking.

Prepare a syrup – proportions are 3 glasses of sugar to 1 of
water, with cloves to taste, a small piece of cinnamon and about
1 tablespoonful of lemon juice. (Lemon juice prevents the
syrup from crystallizing.) When the syrup is almost set, add
the aubergines, bring to the boil, then take the pan from the
fire. Leave to cool in the syrup, then take out the aubergines
with a perforated spoon. Boil the syrup again, let it become
thick, return the aubergines, then bring the syrup 2 or 3 times
again to the boil. Cool, and pour into sterilized jars or jelly
glasses.

A popular recipe in Crete.

SOUR OR MORELLO CHERRY PRESERVE
VISSINO YLYKO

3 lb sour black cherries   ¼ pint water
4½ lb sugar   Juice 1 lemon

Wash and pip the cherries – but be careful not to break them
too much. Put them into a large, shallow pan in layers, sprinkling
each layer with sugar. Add the water and cook rapidly until the
syrup is as thick as honey, then add the lemon juice – this is
to prevent the syrup from crystallizing. Stir gently, skim off any
scum which rises to the top. Test the syrup by dropping a little
on to a saucer. If the syrup does not spread it is ready.

This type of preserve is a very popular spoon sweet.

CHERRY DRINK
VISSINADA

This is included in this section as the recipe is precisely the
same as the previous one – except that more sugar must be added
in order to make more syrup.

To make the well-known *vissinada* take from the *vissino* 1 or
2 tablespoonfuls of the syrup and mix this with a glass of iced
water or mineral water. It is exceedingly refreshing. The preserve can still be used as a spoon sweet or jam.

ORANGE AND LEMON BLOSSOM PRESERVE
LEMONIOU YLYKO

This recipe and the one following are specialities of the island
of Chios.

1½ lb orange and lemon blossoms   2 quarts water
4 lb sugar   1 tablespoon lemon juice

Put the blossom into a basin with a little of the sugar and leave
for several hours, stirring them gently with your fingers – as
with rose petals. Next day boil the remaining sugar, water and
lemon juice until bubbling and the sugar thoroughly dissolved.
Add the blossoms and continue to cook until the mixture
thickens. Pour into sterilized jars or glasses, cool and seal.

Tangerine blossoms are also added when available.

PRESERVE OF BITTER ORANGES OR LEMONS
NERANDZAKI YLYKO

This is one of the favourite Greek spoon sweets and the unripe
oranges or lemons used are dark green and extremely bitter.
They are about the size of a table-tennis ball. This is a classical
recipe and used by most Greek housewives.

To remove the pips Greek housewives have a small gadget
which is like a thinner edition of our marrow-bone remover.
The main idea is to remove the pips by making a small hole

in the fruit and coring it as one does an apple, without destroying the appearance of the fruit.

About 70 or 80 small bitter   4½ *lb sugar*
  oranges or lemons

After removing the pips, soak the fruit in cold water for 24 hours. Drain and put into a large pan, add water to cover and bring to the boil – add a coffeespoonful of bicarbonate of soda to keep the skins a bright green. Boil until soft – test with a needle, if the fruit is soft enough it will slip off the needle. It must not be allowed to cook until too soft, otherwise it will become hard during the cooking in the syrup. Drain the fruit and soak it again for several hours in cold water. Drain and dry in a napkin.

Put the sugar into a large pan, add 1¼ pints of water, bring to the boil, add the fruit, lower the heat and cook slowly for 5 minutes. Take the pan from the stove, cover, and leave the fruit in the sugar until next day. Take the fruit out with a perforated spoon and place on a large platter. Re-boil the syrup and let it become thick. Add the fruit, turn it from time to time and simmer gently until all the dampness of the fruit has been absorbed and the syrup thickly coats the fruit. Cool and seal in jars.

PRESERVED ORANGE ROLLS
NERANTZI YIRISTO

Another very popular spoon sweet and also a classical Greek recipe. For it you must have large, very thick-skinned oranges which are both ripe and a golden yellow.

First lightly grate as many oranges as you require – about 20 – to remove the first bitterness. Wash them well and score deeply through the skin into quarters. Peel these quarters off neatly. Thread a darning needle with strong thread. Roll up the pieces of orange skin tightly as you would a Swiss roll and pass the needle and thread through them – having about 15 or 20 pieces on the thread. Break off the thread and tie the two ends together – you have now a ring or necklace of rolled orange skins. Repeat this until all the orange skin is rolled up and threaded (or 'threddled' as one old countrywoman used to tell

me). Fill a large saucepan with water, add the orange skin rolls
and cook them until they are very soft. Cool, drain and pour
cold water over them. Leave for 24 hours, changing the cold
water several times. Drain, remove the threads and dry on a
napkin. Prepare a syrup as in the preceding recipe – roughly
the same quantity – boil the rolls twice in the syrup, then seal
them in jars.

QUINCE JELLY
KYTHONI PELTES

4½ lb quinces, after peeling and cleaning	Sugar
2½ quarts water	3–4 young leaves from the ivy-leaf geranium

Wash the quinces, then peel, clean, and stone them – save the
skins and stones and put these into a muslin bag and tie it
securely. When the quinces have been peeled, etc, weigh them
to make sure that you have the required 4½ pounds. When
buying the quinces you had better allow for 4–6 ounces wastage.

Cut the fruit into thick slices and put these into a large saucepan or preserving pan. Add the water and the muslin bag,
cover and cook for 1½ hours. (You cook the skins and stones
for their pectin value.) Remove the bag and pour the fruit with
its liquid through a jelly bag or a large piece of muslin. Gently
squeeze the bag but not too much, otherwise the jelly will become cloudy. (By the way, do not discard the pulp, it is valuable,
see following recipe.) Measure the liquid carefully and add
1 cup of sugar for every 2 cups of juice. Add the geranium
leaves and simmer for about 30 minutes. Skim off the foam
from time to time. To test for readiness, dip a spoon into the
jelly, take it out and let the jelly drip back into the pan. If the
last drop sticks to the spoon it is ready. Pour into jars or glasses
and next day cover with wax paper and store. Failing geranium
leaves, which give a delightfully delicate flavour to the jelly,
use vanilla.

QUINCE PASTE
PASTOKITHONA

A recipe from the island of Cephalonia.

The pulp from preceding recipe   4 oz chopped and blanched
1½ lb strained honey   almonds (lightly fried)
1 inch piece cinnamon   *A few halves blanched almonds*
            (optional)   *A few bayleaves*

Rub the pulp through a fine sieve, then mix it with the honey.
Put this mixture in a thick-bottomed pan and cook very slowly,
stirring from time to time, for about 1½ hours. When the paste
comes away from the sides of the pan it is ready. During the last
30 minutes of cooking add the toasted or lightly fried almonds
and the cinnamon – this must be removed when the paste is
ready. Spread the paste on to a wooden board or better still a
piece of marble slab and pat it down, using the back of a
wooden spoon or a spatula. It should be about 2 inches thick or
just a little less. Garnish with the halves of almonds and leave
until cool. Cut into shapes, diamonds, triangles or squares.
This kind of paste can be stored in air-tight containers. Place in
layers, with a bayleaf or two between each layer. Extremely good.
The paste should be kept in a cool place.
    Quince paste is sold wrapped in cellophane paper in the
sweet and pastry shops and the kiosks of Athens and other
towns. It is extremely good. I have used the same recipe with
guavas with equally good results. Instead of honey you can use
sugar, 1 cup of sugar to each cup of pulp.

QUINCE CHEESE
KYTHONI XYSTO

3 lb quinces   *1 teaspoon vanilla or 1 or 2*
3 lb sugar   *geranium leaves*
½ pint water   *1 tablespoon lemon juice*

Peel the quinces and grate them on a coarse grater. Put them
into a large saucepan, add ½ pint of water and cook gently until
the fruit is soft and begins to set. Gradually add the sugar and
continue to cook over a high flame until the syrup is thick – at

this point add the lemon juice to prevent the syrup from crystallizing. Towards the end add either the vanilla or the geranium leaves – the latter give a more unusual and delicate flavour. Test the jelly by dipping a spoon into it – take up a little of the jelly and drop it back into the pan. When you do this several times and finally the last drop sticks to the spoon like a bubble – then the jelly is ready. Take the pan from the heat, slightly cool and then pour into jars, and seal when cold.

ROSE PETAL PRESERVE OR JAM
TRIANDAFILLO YLIKO

You need preferably fresh, large, dark red rose petals, if possible from the homely cabbage rose.

3 dozen fresh roses, making 2 quarts of rose petals	1 quart water
	2 tablespoons lemon juice
2 lb castor sugar	

Pull off the rose petals and cut off the hard white base which is bitter and also spoils the colour of the jam. Put them into a mixing bowl with a little of the sugar. Gently mix them with your fingers and leave covered overnight. Next day boil the remaining sugar with the water and the lemon juice until the sugar is dissolved and the syrup is rapidly boiling and bubbling. Add the rose petals and continue to cook until the mixture thickens. Pour into hot, sterilized jars and seal.

A favourite breakfast of mine when travelling in the Balkans is brown bread, rather coarse and immensely soft, rose petal jam and fresh butter.

Cheeses

TYRIA

The cheeses of Greece are not spectacular and are made principally for local consumption, although some commercially-made Greek cheeses are exported to the vast Greek communities abroad. Most of these cheeses are soft, made either from ewe's milk or goat's milk and traditionally made by shepherds and the peasants. Their quality depends, therefore, entirely on local skill.

The most popular of Greek cheeses is *feta*, which is a dead-white, soft and crumbly cheese, well salted and equally popular throughout the Balkans. In Greece it has its origin in the mountain regions above Athens. When travel writers talk of their meals with peasants, eating soft, coarse brown bread and white cheese, they mean *feta*. It is a farmhouse, so-called pickled cheese, but distinct in flavour and, in the right setting, extremely good to eat. It can also be used in cooking, although not in the same manner as a Cheddar or Italian Parmesan cheese.

Feta cheese is made in the same way as all farmhouse cheeses, milk curdled with a starter and rennet, allowed to drain until firm (the whey is kept) and then heavily salted before being packed into wooden kegs. It is left for a month. *Feta* is not a good traveller, mainly because its water content is too high. It is usually brought into the cities in the large wooden kegs.

One can make a reasonably passable *feta* at home by curdling milk with rennet and allowing it to drain until the cheese is very firm. When the curd is firm enough to cut into thick slices, it should be generously sprinkled with salt and left for 24 hours, then packed into a wooden keg and left for about 4 days, when it is ready for use.

There is also a slightly more refined *feta* cheese made from pasteurized milk which is usually exported.

Touloumotyri
A *feta* cheese packed into goatskins and weighing between 60 and 70 pounds. It has a slightly different flavour and the effect is fascinating when the skin is opened, exposing its pure white inside.

Telemes
Another *feta*-type cheese made into squares, weighing around 2 pounds each and rather more heavily salted. It ripens more quickly than *feta* but the two are often confused.

Kopanisti
This is a 'blue' *feta* cheese which has been allowed to coagulate longer and is, therefore, of a finer texture. It is also allowed by certain processes to gather a blue mould which, in time, is kneaded into the cheese. It has a sharp, rather peppery flavour and is recommended to those who like to try different cheeses.

Myzithra
A soft, cottage cheese made from the whey which is drained from the *feta* and mixed with fresh milk. The Greeks find many more uses for cottage cheese than we normally do in Britain and one of their specialities is the cottage cheese and honey pie (see page 177) which I highly recommend.

Kefalotyri
A hard cheese, very salty with a hard rind, used as a Parmesan. It is made in various parts of the country and known under several names. It is used mainly as a cooking cheese and can be easily grated. Its name comes from its shape, which is like a hat, or *kefalo*.

Pinthos
A better-class *kefalotyri*.

Kasseri
A firm, white cheese, mildly flavoured but somewhat softer and much used in cooking as a grating cheese. Also eaten fresh.

Gruyère
The Greek version of the famous Swiss cheese. It is made from ewe's milk and, when it is good, it is very good. When not – well – it is just a poor imitation.

Agrafa
An improved version of the Greek Gruyère and usually of high quality.

Anthotyro
A goat's cheese from Crete, eaten at all times of the day. Firm, with not too strong a flavour, it is extremely popular with Cretans, who like it served with grapes.

Antholyti
This is a round, pale yellow cheese which comes in two or three sizes. It has a mottled, thick rind as wrinkled as a relief map.

Anari
Goat's or ewe's milk cheese which, when kept, looks like a ripe Gorgonzola. It can be bought in salted squares or round like a pudding. Greek-Cypriot.

Halorini
A cheese made usually from ewe's milk folded over like dough and filled with pounded coriander. Greek-Cypriot.

Manouri
A sweet, soft cheese when it is fresh but hardens as it ages.

Gravieri
A similar cheese to Gruyère and made in Crete. Like the Greek Gruyère it can be extraordinarily good.

Parnossus
Another of the white cheeses made from ewe's milk.

Sundries

THIAFORA

COFFEE
KAFES MAVROS

Actually Greek coffee is Turkish coffee. Coffee is said to have
been introduced into Europe, via Turkey, during the reign of
Suleyman the Magnificent (1520–66) by a merchant of Aleppo
who returned to his home city richer by 50,000 ducats. The
Arabic name was, and still is, *kahveh*, signifying the queller of
appetites. At first it excited the suspicions of the more puri-
tanical Moslems and the new coffee houses, which were opening
up throughout the Ottoman Empire, were viewed with appre-
hension. But Suleyman was as wise as he was magnificent and
allowed them to continue.

Since then coffee drinking in special coffee houses has been
a habit of the Balkan peoples. Sitting for hours in a coffee
house staring into space and sipping a small cup of coffee is a
recognized way of living. The waiter brings the customer glass
after glass of water, sometimes yet another cup of coffee, and
the classical coffee drinker sits and stares, or talks politics, or,
if he is old-fashioned, gurgles leisurely through his *nargileh* or
hubble-bubble. If you want to see something typical of the
Balkans while in Athens, simply wander along to the coffee
shops – *kafenion* – in and around Ommonia; there sit men up
from the country, each in his favourite coffee house with his
cronies.

However, if you prefer it, you can order French coffee in
Athens and in other larger cities and this means coffee with
milk. Athens has many coffee bars, they grow up overnight.
I was there when the first Sputnik completed its successful
orbit around the earth; overnight Athens had its 'Sputnik' coffee
house.

When ordering Turkish coffee you need guidance. You

must know whether you want it with sugar, a little sugar, or no sugar at all. And then you must know whether you want it well-boiled or not. Most people who are unused to Turkish coffee prefer it medium boiled and medium sweet, and for this one asks for *metrio vrasto*. Those who like their coffee very sweet should ask for *vary ylyko*, strong and sweet. But those who, like myself, prefer all coffee, even Turkish, without sugar must ask firmly for *sketto vastro*.

Making Turkish coffee is not difficult. First consider the coffee: this must be finely ground, pulverized in fact, and in this state can be bought in several of the better coffee shops in Britain. On the other hand it is rather fun to have one of the Balkan-type coffee grinders, they can be bought in Soho and probably elsewhere. They are quite elegant, long and cylindrical, made of brass, and they grind coffee beans to a fine powder.

Next, for better effect when serving the coffee, it is nice to have a long-handled, lipped copper or brass coffee pot in which to boil the coffee. These, too, are available in several of the Soho shops and in many of the coffee shops dealing exclusively with coffee.

For each cup of coffee (small *mokka* cups) you require one cup of water, one heaped teaspoonful of coffee powder and sugar to taste. It is usual not to make more than three or, at the most, four cups of coffee at a time. Put three coffee cups of water into the pot and bring this to the boil. Add the coffee and let it rest on the top of the water, then add sugar to taste. Bring the water once more to the boil, take it from the heat, let the froth which has risen die down and then return the pot to the fire again. Let the water boil and froth again, take it from the fire and when the froth has died down repeat the process. But this time stir the coffee well into the water as it boils, at the same time trying not to lose too much of the froth. Pour the coffee at once into the coffee cups, evenly distributing the froth, for this brings luck. The more froth you have the more luck.

Among the Greeks in Istanbul there are those who can read the future in the coffee grounds left in the cup after drinking, but I found less of this in Greece. Which is sad, for such fine futures are foretold from the thick mass of coffee grains left in the cup after being turned upside down and allowed to cool.

SALEPI

This is a drink sold in the early hours of the morning or very late at night. It is a hot, sweet infusion of orchid tubers, rather like milk in appearance, but to my taste quite insipid. The vendor carries his equipment in a brass container which includes a charcoal stove to keep the *salepi* hot. It was once a popular British drink, but is today quite unknown.

TISANES

In most parts of Greece as well as in the islands the people use all the herbs of the fields as well as those of the gardens. Each herb has its own special quality and flavour and many are turned into a *tisane*, or tea, for curing this or that complaint. Many Greek housewives have herbal recipes for all domestic ailments.

PUNCH OR WINE CUP
BOWLE

1 *bottle champagne*	1 *sliced orange*
2 *bottles white wine*	1 *sliced banana*
1 *large glass brandy*	1 *small tin cubed pineapple*
2 *bottles aerated water*	

Mix the champagne, brandy and wine, add the fruit – together with the pineapple juice. Put the bowl in which you have mixed the ingredients on a bed of crushed ice. Add the aerated water just before serving. If a sweeter wine cup is required, add about a cup of syrup, but this would make a very sweet punch even sweeter.

Instead of champagne a sparkling wine can be used.

YOGHOURT
YAOURTI

Yoghourt belongs to the species buttermilk, sour milk and cottage cheese and is made by adding a bacterial culture or bacillus to fresh milk – in Greece this means, usually, sheep's milk. There are several stories concerning its origin. One is that the Turks discovered it when they were wandering nomads and carried their milk in gourds slung over the backs of camels. The sunshine and the constant jolting turned it thick and sour – and made the first yoghourt. Another story is that the early inhabitants of Greece used to leave their goat and sheep milk exposed to the bacteria of the open air and it developed a new character which they liked. So yoghourt became a staple part of the people's diet.

Many things are claimed for yoghourt; it is a cure for stomach troubles of a minor kind; it helps dyspeptics and those afflicted with dysentery. A large bowl of yoghourt taken after an evening's heavy drinking will, it is claimed, avert a hang-over, while others claim that if you already have a hang-over a bowl of yoghourt will go a long way towards sending it away. Many of the really old people living in the mountains of the Balkans claim that yoghourt is the secret of long life.

In cooking it has many virtues; food can be marinated in yoghourt, it blends with almost all vegetable dishes and can be used in gravies, in cakes and scone-making, in fact, its virtues are almost endless.

Today, both in Britain and the United States, yoghourt is sold with the morning milk and comes in all kinds of flavours, especially in America which produces a prune whip yoghourt, or yoghourt flavoured with pineapple, orange, strawberry, etc. Personally, I find these flavoured concoctions cease to be yoghourt and they certainly bear no relationship with the thick, tangy, sour yoghourt sold in the Balkans and in some of the dairies in Britain.

Yoghourt can be made at home quite simply. All that is required is a teaspoonful or so of the commercially prepared yoghourt mixed with milk.

Recipe. Bring a quart of milk to the boil, pour it into small earthenware dishes or cups and leave until it is blood hot. Dilute 2 teaspoonfuls of commercially made yoghourt with some cold milk and pour a little of this into each dish or cup, disturbing the milk as little as possible. Cover with a flannel cloth to keep warm, or put into a warm oven, without the heat turned on. Leave until the yoghourt is very thick. Serve cold.

CHEESE PIE
TYROPITA

1 *lb feta cheese*	20 *sheets phyllo pastry*
(see page 196)	(see page 162)
1 *lb myzithra, or cottage, cheese*	2 *oz sifted flour*
(see page 197)	*Chopped parsley and nutmeg*
½ *cup cream*	*to taste*
4 *eggs*	*About* 3 *or* 4 *oz melted butter*

Test the *feta* cheese. If it is too salty soak it in water for a while, drain and put it in a mixing bowl. Add the *myzithra* (or cottage cheese) and blend. Break in the eggs, one by one, beating each well into the cheese. Mix the flour with the cream, then stir this into the cheese mixture. Line a large, shallow baking-tin with butter and lay in it 10 sheets of *phyllo* pastry, each sheet brushed with melted butter. Spread the cheese mixture on the top sheet, then cover with the remaining *phyllo*, spreading each one lightly with butter. Turn in the edges of the pastry to keep the filling from oozing out and sprinkle the top sheet lightly with water to prevent this from curling upwards. Score the top through the first 3 or 4 layers of pastry into serving-size pieces, diamond or oval shapes. Bake in a moderate oven for about 45 minutes. Cool a little before serving. Serve warm for Greek taste; hot for British.

This is a popular Lenten dish and also eaten during *tyrini*, or cheese week, the last week of the pre-Lenten carnival, locally called *apokries*. The word *apokreo* literally means fast from meat and applies to the many days of fasting which the Greek Orthodox Church ordains. In its plural form *apokries* has today come to mean two weeks of meat fasting, called *kreatines*, and one of cheese eating called *tyrini*. These three weeks constitute the Greek Carnival, much entertaining, masked balls, streamers, noise, and confetti, in fact, all the fun of Carnival and certainly a time to visit Greece.

Tyropita can also be made with all cottage cheese instead of half cottage and half *feta* cheese.

RICE OMELETTE
OMELETTA ME RIZI

5 eggs

3 tomatoes

6 tablespoons boiled, salted rice

Butter

Salt and pepper

Breadcrumbs and flour

Sugar

The tomatoes should be large and firm. Peel, and slice them thickly and sprinkle them with salt, pepper and sugar. Mix enough fine breadcrumbs with flour to make a coating for the tomatoes. Dip each slice of tomato into this and fry them on both sides in hot butter or other fat. Put aside and keep hot.

Beat the eggs, add salt and pepper and then the rice. Spread this out in a frying pan and cook slowly until the egg is set. When it is cooked put the omelette on a dish and garnish it with the fried tomatoes.

Sometimes finely chopped, fried onions are added to the rice and eggs before cooking. A most substantial kind of omelette.

SCARLET EASTER EGGS
KOKKINA AVGA

There are many ways to colour eggs. They can be painted or dyed in a harmless powder dye, or you can simply cook the eggs until hard in water which has been treated with cochineal or other commercial cooking colouring matter.

ANISEED
ANISE

The seeds of a small aromatic plant and a member of the parsley family. As children we first meet the flavour in liquorice sweets. It is greatly used in Oriental and Balkan cooking and is popular as a pickling spice.

In ancient Greece a sprig of anise was hung over the bed to prevent bad dreams and nowadays herbalists prescribe a teaspoonful of anise seeds in a glass of hot milk sweetened with honey as a cure for insomnia. Anise is also made into a *tisane* and served as a cold tea in hot weather.

CUMIN
CUMIN

An aromatic fruit, so small it is usually referred to as a herb. It has a slightly bitter flavour and when it is not available it can be substituted by the caraway seed. Cumin flavours much of the Oriental cooking and is highly prized as an appetite stimulant. Jesus spoke of it when he was exhorting the Scribes and the Pharisees . . . 'ye pay tithe of mint and anise and cumin and have omitted the weightier matter of the law, – judgment, mercy and faith.'

SESAME SEEDS

The product of a small annual plant grown extensively in various parts of the Balkans, Russia and the East. The seeds are small, honey-coloured (sometimes called white) and are used in Greece in flavouring breads, rolls, biscuits and cakes. It is also a main flavouring in the commercially made *halva*. Gives a rich toasted flavour to breads, etc.

MASTIC
MASTIHA

Small, clear crystals coming from an evergreen, resinous shrub. It is used a greal deal in Balkan cooking. Mastic is one of the important Greek exports and in the days of the Turkish occupation the ladies of the Sultan's harem were allowed as pocket money the proceeds from the mastic gum sales. In those days the sales were considerable and the main growing area was the island of Chios, which became important as a money-earning island through its mastic, so was granted its own parliament. There are some four million mastic shrubs still in the island of Chios, but no longer a separate parliament. The flavour is faintly like liquorice – a word of Greek descent – which means sweet root.

Mastic gum is produced by making incisions in the bark of the main trunk and branches to make the shrub 'cry'. On the ground around the shrub is sprinkled a layer of fine sand on to which the 'tears' of the tree drop. These tears are the crystals and the work of sorting them out for size, colour and quality is still done by hand.

ROSEWATER

The best rosewater came formerly from Bulgaria from the famed rose gardens. It is an important ingredient in Balkan and Oriental cooking and used to be so in British cooking. Imparts a fragrant perfume and flavour when used with discretion.

ORANGE FLOWER WATER

Nerole or *Neroli* is an essential oil distilled from orange blossoms and used in flavouring confectionery. Orange flower water is the fragrant liquid collected from the distillation of the oil.

Wines

KRASSI

Wheat, olive oil and wine compose the holy trinity of the Greek
diet. Of these only olive oil is obtained without sweat and labour.
The goddess Athene was generous in her gift of the olive tree
to the people of Greece as i t requires so little attention. But wheat
and wine, these mean hard work and so, perhaps, it is logical
that both Demeter, the Goddess of Grain, and Dionysus, the
God of Wine, in the old pagan days should have been closely
associated with the religious rites and ceremonies of the people.

Bread and wine form the components of the greatest mystery
in the Christian Church and, therefore, it is fitting that the
harvesting of wheat and grapes should be the two main harvests
of the year, taking precedence over the profitable olive harvest.

Bread and cheese with a bunch of grapes (or a glass of wine)
is the usual meal for many Greek peasants and, according to
doctors, this is a full diet – the grapes alone are enough. In days
gone by the rules of health and hygiene were closely allied to the
teachings of the Church and its religious rituals. For example,
the first eating of the grape in Greece is on the day of Our Lord's
Transfiguration, August 6th. On this day the grape-growers
bring a basket of their choicest fruit to the priest, who blesses
it with the words: 'O Lord, bless this season's fruit of the vine
so that it may bring health and joy.'

In still more ancient times, the god, Dionysus, was worshipped
and the grape harvest (*tyrgitis*) was a time for the gathering
together of the agricultural workers, and began with an incanta-
tion to the god, Dionysus.

Greeks have drunk wine since the beginning of time. Their
present habit of dipping bread into wine and olive oil, even in
the early morning, is a survival of an ancient custom. Wine is a
part of the Greek heritage. To quote Hesiod: 'After the toil
of the day is over, should your desire be to eat your food in

peace and drink a glass of wine to settle yourselves, it is a worthy ambition.'

The Greeks believe they have the finest grapes in the world and, say they logically, the best wine. In earlier days Greek wines were sent throughout the known world, even as far as India. Unhappily the Indians long ago lost their taste for wines.

Greek wines vary enormously, principally because the grape growers do not confine themselves to a particular brand of grape, of which there are at least five hundred different varieties. This means that the wine producers must make their wine from the grapes as they come in. One vineyard alone will send six or more different kinds, so that it is impossible for the wine-producers to conform to a uniform quality. The only possible exception to this is the wine produced in the Mesogeia, that is, the interior of Greece as opposed to the coastal areas. Here there are quite large tracts of land under cultivation producing one variety of grape, the Savvatiano. This grape in turn produces a *retsina* wine of a fairly uniform quality, said to be the best in the country.

To show the diversity of Greek wines, at the 1958 Daphni Wine Festival fifty different kinds of wine were offered for exhibition. However, the ancient Greeks could doubtless have produced as many or even more. Then, as now, there were white, red and rosé wines, dry and sweet, and light and heavy.

This wide choice of wines adds pleasure to the tourists' eating and drinking. But such is the diversity that when one finds a wine especially to one's liking and notes with care the name and the year of its vintage, another bottle of the same type might be a sorry disappointment. Equally, a bottle of wine which may seem displeasing can have a sister bottle which is quite good.

Probably the most controversial wines of Greece are the *retsinas*, which, although the national drink of the Greeks, are wines which many people, including Greeks, find overpowering. A *retsina* is a wine (either white or red, but usually white) which has been deliberately and heavily resinated. To those who acquire a taste for it, it can be a wine of pleasant distinction and one soon learns to be knowledgeable about it.

The origin of *retsina* wine is interesting. In the days before casks and bottles the Greeks kept their wines in goatskins and

then poured pitch-pine on top in order to caulk or preserve
them. The Greeks, therefore, expected their wines to taste of
resin or pitch-pine and continued to add this flavouring after
both casks and bottles had been invented. Many critics say that
adding resin to wine is spoiling it. I do not agree. Drinking *retsina*
wine on a sea shore beneath the pines, or in the pine woods
themselves, is a pleasure which remains long in the memory.
The fragrant scent of the pine needles mingles with the taste
of the wine and enhances the flavour of what one is eating.

Retsina wines belong to the *tavernas* of the cities and countryside, and it is on the quality of the *retsina* that the reputation of a
taverna is made or lost. The new wines arrive in the *tavernas*
in the middle of September, when waiters can be seen busily
scrubbing out their barrels to receive them. On October 26th,
St. Demetrius' Day, these new wines are served and thousands
of barrels of *retsina* are tapped. Regular *taverna*-goers are invited
to attend the first tasting of the new season's *retsina*. This first
evening is an anxious one for the proprietors for, on this first
tasting, depends the custom of the following year. If the *retsina*
is good the word flies swiftly throughout the district; if bad or
indifferent, then with equal swiftness everyone is told. And at the
end of a convivial evening the patrons may sing:

> *Retsina wine,*
> *With you I'll die,*
> *No earthly joy,*
> *With you can vie.*

To visit one or other of the private wine presses is for most
people a definite holiday attraction. Just outside Athens, at
Markopoulo, there are several private presses and it is here
that some of the best *retsina* is produced. At the time of the
grape harvest the roads in the area are cluttered with a constant
stream of traffic of all kinds, horse-drawn carts, donkeys and
donkey carts, mules and lorries, all loaded with grapes, all
making their contribution to the flow of grapes destined for the
commercial wine presses or the smaller, private ones.

Those grapes which come to the private presses are un-
loaded through an opening in the wall and tumbled on to the
cement floor of the pressing room. Here several men will be
waiting ready, with feet bare and trousers rolled up to the

thighs, to stamp the grapes. Some, with the aplomb with which a Spanish dancer wears a rose, will fasten a bunch of grapes over their ear and, as they begin to work with precision and skill, they sing songs of the grape, their voices getting louder as the tempo of the stamping rises. As the grapes are loosened from their skins the precious liquid flows through an opening into a vat below and the mass becomes denser and denser until only the stems and skins remain. As each batch of grapes is finished, the skins are swept away and another supply of grapes is attacked. The juice is then tested for its sugar content and pumped away into the tank-like lorries which are standing by. Over the district the faint but pleasant smell of must hangs for days.

For those who might like to indulge in a little amateur grape-trampling there is a *taverna* at Liopessi which has its own press and has become popular with patrons on this account. Carved on the barrels here are many famous names of those who have allowed themselves a little fun.

But not all the wines of Greece are resinated. Far from it. In the average restaurant the wine list will contain at least twenty or more different names and, if you want advice, the best people to ask are the *taverna* or restaurant owners or waiters. They will be refreshingly frank on the subject. Most Greek wines are extremely cheap so that it does not cost much to buy experience. The resinated wines are usually golden, although there are red and rosé *retsinas*. Most Greek wines of any character are white, with the main exception of the well-known Nemean.

There are one or two wine-drinking *tavernas*-cum-shops in Athens where you can sit and nibble at *mezethakia* and try wines from the cask for as long as you like. It makes a delightful holiday occupation for the tourist. One such place is Kanakis, at the corner of Skoufa and Kolonaki Streets, and the other, Orphanides, immediately opposite Zonar's.

The following list of Greek wines is by no means comprehensive. It is meant merely as a guide to the more popular wines, a starter for the wine drinker who should, after his first local initiation, go adventuring into this field of research alone.

Retsina
This comes from many parts of the country and is of three types but many varieties. Generally *retsina* is a golden wine but there is *kokkinelli* which is rosé colour, and *kokkino* which is red. Towards the end of an evening of eating and drinking, many Greeks like to take a glass of *retsina* wine mixed with soda or mineral water. It is not unlike a light champagne in taste and is said to help against having a hangover.

Mantinea
A light wine of the Riesling type and popular with most foreigners. It comes from the Peloponnese which produces what the French call *petits vins*. From the same area is a type of Hock called Tour La Reine.

Domestica
Both red and white and considered as a reasonably priced good table wine.

Hymettus
A very inexpensive wine of the Pouilly type.

Kamba
A rather dry white wine.

Zitsa
Very pleasant sparkling wine, somewhat grandly called a champagne.

Nemean
A rich, red wine known locally as 'Lion's Blood' because of its alcoholic strength. Comes from the Peloponnese.

Mavrodaphne or Maurodaphne
An exceedingly sweet, heavy wine for serving with fruit or dessert. It is also used as a main ingredient in a wine cup or bowle.

Castel Danielis
A red wine of the Burgundy type, belonging to the slightly higher priced groups.

Naoussis Boutari
An almost black wine, very powerful and considered by many
to compare with the Medoc wines. Very dry, 'as dry as a wood-
file,' I was told as I tried it. And how right this was: it almost
rasped my tongue.

Broussiko
A sweet, port-wine type from the Cyclades.

Romola
A rosé wine of the Anjou type, coming from the islands of Zante
and Cephalonia.

Château Decilie
A wine which has the distinction of being made from grapes
grown in the royal vineyards.

Chevalier di Rhodi
A medium-priced red wine from the Island of Rhodes.

Samos wines
Samos has long been famous for its rich and golden wines,
somewhat sweet and very strong. Those who care to follow the
excellent advice of Lord Byron and 'Fill high the bowl with
Samian wine', might also emulate the islanders and add some
water to it. Greeks have added water to their wines for centuries. We read in the *Iliad* that when Aias and Odysseus called
on Achilles in his tent at Troy, the latter, wishing to show real
hospitality, called to his attendants, 'Let there be stronger wine –
wine without water.' There is also a widespread superstition that
water must be added to wine during those months without an 'r'
in them. Probably a wise precaution against too much alcohol
during the trying hot months.

Santorini
The wines of this volcanic island are favoured by the Vatican
for its communion wines. They have a strong, brackish flavour
which comes from the minerals in the ground. These same
minerals also add to the potency of the Santorini wines and
most islanders insist that their glasses must be diluted by one-

fourth of water. But, even so, the islanders, with a sly smile, insist too much of their wine turns a man crazy, a fact which appears to concern them not at all.

Rhodes
An island strongly influenced by the Italians, who occupied it for a long time. Most of its wine is even cheaper than that on the mainland and follows an Italian pattern, more especially the liqueurs and aperitifs.

Crete
King Minos is probably the best of the Crete wines, or at least the best known. It is a pleasant, golden wine best served ice-cold. Kritica, a dark, red wine, rather dry, like the Naoussis, also comes from Crete.

Commanderia
A heavy Madeira-type wine from Cyprus, one of the best-known Cypriot wines.

Brandies and Cognacs
There are several Greek brandies, some of which are very good. Probably the best-known brands are Varvaressou and Metaxas.

Ouzo
A clear spirit, distilled from the grapes, usually the by-product of the wine-making. It can be taken neat or with water as a chaser. Most foreigners find it more palatable to mix *ouzo* with water and add a cube of ice. This sends it cloudy and white. The Turks, by the way, call *ouzo* 'Lion's milk'. It has a strong aniseed flavour and is not only the drink of the Greeks but of the neighbouring countries. It is taken as an aperitif and has the advantage that it does not paralyse the palate for anything to follow. In hot weather it is one of the very best of drinks. *Ouzo* drinkers insist that one should always eat when drinking.

An evening's over-indulgence in *ouzo* (or *arak* or *raki*), British troops claimed, produced the morning after, a blackout after drinking a glass of water: as though this were an economic drink for a drunk. I have not myself experienced this and my husband, who has consumed *ouzo* in large quantities in his time, says this story is pure fantasy.

Ouzo is both privately and commercially made and varies in quality. The best is distilled from grapes and filtered several times. In some parts of the Arab world, in Iraq for instance, *ouzo* is distilled from dates and has quite another taste. Village-made *ouzo* is really fiery stuff, rough, and to be treated with real respect. You do not add water when drinking *ouzo* with a Greek peasant, he would think this incredibly cissy.

Mura

This is a somewhat startling drink, a pure white liquid which the drinker is supposed to toss off in the nonchalant manner of the vodka drinker.

Mastiha

This is sometimes described as 'a liqueur flavoured with gum mastic'. Mastic is a low-branching tree with shiny leaves and belongs to the pistachio family. It grows in several parts of the world, but mostly in Chios, which has over four million trees. I have not been able to like this drink but there are many who do, including foreigners.

Beer

Greek beer is very palatable and based on German beer. Like many things in Greece, this is a monopoly of the firm Fix, which is a corruption of the German name Fuchs. Herr Fuchs was a Muenchener who followed one of the Bavarian princes chosen for the Greek throne. He started to make beer and the family, now Hellenized, have been making beer for several generations.

Restaurants

TAVERNAS

Greek *tavernas* represent a way of living, for Greeks like to eat out and a visitor to Greece is more likely to be asked to a meal in a *taverna* than in a home. *Tavernas* exist for every type of appetite, every type of purse, every type of temperament, even for every type of food.

It is important to know exactly what is a *taverna*. A good *taverna* must be hidden away in side streets – just why I am not sure, except perhaps that a *taverna* on a main street would cease to be sufficiently intimate. A *taverna* is to the Greek what the pub is to the Englishman and the *bistro* to the Frenchman, convivial, full-blooded, and noisy with the buzz of talk and the clatter of waiters. And every Greek, certainly every Athenian, holds passionately to his own views concerning his favourite *taverna*. They will drive or go by bus for miles to visit one of their choice and their mood.

However, to find a good *taverna* one does not have to make a journey out of town, particularly in Athens, which boasts every type.

If you seek bright lights, some dancing or a singing girl, well, some *tavernas* have both, but such *tavernas* are for the tourist. The traditional *taverna* is small, with one room which is kitchen and dining-room combined, or in the summer a walled-in garden or a paved courtyard with just a few tables and just enough customers to make it amusing. The food is good enough to be enjoyed, if not memorable. There is good *retsina* wine, a stray cat or two, a faint breeze and the smell of night-blooming shrubs. Some *tavernas* are even less than this – a few tables on a gravel path or under a mimosa tree. Here *retsina* is served, as it should be, in copper mugs and there are simple salads to eat, with brown bread, cheese and olives, or *kebabs* which are placed on the table without much ceremony. Not food for the fastidious, I agree, but pleasant nevertheless.

In the summer all the *tavernas* seek the open spaces and fresh air and the cook follows, happily bringing his stoves and pots into the courtyards or on to the pavements.

In the winter, which is mercifully short, the *taverna* stays inside its one room with the tables crowded together hug-a-mug, requiring no heating other than that which comes from the cooking stoves set in a corner and that generated from the bodies bunched around the tables.

A *taverna* will only serve Greek food. Copper pans filled with food simmer on top of the stove, and in the ovens are great pans of tomatoes, macaroni, meat and chickens. Cold dishes are on display in a glass case and fish is kept in the refrigerator which the obliging cook will open to let you decide which fish you will eat. He pulls out large trays and you gaze entranced at rosy mullet embedded in crushed ice, glassy eyes peering out through the crystals, or at great, fat fish recumbent on icy couches – I always think of Madame Récamier. There are prawns, mounds of smelts (*marithes*) or baby shrimps (*garithes*), all of which are sold by the weight, not by the portion. You choose your fish and plead with the cook not to cook it immediately, which is the usual custom, but to await your pleasure and cook it only when you have reached the fish stage of the meal so that it will be served hot.

Having made your choice of a fish and main dish you return to your table to sip your *ouzo* and nibble at the *mezethakia*, or appetizers (see page 17) and decide on the wine you want.

If you are not too keen on olive oil, you must do some more explaining. A common complaint of foreigners is that Greek food is not served hot and is always smothered in too much oil. Try saying, '*ochi poli lathi*', which means, more or less, 'not too much oil'. Restaurant and *taverna* proprietors are becoming so used to this complaint that however bad your pronunciation is, it will be understood in essence, if not in words.

Incidentally, inspecting the kitchen has nothing to do with not understanding the menu or proving that the kitchen is clean. It is simply to see what is cooking and, if later, you don't like what you have ordered then you have no one to blame but yourself. Everyone chooses from the stove, Greeks included.

Along one wall of most *tavernas* are barrels of *retsina*, forming a mural and offering a welcome. The furnishings are not smart and the tables are often spread with a shabby cloth. The waiters may be part of the family which runs the *taverna*, husband, brother or cousin, or employed from outside. They all take a friendly interest in everything and everyone. And no one hurries. If you want to eat quickly, then don't go to a *taverna*.

It is not difficult to find a *taverna* anywhere in Greece except perhaps in the really remote regions. But in Athens you simply wander through the Plaka, where Byron lived and loved, which is a short walk from the famed Constitution Square in the direction of the Acropolis. In the shadow of this mighty monument you come across a maze of cobbled streets, mentally go back a little in history, look around you and choose your *taverna*. This you can do largely by its smell and general atmosphere. And if you are a woman, do not wear really high-heeled shoes or you are likely to end up with a broken ankle. I found few women in most of the *tavernas* and these were mostly foreigners. Greek men, it seems, love to spend their evenings away from their wives happily clutching a mug of *retsina* and noisily solving the political problems of the world. As I have not heard complaints from their wives, I suppose everyone is happy. In the brighter *tavernas*, especially those with neon lighting, there are more women, but these are not 'true' *tavernas*.

Few of the Plaka *tavernas* boast their own musicians. Some proprietors, like Zafiris, refuse to have any kind of music. Zafiris declares that you can either eat and drink or listen but you cannot do all three at the same time. Other *tavernas* have strolling minstrels or guitarists. Patrons are expected to drop a tip in the plate, thoughtfully provided, before they leave.

Within a short drive from Athens are several coastal suburbs with some very popular *tavernas*. (Failing a car you can travel in a bus or on the underground railway.) The *tavernas* here quite naturally specialize in fish dishes, for the sea comes literally to their doorsteps. Most of the *tavernas* have tables set on the sands or straddled across the road but looking out to the sea. When it rains the tables are protected by a tarpaulin. Only a very severe downpour sends one scuttling inside for shelter. As one wanders along the sea-front waiters dart out and swoop upon one, declaiming the virtues of their fish and their cook, almost dragging one into their particular lair. A firm hand is required to continue in search of a special *taverna*, and if one has no prior

information, then it is best to look for a *taverna* which already
has a good sprinkling of Greeks inside. They will not patronize a
taverna where the food and wine is either inferior or too expensive.

In the country the *tavernas* are often simply a few tables and
chairs set in a small garden or in the kitchen which is the living-
room of the proprietor's family. The garden is walled and
usually there are vines climbing the walls and spreading over
trellis-work. Inside the main room, which is also the store-
room, will hang strings of drying onions and garlic or festoons
of home-made sausages. Sometimes there will be an old-fashioned
marble sink and often an equally old-fashioned Victorian-style
marble-topped washing table. This holds not only a basin and
soap dish but bowls of drying pomegranate, sunflower or melon
seeds, or jars of preserves. In a corner probably stands a large
jar, like those in which Ali Baba hid his forty thieves, filled with
oil, produced, more likely than not, from the olive trees owned by
the proprietor and pressed in his own primitive press. Here and
there will be a bunch of flowers packed tightly into a jar or bottle.

There are also remote *tavernas*, snuggled under cliffs, where
you can look out across a sea sometimes so dark that you realize
what Homer meant when he called it 'wine-dark'.

In Athens there are *tavernas* where the *bouzouki*, a mandolin-
type of musical instrument, is played. These are down-to-earth
establishments (literally so, as most are small basement rooms
in and around the main squares) although some of the larger
bouzoukia tavernas are situated along the Syngros Boulevard,
the main road leading from Athens to Piraeus. Like other *tavernas*,
in the summer they are in the open-air and in winter inside. They
vary slightly but if I give a description of one of the larger type,
winter style, it will more or less cover them all. The room is really
large, with tables everywhere, around which men sprawl. In the
bouzoukia tavernas, especially the very small ones, women are
not welcome, although naturally allowed. At the end of the room
is a platform where the *bouzoukia* band plays. There is also a
singer, a girl, coquettish and decidedly plump by our standards.
Accompanied by the *bouzoukia* band she sings of love, of lovers
lost or vanished, of others hot and new. Sometimes one member
of the band will join her in the singing, sometimes two. The style
is Oriental and the aim of the musicians is to inspire the listeners
either to sing or dance.

The repertoire of the *bouzoukia* singers is fairly limited and the type of composition is called *rebetika*. Married to the song is a dance called a *zebekiko* and this has been much developed in this kind of *taverna* in Athens and throughout Greece. When the band and the singer have really warmed up, a group of men at a table will begin to sing and to clap in rhythm; usually one of the men will get up and dance the *zebekiko* in perfect rhythm without any self-consciousness. Some of these solo dances are very good. The solo over, the dancer will give the girl singer some money – and the amount should be generous. She shares this later with the band, and most of the girls have an endearing habit of putting these hard-earned notes down their bosoms for safekeeping.

There is no note of refinement in this type of *taverna*. The singing girl is usually gaudily dressed and most of the patrons do not come from the upper income bracket. The singing is of a throaty kind, in an imitation of the first singer who made this type of entertainment popular. An evening spent at a *bouzoukia taverna* as a rule starts around eleven o'clock at night, for it is only by then that the atmosphere begins to warm up. Singing and dancing can, and does, go on throughout the night. Just how Greeks manage to go carousing through the night and yet rise early is always a surprise to me, but I suppose it is the good use they all make of the afternoon siesta. Almost everything is shut during the afternoon and starts up again around 4 p.m.

The *kafenion* or coffee houses are popular, for any time is coffee time to Greeks throughout their country. At times Athens' Constitution Square is so filled with small metal tables and chairs that it looks like one vast coffee-garden. Outside Athens or in the islands you can spend lovely, solitary mornings sitting in front of a stray fisherman's house drinking coffee, or under the trees – three chairs and a table make a coffee house anywhere in Greece, just as in Cyprus or in Turkey.

And if all this is not enough there are the small 'dairies', called *galaktopolia*, where you can order a small bowl of rice or cornflour pudding or yoghourt. And, before you smirk, let me add that on a hot morning, or when you have had too much museum-walking, a dish of ice-cold rice pudding is extraordinarily good. So is the cornflour mould flavoured with rosewater and sprinkled with chopped nuts.

One cannot talk of Greek outdoor eating without mentioning the corn-on-the-cob man and the chestnut man, and the many kiosks where you can buy cheesecake or pie, etc. All have their place in the Greek way of living and this place is usually at the street corner.

Tavernas *in the Plaka district of Athens*

ZAFIRIS. The doyen of the Plaka *taverna* proprietors, Zafiris, who is no longer young, has some firm convictions about food and wine. In his opinion you cannot enjoy both these things and a third, music. So he permits no music in his *taverna*, which is treated with great respect by most Greeks. It is considered almost sacrilegious to dispute the cooking. Not very large, Zafiris' *taverna* is usually full without being over-crowded.

XENOS. Old and charming, this is considered by experts to be the best *taverna* after Zafiris, with a reliable reputation. Usually there is one guitarist who also sings.

EFTA ATHELFIA. The name means 'seven brothers'. The *taverna* at one time belonged to a man who had seven sons and, if my story is correct, he bought it for his seven sons, all of whom naturally worked in the *taverna*. When the father died, the brothers split up in the friendliest possible way and now they have *tavernas* scattered throughout the city. At least, this is the story I was told. Facts have a way of being changed. The Efta Athelfia is very popular, noted for its *retsina* as well as its other wines, and the food is considered good.

KASTRO. This is rather a more tourist-minded *taverna* than most, but even so there are enough Greeks who frequent it – both to eat and drink as well as to play backgammon – to make it interesting. You have to climb a fairly long flight of stone steps to reach it.

VACCHUS. A small, intimate *taverna* where the wine is excellent and the food 'plain' but good. It is in Vacchus Street.

Ton Theon. Situated at the far end of the Plaka, it has become rather well-known to foreigners, probably because the translation of its name is so enchanting, 'The Tavern of the Gods'.

Palea Yitonia. Another of the simpler *tavernas* with a good reputation for wine and good, but plain, food. The translation of its name is 'Old Neighbourhood'. It is in Thaidalon Street and is a night-club, but not of the smart type. You can eat and drink until late in the night.

Methysmeno. The name means 'Drunken Boat' and the owner is a poet of local repute with some published verse to his credit. I believe he is one of the seven brothers. The *taverna* got its name from a poem of Rimbaud. All the tables have names such as 'The Lovers', or 'The Intellectuals'. One hopes that guests are not assigned to tables which are supposed to match their mood or their intellect for it might be embarrassing. Quite pleasant without being too quaint.

There are other *tavernas* with similar names. The Drunken Moon is one.

Saitis. This is typically Greek – all are this, of course, but some more so. The prices are reasonable, the food plain but good, and the wines have a good reputation.

Plakiotopoula. The translation runs, 'The Girl from the Plaka'. It is very small, very romantic and usually has one guitarist and a singer. Food and wine is good and the prices are not high. Romance and low prices should be recommended.

Palia Athina. This is a night-club *taverna* with a Greek floor show. According to my Greek friends it rates one star – but remember, all these night-club *tavernas* can change or disappear overnight.

Sarandithis. This is highly rated by seasoned Greek *taverna*-goers.

Tavernas *in the Ommonia Square District of Athens*

In this area are many of the so-called provincial *tavernas*, some of which are large and noisy and filled with men up from the provinces. They are also often localized – by this I mean that if a man from Salonika is feeling lonely in Athens he knows where he will find a *taverna* frequented by men from his own town. Generally you have to step down into a tiny basement-like room, heavy with the smell of smoke and food, *ouzo* and bodies, stopping *en route* to your table to take a knowing glance at the *kebab* or *kokoretsi* or the lamb slowly roasting. The waiter, rough and ready, literally plonks a small bottle of *ouzo* on the table, an *ouzo* more rough and ready than the waiter, and you wait for the grilled meats and sausage to appear smothered in onions, raw and rasping.

In this area are the *klephti tavernas* which are owned and managed by shepherds from the mountains who have come to try their luck in the big city. They have lost nothing of the cooking skill they practised in the mountains. If you are near Ommonia Square you hardly need directions to reach these *tavernas*, just follow your nose.

Not far from Ommonia Square are a couple of Roumanian *tavernas*. Both produce excellent Roumanian-type food. One, the Norok, specializes in a swordfish dish which is really worth trying. Swordfish has a rich and firm texture not unlike veal, and grilled over a charcoal fire is decidedly good. The second Roumanian restaurant is the Bucharest. Both are run by Roumanians but are popular among Greeks too. The Roumanian-style *kebab* is delicious. The atmosphere is gay and wine flows.

Rather more in the centre of Athens are two *tavernas* with the same kind of décor, and both are good. The Kalamia, which is to be found tucked away in a passage opposite the Tamion Building, is worth looking for, especially if one's pockets are not lined with gold. The food is essentially Greek and the cook is noted for his pork roasts. The table cloths may not be over-clean but the food will be. In this category comes another simple but excellent *taverna*, the Ideal, which caters for the lower-income-bracket Greeks. The other bamboo-decorated *taverna* is the Pindaron, known locally as the Yero Phiniki, which means the 'Old Palm'. This is in Pindaron Street. Once you have discovered

it you will go again. The food is good and they specialize in a
pork and celery dish (recipe in meat section) as well as *youvar-lakia*. At least they did on my last visit to Athens. You will find
mostly Greeks here and foreigners who live in Athens and know
their *tavernas*.

Outside Athens there are numerous *tavernas*: the coastline,
for example, from Athens to Sounion is dotted with them, of
all kinds and to suit all purses, and by this I mean what I say,
including the purses of those who travel by third-class bus.

Kifissia, the Hampstead of Athens, is a favourite haunt of
the *taverna* clientele. Here *tavernas* are both easy and hard to
find for some are tucked away and known only to the discerning Greeks, who, while they delight in tourists, do not want to
have all their more precious haunts discovered, for even the
poorest tourist can step up prices. These Kifissia *tavernas* I am
listing are the rather better known, Greek-frequented, naturally,
and, I think, should be popular with the average and non-
average tourist to Greece.

SAMANDANIS. A *taverna* which specializes in liver dishes, small
game-birds and, in general, good food. It is rather quiet although
quite large and, like most *tavernas*, in the summer goes into the
garden.

MITILINEOS. Definitely one of the favourite Kifissia *tavernas*
with good *retsina* wine as well as good food.

KALAMBOKAS. There are two *tavernas* with this name (the same
owner) and they are rather fashionable, with dancing, and
Western as well as Greek food.

THIMAS. Once extremely fashionable but less so these days. Even
so to be recommended.

HATSAKOS. The *taverna* of the singing baritone, the proprietor.
Hatsakos has a powerful voice and after midnight, when he
thinks his guests can relax from both eating and drinking, he will
entertain them with his repertoire. His *taverna* is very popular
and the food I found not only good but served hot. Outside the
gate, very patiently, sits a nice, wrinkled old lady who turns the

spit over a charcoal fire. She turns about twelve chickens at a time. Not even the chill November evenings seemed to disturb her, although by then all the *tavernas* had gone into their winter quarters.

KORES. This *taverna* specializes in grilled chickens (unless things have changed since I was last there) and has been known to serve as many as 500 chickens on a good night. Kores is very difficult to find, it is somewhere amidst some ruins, I remember. But take an Athenian with you. They are always willing to be 'dragged' to a *taverna* meal.

NEA ZOI (*New Life*). A little further along the road after Kifissia, this *taverna* is especially popular with the foreign population, most of whom claim to have 'discovered' it. I was prepared to be disappointed with it because of this, but I found the food good and the atmosphere gay and relaxed. The *taverna* started simply as a wayside kitchen where men could drop in after shooting for a small meal and a glass of wine. Gradually it developed to a *taverna* of some size.

ZERVAS. Along the coastal road in Glyfada. The food is excellent. A *taverna* that is known as the meeting place of Greek ship-owners, and Greek shipowners are seldom poor.

ASTERIA. This elegant *taverna* and night-club also requires the escort of a shipowner.

In the district of Turcolimano *tavernas* abound and in good weather are arranged on the sands. Here you will get sea-food of all kinds, some from the *taverna* itself and some from the itinerant hawkers who gaze at you hopefully, clutching a basket of sea urchins or sea quinces or anything they happen to have bought or caught. If you buy these, the vendor will open them up for you and the waiter will not be annoyed. If you feel squeamish about eating all this, remember that wine is said to kill all germs in no time at all. This may not be entirely true, but it is a helpful thought and one I cherish. So, take wine with your food.

And now Piraeus. Of course, the sea-front where the boats

anchor is chock-a-block with *tavernas* of all kinds. Once I remember learning to cook *arni exotica* from a *taverna* cook. Why I chose this *taverna* for my lesson I am not sure; probably because I was there and the cook was a charmer who wanted to show me something new. As he was Greek and I had no word of his language except for the names of food, our conversation was amusing. I took a note of it.

'You parle Française?' asked the cook. I nodded. He grinned. 'Me ein bischen,' he said. 'Gut,' I replied, wondering just which language we were going to pursue.

Cook took an onion, medium size: 'Take, cut, cut,' he said as he chopped away at the onion. I nodded. 'Put in boat.' I looked bewildered but he fortunately took up his saucepan. 'Spik Italiana,' he questioned. I nodded. 'Un peu,' said he. 'Aqua in boat. Agneau,' and he picked up the lamb, then salt and pepper, waved them at me, spilling pepper all over the kitchen, sending the kitchen staff and myself into sneezes. 'Sorry,' he apologized. 'Petit pois or Kartoffeln or vino – maybe.' His black eyes gleamed beneath his tall chef's cap and his hands flew into the air. 'Una ora au four,' he almost shouted. I grasped that he meant all these ingredients were to be popped into the pan and then baked in the oven for one hour. I nodded my head vigorously. He took a cloth filled with *phyllo*, the Greek pastry. 'Uno, deux, drei . . .' He gave up counting, picked up the saucepan . . . ' 'ere, agneau, onions – all t'ings,' and wrapped all the ingredients in sheets of pastry, five sheets in all. 'Au four, eine ora,' he added, no less exhausted than myself with all this language effort. But still feeling more detail was required, he added, 'Au four, molto force.'

We parted, the lesson over. I had learned to make lamb and peas, with onion and potatoes in pastry. As I left his astonished *piccolo* cook (assistant), sweating and wondering, flapped a steaming hot chicken in the air, just missing me. He insisted that I see his side of the kitchen, where chickens lay cooking in a thick sauce, the macaroni and spaghetti, the heaps of fried potatoes and those 'English roasts'. He was certainly a versatile *piccolo* cook.

However, apart from the general run of *tavernas* in Piraeus there are two which are famous. The first, Vasilenas, named after its owner. Vasilenas is a man of parts. For years he was

butler to a well-known Greek admiral and then, late in life, he
married, his wife bringing as part of her dowry a small wine
shop. Financially this was not much of a success. The admiral's
ex-butler decided that he would turn it into a *taverna*, but being
a man of his own ideas he also decided what he was going to
serve. It started with small eats and *retsina*. Then gradually,
since he was also a man of imagination as well as silence (unusual for a Greek), the choice of small eats extended until the
day came when he was serving as many as twenty or more different *mezethakia* followed by a main course consisting of a
soup, often a large baked fish garnished with rosy pink crabs, or
crayfish, and a meat or chicken dish, all depending on the season,
followed by a bowl of fruit. And all through the meal the carafe of
retsina is replenished, no questions asked, none answered. In a
corner Vasilenas stands and watches, silent, almost morose. If
the guests show interest there dawns a light in his eye, he thinks
up a new small eat and dashes into the kitchen. If they eat well
he gives them more. If they falter or pick at their food, which is
also his food, he loses interest and his eyes gaze dully into space.
Such people are, according to Vasilenas, not worth bothering
about. The meal finishes with coffee and the price, inclusive, is
sixty drachma which, when I was last in Greece, worked out at
about 60p per head. One evening I dined there with a Greek
friend, one who had by chance (because of visiting firemen)
dined there twice in the same week. Vasilenas, who knew him
well, admonished him, growling curtly, 'General, you have
dined here already twice this week. Are you trying to kill yourself?
Once a week is enough for any man in my taverna.'

Here is a typical Vasilena menu. *Lakertha* (pickled fish),
brawn, anchovies, *taramo salata* (botargo), shrimps and prawns,
with shredded raw carrots and a mustard sauce, lobster rissoles
flavoured with ground ginger and lemon, smelts fried to biscuit
crispness, tomato and capsicum salad, octopus in a red wine
sauce, sausages of various kinds, *bourekia*, which are small fried
savoury pastries, meat balls and *kebabs*, large green olives and
pointed black olives from Kalamata, all kinds of cheese including Roquefort, mussels, *dolmathes*, octopus fried in oil until
crisp, and cuttlefish. As this is followed by soup and a main
course I quite understand that Vasilenas prefers his guests to

limit their visits. After my first visit I felt there never was such a meal, to misquote Mr Dickens.

It would seem there could never be another such *taverna* either, at least not as good, in the district. But it has a rival in the Grotto or the Cave (Spilia Paraskeva) which is, as its name might suggest, half *taverna* and half cave. Its adherents are as vehement as those of Vasilenas in praising its cuisine, which is, however, more usual. Both are worthy of a ride in the cosy underground from Ommonia Square to Piraeus. And for those who land in Piraeus by ship, well, it's just 'around the corner'. Everyone knows both and dinner is the meal to patronize – although lunch is available.

As if Piraeus had not enough in these two *tavernas*, there is yet another, Thiassimos, which means 'famous'. And it is indeed famed for the quality of its seafood. 'Go there once,' said a Greek friend, 'and you will go again.' He was right. But Thiassimos is not actually in Piraeus, it is round the coast at Passalimani. But only just round the corner.

This is but a beginning to *taverna* hunting. Try these and then find new ones yourself. But for those who prefer, or also want to try, restaurants, I will list a few. These are more expensive than the *tavernas* and more westernized. You will find Greek food, but rather 'watered down' as it were.

Of these I think Zonar's must lead, for it is certainly the most important. You could spend a whole day here quite easily, starting with breakfast and running cosily through the day's meals. Zonar's, together with its neighbour, Floca (this specializes in light snacks and most particularly pastries and coffee) constitute the Café de la Paix of Athens. To the visitor who passes the long rows of closely-packed chairs the two restaurants are scarcely distinguishable. On good days – and most days are good in Athens – it is hardly possible to find a chair at either. Everybody who is anybody is sitting in the metal chairs (Zonar's) or the bamboo ones (Floca's) sipping coffee, eating pastries or mounds of chestnut *purée*, gossiping and watching the passers-by. And, if you are a stranger, you will not be lonely for long, always supposing that you find a chair. There is the sponge seller, his sponges tied round his middle like some odd pneumatic tyre. He wants to sell his wares, so hardly obtained, cheaply.

Somebody nearby is sure to tell you the tragic stories of the sponge seller, stories which tear at the heart and produce a schizophrenic thought. Because it costs so much labour and heartbreak diving for sponges one feels one ought to buy them, yet, because they cost so much in lives and health, one wonders whether one should buy nylon sponges and so kill the wicked trade. Difficult to decide.

So one turns to the nut vendors, not only to the *passa tempo* man but also the little man who comes along with his tray of nuts and almost thrusts paper bags of his nuts into one's hands. Then the flower sellers and the man with postcards – not feelthy – and the man who has a line on the tourist trips and buses, rather good in limited doses; the small boys who look with scorn at dusty shoes and proceed to clean them whether one will or not. And so on. By the time all this has happened one is head-over-heels in conversation with the man or woman in the next chair. How can one be lonely? So Zonar's or Floca's, both, are not to be missed.

Immediately opposite Zonar's is Orphanides, nicely old-fashioned and selling beer and wines. It also has a counter where you can buy all kinds of delicacies. And if you sit and drink inside you can watch the shopping going on as well. Rather amusing and one learns a lot.

After this there are the hotels, the three main being the Grande Bretagne, the King George and the Athenée Palace. Some Athenians says that the latter has the best kitchen in Athens. There is also the National.

Of the restaurants: well there is the Corfu, which is in the centre of Athens, in a side street, and has an almost exclusively Corfiote cuisine. Its owner, who sits in his restaurant throughout the evening, told me that all his fish and meat comes from his mother island. I must have raised an eyebrow, for he explained, 'Our fish and meat is the best, especially our meat. Both are handled by girls who are working hard to earn a dowry. For example, they earn enough money to buy a calf, this they fatten for meat of good quality. They sell this and earn enough money for a dowry – and so buy a husband. It is as simple as that.'

Costi has a good reputation and specializes in some lesser-known Greek dishes such as *trahana* soup. Averoff – I wonder if I should mention this. Most of my Greek friends tell me it is good. I tried it once, and it could be that I chose badly, but I ate very indifferently there. But that does sometimes happen, even in the best of restaurants. One of my most discerning Greek friends rates it as two star. Pantheon, a large, typically Balkan-type restaurant on University Street, has good food, both Greek and Western, and the owner, an old soldier, does his own marketing. I like it, always ate well there and found the wine list most interesting. By no means expensive but more expensive than the *tavernas*.

Elenikon, owned by the proprietor of the Pantheon, is ex-exclusively Greek provincial. Very large and to be found just off Ommonia Square. The food is good and for those interested in Greeks as well as their food it is an excellent place for a quiet (or not so quiet) study of Greek nationals.

And finally, the question and headache of all tourists. Tipping. On the bill one is charged 12 per cent of the total and this goes to the waiter. If you feel he has earned something extra by his attentions, then you may give him more, but he does not look for it, not even among the tourists. The ever-open hand is missing in Greece. But you should remember the water boy, who is a waiter trainee and unless tipped gets nothing at all. He re-fills your glasses with water again and again, empties ashtrays and picks up napkins. For him the patron should leave a small tip on the table – not in the hand or on the tray, but definitely on the table. No one but the water-boy will touch it.

Index

A selection of Mayflower Handbooks

Cooking and Drink

HOME WINE-MAKING	H. E. Bravery	40p	☐
SUCCESSFUL MODERN WINE-MAKING			
	H. E. Bravery	40p	☐
NATURE'S WAY TO HEALTH	Justine Glass	35p	☐
COOKING WITH FRUIT	Ursula Grüninger	50p	☐
BEE NILSON'S KITCHEN HANDBOOK	Bee Nilson	50p	☐
DEEP FREEZE COOKING	Bee Nilson	40p	☐
LET'S PRESERVE IT	Beryl Wood	40p	☐

Sport and Health

UNDERWATER SWIMMING	Michael Brennan	35p	☐
YOGA MADE EASY	Desmond Dunne	50p	☐
YOGA AND YOUR HEALTH	Sonya Richmond	40p	☐
KARATE	Bruce Tegner	50p	☐

General

COIN COLLECTING	Laurence Brown	35p	☐
THE ORIGINS OF EVERYTHING (Encyclopaedia)			
	Gordon Grimley	50p	☐

All these books are available at your local bookshop or newsagent, or can be ordered direct from the publisher. Just tick the titles you want and fill in the form below.

Name ....

Address ....

....

Write to Mayflower Cash Sales, PO Box 11, Falmouth, Cornwall TR10 9EN. Please enclose remittance to the value of the cover price plus:
UK: 18p for the first book plus 8p per copy for each additional book ordered to a maximum charge of 66p. BFPO and EIRE: 18p for the first book plus 8p per copy for the next 6 books, thereafter 3p per book.
OVERSEAS: 20p for the first book and 10p for each additional book.
Granada Publishing reserve the right to show new retail prices on covers, which may differ from those previously advertised in the text or elsewhere.